Sails of the Herring Fleet

THEATER: Theory/Text/Performance

Enoch Brater, Series Editor

Sails of the Herring Fleet

Essays on Beckett

Herbert Blau

Ann Arbor

The University of Michigan Press

First paperback edition 2004
Copyright © by the University of Michigan 2000
All rights reserved
Published in the United States of America by
The University of Michigan Press
Printed and bound by CPI Group (UK) Ltd, Croydon, CR0 4YY

2007   2006   2005   2004   5   4   3   2

A CIP catalog record for this book is available from the British Library.

Library of Congress Cataloging-in-Publication Data

Blau, Herbert.
  Sails of the herring fleet : essays on Beckett / Herbert Blau.
    p. cm. — (Theater—theory/text/performance)
  Includes bibliographical references (p.) and index.
    ISBN 978-0-472-11149-7 (alk. paper)
    1. Beckett, Samuel, 1906—Dramatic works.   2. Beckett, Samuel,
1906—Dramatic production.   I. Title.   II. Series.
  PR6003.E282 Z576   2000
  842'.914—dc21   00-008325

ISBN 978-0-472-03001-9 (pbk. :alk. paper

The following essays and interviews in this collection were originally published as
indicated:

"Notes from the Underground," in *The Impossible Theater: A Manifesto*. New York:
Macmillan, 1964. 228–51.
"On Directing Beckett: An Interview," in *Directing Beckett*. Ed. Lois Oppenheim.
Ann Arbor: University of Michigan Press, 1994. 48–65.
"The Bloody Show and the Eye of Prey" and "Barthes and Beckett: The Punctum, the
Pensum, and the Dream of Love," in *The Eye of Prey: Subversions of the Postmodern*.
Bloomington: Indiana University Press, 1987. 65–103.
"The Oversight of Ceaseless Eyes," in *Around the Absurd: Essays on Modern and
Postmodern Drama*. Eds. Enoch Brater and Ruby Cohn. Ann Arbor: University of
Michigan Press, 1991. 279–91.
"Quaquaquaqua: The Babel of Beckett," in *The World of Beckett*. Ed. Joseph Smith.
Psychiatry and Humanities, Vol. 12. Baltimore: Johns Hopkins University Press, 1991.
1–15.
"The Less Said," in *Performing Arts Journal* 35/36 (1990): 11–13.
"Remembering Beckett: An Interview," in *Sources: Revue des études anglophones*
2(1997): 31–54.
All photographs of productions at The Actor's Workshop of San Francisco were taken
by Chic Lloyd.

ISBN13 978-0-472-11149-7 (cloth)
ISBN13 978-0-472-03001-9 (paper)
ISBN13 978-0-472-02440-7 (electronic)

To Jonathan

Acknowledgments

My only hesitation in thanking, once more, the Center for Twentieth Century Studies is that it will probably have changed its name before this is published, although it's been rather mischievously casual, dilatory about that, while its current research on animals may suggest, to those not familiar with its leading edges, either some millennial atavism or eco-detour around the cyborgs. However that may be, here are the names of those negotiating the Y2K transition as if it were simply a matter of course, which is pretty much how they've made things easier for me before: Carol Tennessen, Nigel Rothfels, Patti Sander; and, when I started putting the collection together, my research assistant, Clark Lunberry.

As for my wife, Kathleen Woodward, director of the Center, she's been acknowledged in so many books by so many other scholars that anything else I might say would be not only partial but redundant, though I rather like the redundancy of her unabating support.

At the University of Michigan Press, LeAnn Fields has long been receptive to suggestions I've made about other books published there, and I appreciated her enthusiasm about this one from the moment it was proposed.

I won't repeat here what I've written about within, but for this particular book my deepest and longest gratitude goes to some who worked with me back in the 1950s, out in San Francisco, in and around those early dubious productions of Beckett's plays. There were times when Robert Symonds was so deep in—as before the unveiling in *Endgame*—that it seemed he'd never get out, but forty years later, usually now in Paris, I'm delighted to be seeing him still, lively as ever, good-natured, even performing there and, as if heartened by all adversity, next to "inexhaustible"—a word he may remember from the waiting for Godot. As for one who never forgets, I must mention Alan Mandell, first of all because he asked me to. "Mention my name," he said, in his imperious way, when I told him I was doing the book, "and don't forget to send me a copy." That will be duly done, and with love for long devotion. I might add, meanwhile, that in the aftermath of our production of *Godot* at San Quentin prison nobody did more to perpetuate the Beckettian ethos there, which he did by advising and supporting the inmates in their own theater work. When some of them were paroled and the San Quentin Drama Group was reformed outside the prison, Alan acted with them, and later, too, in productions directed by Beckett.

Another I want to mention, though I can only wish to send the book, is the late Tom Rosqui, who came to The Actor's Workshop, young and handsome, while still a sailor at Treasure Island (below the Golden Gate Bridge), only to find himself, eventually, sealed into leather as Clov, in the claustrophobic chamber of *Endgame,* too relentless an actor not to find it exhilarating. And then, of course, there's my partner in the theater for many hectic years, Jules Irving, who directed *Krapp's Last Tape* after playing Lucky in *Godot* but who in the much too early end should have been—he who loved to gamble and almost always won—far luckier than that. I will be saying more about him in one of the essays.

There are age-old personal reasons for (again) acknowledging Ruby Cohn, but what I'm remembering at the moment is that, amid her irreplaceable contributions to the criticism of Beckett, she also organized, some years ago, what may have been an unprecedented panel at the MLA, consisting of my (former) wife, Beatrice Manley (who had played Winnie in *Happy Days),* my son Dick (then a student at Harvard, where he directed Beckett plays), and myself—thus bringing to the subject a familial perspective. Shifting somewhat within that perspective, let me explain something about the dedication.

Three of my children, back in San Francisco, grew up with Beckett in the theater, two of them (Tara and Jonathan) virtually in the cradle when we started producing the plays. Much too late for that, my youngest child, Jessamyn (by a second marriage), somewhat reproachful about my having left the theater, nevertheless read Beckett when she was just in her teens, in a summer creative writing program—which shows, too, the canonical status achieved in less than a generation. Before that status was certified, however, my son Jonathan wrote a remarkable paper on *Endgame* when he was a freshman at UC–Santa Cruz. It was apparent from the first paragraph, its charged and foreboding abstraction, that he knew the play in his bones. It "does not describe an event," he said, but is rather about the human mind looking upon itself and seeing nothing, "only the suffering of a mind uncalled for." What was surely uncalled for was the attitude of the instructor who—with a sort of obtuse literality and little feeling for a searching thought—made dismissive remarks in the margins of a quite extended essay. As it turns out, I still have the essay and read it again recently. It still seems to me extraordinary, even by graduate standards today. The dedication is belated justice for an ill-considered grade.

Contents

Preface

I seem to remember something earlier, but the first letter I saved from Beckett was typed, dated 21.9.59, and sent from 6, rue des Favorites, where some days later we met. In the small courtyard to entrance C, there was, as if from a picture I had seen, the bicycle next to the trash can, perhaps the model for Nagg's and Nell's. A woman answered the door, reddish hair, ill-fitting suit—I knew nothing then of Suzanne—and said Mr. Beckett was still at his desk. She quickly disappeared, but there he was, rising, wearing a white shirt, tie tucked, face long, graven, thin-skinned, hair severely brushed, standing high in resistance, looking, I thought, like Clov, with the same aggrieved passion for order. In a moment he was impatient with his own slightest negligence, apologizing, muttering, after seating me on the day bed, about something that had been misplaced. The typewriter was off to one side, a new portable used in its case. What he had typed began with the formulary, "Thank you for your letter." The word *your* was inserted by hand, in blue ink, above the word *my*, which had been crossed out. The letter was nothing more than a note, giving me his phone number—all the world can have it now: BLOMET 09.11—and saying he'd be glad to see me. I like to think, however, there was something proleptic in the correction, as if the *my* were *sous rature* (under erasure, as they'd be saying in emergent deconstruction) and—as with a couple of essays in this collection—identities conflated in the slippage of pronouns, his voice momentarily in the grain of my voice.

As I suggest more than once in the essays, Beckett was not only aware of the slippage but sometimes agonized over the perfidy of pronouns, as he was later baffled and even outraged by the presumptions of performance, particularly when they entailed taking liberties with his plays. I will have something to say about that in remarks on directing Beckett, one of two interviews in the collection, gathered otherwise from writings over more than forty years, beginning with the program notes for the productions of *Waiting for Godot* and *Endgame* that I directed in the fifties at The Actor's

Workshop of San Francisco. If my engagement with Beckett came through the theater, it has in recent years taken a theoretical turn, yet personal, equivocal, virtually a habit of mind that, almost from the beginning—in the shift from thinking *about* him to the sensation of thinking *through* him, by means of his thought, such as it was, in the extremity of meaning's absence—also resists the habit. I stopped seeing Beckett for some years (foolishly, no doubt) because everybody was seeing him, and I hesitated for some years to collect these essays, or write anymore about him, because he was overwritten. But among the reasons for the collection, aside from bringing it all together from diverse sources over time, is that time has made it apparent ("that time you went back to look")[1] that nobody who has directed his plays has sustained, from the rehearsal into the writing, with the writing as a kind of rehearsal, such intimately extended reflection upon the unsettling substance of Beckett, turning it over and over, what and how he thinks, its aporetic expertise in "the science of affliction," and—suspended painfully to the point of laughter in the aphasia of desire: "quick grab and on"—its peculiar mixture of stringency and nostalgia.

The title of the collection, moved by the nostalgia, is prompted by a passage from one of the essays, which expresses a recurring theme, though here the titular phrase (from *Endgame*) is floating in a stream of thought initiated by "the constant process of decantation," as well as the intricate language, of his early meditation on Proust: "If Beckett, despite himself, is still turned toward origins or the moment *forgotten as an appearance* in the fluid of future time, from things about to *disappear*—like the sails of the herring fleet or all that rising corn, the mordancy rising with the myth of rebirth, all that *corniness*—he turns away in time, like the painter or engraver: 'Appalled.'" Which is what makes him modern and postmodern at once, or merely confounds the categories.

To stay with what's appalling in Beckett, which even the laughter can't relieve, is to realize too that "category confusion" or the subversions of

---

1. The phrase is from Beckett's *That Time,* but if there's no full reference here that's because what comes to mind in this preface, not quite a memoir, but remembering nevertheless, feels better to me as thought—including texts remembered—without the documentation. Certain of the essays, too, were originally written without it, while others have a more scholarly look, replete with annotations. In any case, I've left them, with only the slightest revision, pretty much what they were, since the range of writings, over many years, will represent the way I was thinking of Beckett through changing occasions and contexts—to begin with, not scholarly. I will not, thus, be providing annotations where there were none.

identity politics or the transgressions claimed by one or another discourse are occurring somewhere in a different order of being. In this regard, the essays point now and then to what in his work escapes or frustrates the ideological leanings of cultural studies today. To the extent, however, that Beckett's writing has foreshadowed or mirrored various theoretical developments, it has become absorbed, again, almost as a matter of reflex, into my own thought, which tried to preserve in theory, after I left the theater, the heuristic energy of what I'd been doing there. The collection includes an essay on Barthes and Beckett (both of whom I met in the same week, when I first went to Paris), while the one quoted from above, "The Bloody Show and the Eye of Prey," is on Beckett and deconstruction, which I'd been asked to talk about at a meeting of the Beckett Society, at a time when theory was just making its way into theater studies (and, as with literary studies, against considerable resistance). As it turned out, the essay was conceived around the rather difficult birth of my daughter, which seemed to literalize the issue of the paternity of the text, in language moving from the Mouth of *Not I* through the Derridean "trick of writing" in the notion of *différance* to the imagining of imagination in the declaration of its death, as if the transcendental signifier were rescued by the gravedigger putting on the forceps.

The immediate source of the performative impulse in this essay was the experimental work I did in the seventies with the KRAKEN group, from which I've derived in a series of books a sort of ontology of performance, what I've come to think of as a subatomic physics, in a circuit of indeterminacy once charged by the work on Beckett. I first wrote about that, from another perspective entirely, as part of a long chapter in *The Impossible Theater: A Manifesto,* which became notorious in the sixties, in its call for decentralization, for the ferocity of its attack on the state of the American theater. That sometimes obscured what the book was also about: a conceptual summing up, after ten years of embattled operation (starting in 1952), of what we'd accomplished, or not, at The Actor's Workshop of San Francisco (which continued till 1965, when Jules Irving and I took over, from Robert Whitehead and Elia Kazan, the directorship of the Repertory Theater of Lincoln Center in New York). Among the reasons for our being embattled were the seminal productions of Beckett, who was by no means then the venerated figure he became. The most remarkable production, for me, was the staging of *Endgame,* but the most legendary is surely the production of *Waiting for Godot* that, after its performance at San Quentin Prison, became the talismanic referent for the Theater of the Absurd, as that was defined by Martin Esslin in his now classical book, which invoked that performance as its prologue.

"Notes from the Underground" rehearses the work we did on both of those plays, while reflecting on the really troubling strangeness of Beckett in the Eisenhower era, with its Cold War rhetoric and Silent Generation, before he was certified by the Nobel Prize. It also discusses what he came to mean in our company, which, despite our growing reputation for taking on unusual plays, resisted him at first. Two of our best and most experienced actors, cast in *Waiting for Godot,* thought I was crazy for doing it and dropped out, one before, one after the first reading, though by the time we did *Endgame* they were ready to jump into the trash cans. By that time, of course, Beckett had been authenticated by the surprising response to *Godot,* with the actors persuaded, as ever, by what they read in the newspapers and the mounting celebrity of Beckett. As for the performance at San Quentin—the first production of any play in a maximum-security prison—when it was first proposed, the prison psychiatrist was vehement about its not being done, because potentially harmful to the inmates, and it was only permitted after a debate before the warden (who listened to the arguments, then tapped me on the chest and said, "This guy's okay, let's do it"). After productions of other Beckett plays—*Krapp's Last Tape* and *Happy Days,* as well as workshops within The Workshop, and a second, quite different staging of *Godot*—his images and language became something like second nature, determining the way we thought about theater in what was during the sixties a dialectic with Brecht, whose *Mother Courage* I had staged in 1957 (its first American production). That was the same year I directed *Godot,* while our production of *Galileo* was almost concurrent with *Endgame,* in 1959.

If Beckett was virtually unknown in San Francisco when we started to produce his plays, the plays would seem to have been a far cry, too, from the burgeoning student protest over the Bay Bridge in Berkeley and the incipience of a generation of dissent with which, given the emerging repertoire, our theater seemed affiliated. But for some on the radical Left—among whom we had developed an avid following—Beckett was not only a departure into the obscure or nonsensical avant-garde, always by nature suspect, but in our case an ideological betrayal. This was especially true after a sequence of productions—*Mother Courage,* Arthur Miller's *The Crucible* (a quick failure in New York, a sensation in San Francisco), and Sean O'Casey's *The Plough and the Stars* (proletarian life-as-it-is on the raucous fringe of the Easter Rebellion)—which seemed to declare and legitimize our politics. That was a period when San Francisco had a Labor Theater and a strong working-class tradition. It was the only city in the country that had assembled a General Strike in the thirties (led by Harry Bridges and the Longshoreman's Union), and it was still the only city, aside from New York, to have a Communist newspaper, in which we were local heroes. Others may have been bewildered or outraged by the non sequitur boredom or—in that sparkling, hilly Baghdad by the Bay—gratuitous bleakness of the plays, but *The People's Voice* was critically more severe: the turn to Beckett was taken as evidence of our recidivism, something of a sellout, which became all the more palpable when, unexpectedly, the production became not only the talk of the town but also (on a scale quite meager in Broadway terms) a considerable success at the box office.

This was in the wake of the McCarthy purges, when California doubled up, with the invidious Levering Act, on the federal loyalty oath—about which I published an angry article, assailing beyond the legislation the leveling acquiescence to a pathology of conformity. Protest could rally around *The Crucible* (audiences were thrilled by the melodrama, though it was one of our weaker productions) but where sentiment turned militant *Godot* was an arty indulgence in European despair, the worse for being effective, the waiting a dead end. I had my own mixed feelings about it—about which, more in a moment—but what our leftist friends saw in Beckett's pessimism, laughter notwithstanding, were symptoms of decadence and evacuated will, its opening line ("Nothing to be done") nothing but the slogan of political impotency. Yet, despite its apparent passivity (the nothing that happens, twice), *Waiting for Godot* turned out to be not merely a freak success but, as I've said about it since, the most consequential *political* drama of the fifties, far more so than the activist drama of Brecht.

This is despite Beckett's having remarked (what's been referred to now and again since it was quoted in *The Impossible Theater*) that "political solutions to social problems are like going from one insane asylum to another." That was many years ago, at a restaurant on the Île Saint-Louis, where—discomfited by his escalating impotency to a principle of being—I pressed him on the issue of theater and politics. He was sipping a dry white wine and I a Dubonnet as we approached the issue at lunch, where (memory refreshed by a journal now), after a mussel soup that he ordered for me, we both had omelettes. If this was not exactly the setting for European despair, the room suddenly became crowded, and a guitarist came up behind him and, when I saw a look of panic, I asked if he wanted to go, and he said it was driving him crazy, then quickly paid the bill, and we adjourned to another location, suitably dank and grim, a film noir café across the Seine. Over beer for him, espresso for me, he came back to the mixed feelings, and I tried to explain why, out there in California during rehearsals of *Godot,* though I directorially kept the faith, it felt anomalous too, that is, a view of the human situation as almost genetically disordered, incurable, without consolation: behind the buffoonery, no fooling, the intolerable downside of existential angst.

The upside, defined by Camus in the image of Sisyphus ascending the mountain with his rock, nevertheless began with a question actually taken up by the tramps in the inept attempt on the tree: "Why not suicide?" The suicidal impulse, and the compelling grounds for it, were certainly there in Beckett's work, however deflected by laughter. But when pressed to the sticking point by another ubiquitous question, "Why don't you let yourself die?" Beckett—like A in *Rough for Theater 1*—can't, though he's thought of it, muster the will. And he could very well have said, if Camus had posed the question directly, what A did: "I'm not unhappy enough!"—the implication being that, in the accretions of misery, he may be so in due time. Meanwhile—as from the very beginning, right after *Assumption,* in the second of his stories, *Sedendo et Quiescendo*—"what more miserable than the miserable being who commiserates not himself, caesura, with a new grief grieves not for his grief." Whether or not we were ready for the ceaseless renewal of grief, our early engagement with Beckett came at a time when engagement, existentially, was the going thing, providing the psychic environment and moral mandate for the work described in "Notes from the Underground." If commiseration wasn't quite the order of the day, we did what we could to justify ourselves—hardly an issue in staging Beckett today—by finding some promise or solace in the hopeless imminence of Godot, or in the paradoxical animation of what would seem a crippling despair, as if the entropic behavior of the tramps were really, like Pozzo's balanced equation of bereavement (someone cries, another stops: "The tears of the world are a constant quantity"), something like a defiance of the Second Law of Thermodynamics.

One might hardly think of Beckett as compatible with D. H. Lawrence, but after describing Didi and Gogo in terms of Lawrence's notion of character, as allotropic states in a physiology of matter, I go on to say—in an exhaustive enumeration of the resources of exhaustion—that "Beckett is out to recover *wonder,*" like Lawrence, too, except for the dismal things Beckett was wondering about. If, at the time we were doing *Godot,* there was a cause in the cause célèbre, "Notes" makes it everywhere apparent—but particularly in my letter to the actors when they were performing in New York—that it was no small matter to rescue our commitment to Beckett from a forbidding despair. By endowing Didi and Gogo, however aimless, with the undeterred patience of the courage-to-be, and letting it be, moreover, in "the absence of a place" (Simone Weil's location for Being-in-itself), *Waiting for Godot,* I wrote, even "restores the idea of heroism by making the universe their slave," as if, somehow, in the merest breath of their (in)existence, it couldn't be imagined without them.

Despite every effort, however, to find something positive and replenishing in the diminuendo of nothing and the debility of the tramps, some feeble prospect in Pozzo's sightless "On!" the immitigable datum was desperation in an elegiac mode. But even the datum seems to sink in the remorselessness of *Endgame,* which Beckett himself called more "inhuman" than *Godot.* (The revulsion against *Endgame* elsewhere can be remembered in critics like Kenneth Tynan, who said he could accept a view of the world as stifling, but not when it came from an "Egyptian mummy"; or Vivien Mercier, who was so repelled that he abandoned a book he was about to write on Beckett.) It may have been some residual naïveté of the time, but even as we were defending the plays, against hostility or condescension, feelings persisted around the company that the psychic content and social implications were somehow out of place, if not exactly un-American—which was actually the view of the State Department (an account of this within) when we were chosen to represent the United States (in 1958) at the Brussels World's Fair and decided to do so with the production of *Waiting for Godot,* as we did again not long after at the Seattle World's Fair. We hadn't yet done *Endgame* when we went to Brussels, but one can only imagine what they would have said at the State Department if we had come up with that instead: "nearly finished" as it began; in its infinite emptiness, "the impossible heap."

When I talked to Beckett about these conflicted attitudes toward the plays, including my own, he listened attentively, looked puzzled, as if by the philosophical error of our confusing despair with defeatism (hadn't he, after all, carried the flag into Roussillon when it was liberated by the maquis, with whom he had served in the Resistance). Another time, when I had made some distinction, relative to his work, about American writers, he said what struck him most in those he'd read (including one I hadn't, and he liked, Joseph Hergesheimer) was the way in which "the will behaves as if it's perfectly free." He saw that too, through the perversity of the will's negation, its *refusal* to act, in Melville's *Bartleby the Scrivener,* a story he linked, with a certain affinity of his own, to Kafka's *The Burrow.* There was probably a further linkage of affinity, though the conversation slipped my mind, when later the KRAKEN group did an extensive project in the labyrinth of *The Burrow,* from which we developed a methodology called "burrowing," about which I wrote in *Take Up the Bodies: Theater at the Vanishing Point.*

We came to "the vastness of the Burrow," I said, describing the manic intensity of that work, "through the circumference of the needle's eye." As it happens, I used that image with Beckett a couple of years later. He had been talking—as he often did (even when he was younger) if asked how the writing was going—about lack of concentration, loss, memory failing, the narrowing down of possibility, which had in the texts that came of it a manic intensity of its own. But the theme again was impotency, which led him to say, however, that there is in some—a Goethe or Yeats, of course— the discovery of other powers out of a sense of loss, or what (though he didn't say it) he came to think of as *lessness.* When I remarked that, as it narrowed down, his work seemed to be extruded from perception as if through a needle's eye, he brightened and said, "Camel . . . ," looked distracted for a moment, as if memory *had* failed, and then he murmured, ". . . wonderful image." As for the creature of the Burrow, which never seems to forget, turning "the mania into the memorable," what I said of it in *Take Up the Bodies,* by analogy with acting process, was in turn pointing to a definition of the actor, or the deep structure of acting, in an always threatened interior space. I might have been talking of the creatures in *Endgame,* or what it takes to enact them, though Beckett might have denied it, as he appeared to when he directed, impatient as he was with the actor who complicated acting. On more than one occasion we discussed this in other terms (and the interviews allude to the issue) but, while he was interested in my speculations on performance, and the work being done with my group, he would have been, for his own decisive purposes in the theater, equally impatient with an idea of acting that draws "upon that part of a self which defines itself by an absence, torn by an awful dependency on an outside which is incessantly disavowed—in that very solipsism slipping away, hiding, disappearing into an absence, its lair, an unfinished illusion of a self." What he denied to the actor, however, Beckett assumed for himself—as I once ventured to tell him—in the lair, burrowed in, the interior space of his prose.

Where the burrowing is Beckettian is in the excruciating exactitude of the "experimental excavations" (Kafka's phrase) that, proceeding upon a fault, are inevitably doomed to failure. Which is, to be sure, if not the fate of acting, almost metabolic in Beckett ("The void. How try say?" as he says in *Worstward Ho.* "How try fail? No try no fail"), an issue to which I return in various of the essays here, as I do to the perceptual cunning that—in every inadequate instance of a self-regarding vision, with its "burnt" "staring," "spent," "famished," "devouring," "clenched," "great moist cleg-tormented," more often than not "accusatory," "unceasing" eyes—comes of failing better, and thus, perhaps for the moment, "the lids occult the longed-for eyes." Indeed, the eyes have it, whether man or woman or beast, as in the case of the gazing Linny, beaten in *All That Fall,* and then again harder, until Mrs. Rooney—who had encouraged Christy to do it, to put another welt on the horse's rump—wants "out of her field of vision" (which reminds me of the great baffled eye of the beautiful wounded horse on the unburnt half of the canvas of Delacroix's *Lion Chase,* from which—that hypnotically anguished look—you wish you could turn away). There may be, deep down, a certain grandeur to it, but no relief from surveillance in the quest of eyes that, with reproach and accusation, is a kind of inquest too.

There may be things in Beckett that are a dubious sight to see, but in "The Oversight of Ceaseless Eyes" I suggest that the eyes have it, too, across the plane of theory into the reification of the visual and, through conceptualism, into performance art. The essay takes off from the observation that Beckett's early, involuted, mandarin reading of Proust had given us a preface (in something of its style) to poststructuralist thought and "the specular obsessions of the discourse of desire." There was also, in the essay on Proust, Beckett's own version of the (now much-studied) technique of the observer, who—as if it were a disease transmitted by Benjamin's flâneur—"infects the observed with his own mobility." Here the compulsion of looking, in a domain of unstable objects, unmoored by the attritions of sight, warps into an almost universal urge for image in the Society of the Spectacle, seen as the consummation of capital by Guy Debord and later as an orgy by Jean Baudrillard. If this "superfetation of image" was replicated by the supersaturated visibility of mixed-media performance, the emergence of conceptual and body art, and related installations, might have been extrapolated from one or another image or sequence or serial occurrence in the theater of Beckett, who also provided prototypes like *Breath* or *Quad.* If much of this, like theory at the time (moving from the late sixties into the eighties) was part of the critique of representation, it was more committed to an ethos of surface than Beckett ever was, though he shared certain misleading appearances with the (anti)aesthetic of minimalism. Nor—despite *Film* and . . . *but the clouds* . . . , and his writing for radio and television—was he quite caught up in the fascination-effect of a world of simulation whose manipulative powers ("obscene" for Baudrillard) were both exploited and exposed in Robert Longo's *The Magic Fog,* to which I refer in the essay, along with Christo's massive wrapping of Pont-Neuf in

Paris. That thoroughly prepared, costly, and prophylactic spectacle may have temporarily protected the bridge, in the age of massive tourism, from the erosion of ceaseless eyes, but it was not exactly the burrowing in which—as if the simulacra were eroded by the liability of solipsism—the work we were doing through Kafka seemed to merge, at least for me (the actors were young), with that done years before on the strange new drama of Beckett.

Solipsism was surely the risk in the experimental excavations of my KRAKEN group, which assumed the liability as explicit subject matter, for which we developed, too, a psychophysical analytic. What required analysis was not unlike that penumbra of value and disturbing sensations in the cylinder of *The Lost Ones,* in which "alone are certitudes to be found and without nothing but mystery." If at times we seemed to be moving through "distinct zones separated by clear-cut mental or imaginary frontiers," the problem was, of course, that they were "invisible to the eye of flesh" (about which, that eye, I want to say more in a moment). There was a period when we found ourselves, in the lower depths of subjectivity, at the limits of performance itself, compulsively tracing an origin that maybe never was crossing in dark and silence to the identity yet to be, which at the point of distinction seemed threatened by something other or—"Who are all these people anyway?" (what I wrote about in *The Audience*)—"other others, invisible, what does it matter?" on whom, nevertheless, you had to keep a cautious eye, all the more when they look like you. That is, "In Short" (the title of an essay here), just about the congenital condition of the never-ending redundancy of Beckett's shorter prose, with its infectious self-reflexion, mordantly self-enamored, rehearsing it over and over (what *it*? *what it?*) because all stories are in vain, or even the stories' dispersion, the ruined or empty words, like his fugitive figures, only futility mirrored, nothing but dispossessed, in the circuitous vanity of their pointlessness.

"All I say cancels out, I'll have said nothing," Beckett wrote in *The Calmative.* But, of course, we don't believe him and look for nothing's meaning, as despite his protestations he was compelled to do himself. There is in certain passages, even Lucky's flailing gibberish, a sort of encrypted cultural history, as when the climbing narrator of *Fizzle 1* declares he is "on the right road, and that he is, for there are no others," though it's hard to be sure—given the menace of others, possibly invisible others—whether he means other roads or other climbers. In any case, about this conundrum, nature has nothing to say: "The fauna, if any, is silent. The only sounds, apart from those of the body on its way, are of fall, a great drop dropping at last from a great height, and bursting, a solidness that leaves its place and crashes down, lighter particles collapsing slowly. Then the echo is heard," going with some re-echo through the recessions of a dying fall. "Then silence again, broken only by the sound, intricate and faint, of the body on its way." If there's any constancy in Beckett, as we look for meaning, it *is* the body on its way, which he could never think of in categories, as merely social construction (racial, gendered, whatever), as we tend to do today. For, like the solid mass that leaves its place and crashes down, the body he listens to through the silence, the intricate faintness of its disappearance, is the body there from the beginning, the deteriorating body, only grown worse with age.

"Die without too much pain, a little," he might say, "that's worth your while." But ill seen, ill said, in whatever ways inept, bereft, or simply out of commission in the drear "comic vast" of this fiasco of a life (and what's the subject here? and if the sentence drifts), the burden of truth is this: "something has to happen, to my body as in myth and metamorphosis, this old body to which nothing ever happened, or so little, which never met with anything, loved anything, wished for anything, in its tarnished universe, except for the mirrors to shatter, the plane, the curved, the magnifying, the minifying, and to vanish in the havoc of images." To the degree that there is a narrative, it is a tortuous parable of origins haunted by end/lessness, in which for the sake of remembrance memory always fails and in which for the searchers or seekers seeing would be believing if there were anything like belief. Which is by no means an exemption from the obligation to *see.* Although the finest particles of observation may also cloud the eye, and the havoc of images is far too tarnished or disenchanted for the tradition of the *voyant,* it's as if what is never to be abandoned in all the "abandoned work" is the modernist mandate itself, which is suggested in the distinctions made between Beckett and Barthes in "The Punctum, the Pensum, and the Dream of Love."

"Is love the word?" asks Words, in *Words and Music.* "Do we mean love, when we say love?" Whatever we mean, in the notorious slippage of the signifiers, or in the self-deluding realm between pleasure and pain, where even sloth and love are elided (as they are in the play), we'd better be strict about it, or as strict as words can be, which is what—as we await the sting of the *punctum,* the fissure to the forbidden, what we're not supposed to see—the *pensum* is all about: the long circuitous, maybe ancestral sentence that, in its double meaning (see the essay for further briefing), carries an obligation too, from which you can't escape, not unlike the Burrow, whatever the fate of grammar. However you think about it, we come back to the "case of eyes," as in *King Lear*—which I staged at The Actor's Workshop, in the immediate fallout of *Endgame*—and as several of the essays do, which I also did in *The Audience,* in a line of descent from the theater work, by way of *Take Up the Bodies.*

Quite aware of the critique of vision in an age of demystification, it was nevertheless in the enveloping site of a specular realm that the burrowing proceeded, as the Beckettian *pensum* did. "As a structure of investigation," I wrote, about the intensely cerebral activity that was a virtual erotics of theater, "the Burrow imposes the puritanical discipline of anointed paranoia," which requires, amid "the indeterminacies of time and motion, an unremitting perceptual vigilance." We can see such vigilance in the obsessional structures of Beckett's shorts, the fizzles or texts for nothing, or around the ladders of *The Lost Ones,* with its nervous searchers and searcher watchers, or those not searching who watch. As for one who supposedly can't, but a "teasing *voyeur*" in his blindness, veiled like a camera obscura, with "stethoscopic ear"—as I wrote of him in *The Audience*—the figure of Hamm, I always thought, was a master of the *art* of vigilance, there in his cell, like Kafka's chief cell, "not quite in the center" but insisting on being there, willfully, furiously, *not* not quite, but exactly *in the center!* as when he's returned by Clov from the hollow in the wall. Prescient, imperious, demonically cunning, there he is, "perfect, a revenant, rooted in a place, rooted in the absence of a place," where—as explored in *Take Up the Bodies*—the idea of burrowing converges with the most basic principle of any acting technique: "Centering." The question remains, however: "What *is* the center? for the actor? for the entire performance? again, approached as a limit, a matter of perception, not a given." Nor quite visible to the "eyes of flesh"—and not only because of the cataracts, on which, when Beckett finally consented, the lasers did their work in a successful operation.

About those eyes, however, Beckett had mixed feelings (see his story *The Expelled),* or might even be contemptuous (*Ill Seen Ill Said:* "Close it for good this filthy eye of flesh," as if it had squinted into the singular), though they were, at least on one occasion, the eyes with which he wanted to see: in this case, my children, whom he had asked about several times and was supposed to meet, and didn't. "The next time you come to Europe," he said, looking at me askance, as if they might not exist, "you must produce them for my eyes of flesh." He never actually saw them, and they (from a previous marriage) regret not seeing him, but as I say in "The Bloody Show and the Eye of Prey"—ravenously vulnerable, fleshed, most complex of eyes—about twenty years later (remarried) I produced another child. Meanwhile, I was wrong in thinking, as in a parenthesis of "The

Bloody Show," that the phrase, "eyes of flesh," had lingered in his unconscious until it was used in *The Lost Ones*.

"You're sure you saw me, you won't come and tell me to-morrow that you never saw me!" Thus, back to the cryptic child who is, in a sense, the seeing eye of Godot, and to Beckett's puzzled look, that day I was raising questions about the politics of his despair. If I've returned to that period again, that's because, nearing the millennium, it's a large part of the century from us and, now that he's become canonical, it may be something more than amusing to recall, aside from derision or dismissal, or even equivocation, certain paradoxes in how Beckett ("Am I as much as . . . being seen?") was being seen at the time. So with the placeless tramps in the vanity of their waiting. It is not irrelevant to the mysteries of the will that, whatever ideological reservations one might have had about *Godot*—its systemic (ab)negations or negative capability or, with the purposeless Didi and Gogo, the curse of a dubious visibility—they seemed to have had the last word on the belabored political issue: the doing nothing, repeated, amounting to something, though in a context far from intention. This might have puzzled Beckett too, but it eventually became apparent that for many young people in particular, some of them sharing its drop-out sensibility, *Godot* was an anticipatory model of what we first saw in civil rights, not the Days of Rage but a simpler endurance, letting it happen, waiting: passive resistance. Many years later, in a talk given at the Smithsonian Institute ("Quaquaquaqua: The Babel of Beckett"), I described his admiration for the letting it happen, when—in his shabby room at the nursing home, Le Tiers Temps, to which he consigned himself in the end—he pointed to the picture in *Libération* of a lone student on Tiananmen Square waiting to be run over by an approaching tank.

That image of the student would appear to have been authentically existential, in the Sartrean sense of identity being confirmed, even exalted, only by its acts. But to return to the Beckettian downside of existential angst: if this were something other, at heart, than Sartre's "existentialism is a humanism," at heart, too, it was not so much inhuman as cruelly humane. When I used that phrase, about what he had called the "clawing" effect of *Endgame*, Beckett—gray face gaunt, stiff hair gray, glasses set in thin steel frames—liked the qualification that distinguished his cruelty from Artaud's, or the exacerbation of it favored by Roger Blin, who had directed *Godot* in Paris. According to Beckett (though, from what I came to know of Blin, this is not quite accurate), Blin considered himself a disciple of Artaud, who—having observed that Western actors have forgotten how to scream—

denounced the theater as we know it because it could never be cruel enough. Whether or not it was sufficient became the subject of disagreements between the two, who were otherwise fond of each other, when Blin later directed *Endgame* and also—though he didn't think it advanced Beckett's work at all ("sentimental," he told me, "like French postcards") and refused to play the role ("it makes me feel old")—*Krapp's Last Tape*. Actually, what Blin really complained about—or did one night to me, after I'd just seen Beckett, and he complained about Blin—was not so much the issue of cruelty but, rather, the unyielding refusal to accede to social and political interpretations of his work, which might have been useful in aspects of staging and stimulating to the actors. Certainly Blin admired Artaud, and so did Beckett, though he didn't approve of the enraptured ethic of ritual violence, with its sacrificial actor signaling through the flames, as if the apotheosis of theater—its naked, sonorous, streaming realization, reimagined from the Orphic mysteries—were nothing but a scream.

Yet much of Beckett's writing, especially when concentrated in the paranoid figments or obsessive iterations of his shorter prose and plays, is an aggravated assault on the nerves. As I say in the final essay, "In Short: the Right Aggregate, the Grand Apnoea, and the Accusative of Inexistence," there are large reserves of violence in Beckett's work, much of it repressed, but there on the surface too, clawing, as part of the ceaseless struggle to give form to the mess that was, for him (with occasional respite, sure, that "lovely laburnum again" or "Alone the odd crocus still at lambing time"), the grievous seriality and sum total of experience. When Harold Pinter spoke of that at their first meeting, perhaps accenting the form, and thus minimizing the mess, Beckett responded by saying he had once been in a hospital when a man nearby was dying of throat cancer. "I could hear his screams continually in the night," he said. "That's the only kind of form my work has."

The first time I heard of the mess—or, rather, heard him use the word—he was writing *Comment c'est,* though it remained unnamable yet, and in that the struggle began, as it always painfully did, since it could never really be named. As he described it then to me, he braced his arms before him to suggest the size of his desk, the containment of that space, containing the violence too, then stared into the table (we were at another café), as if he were writing there, and it were happening then, the going "way down, down, in complete dark, into the mud," alluvial site of the mess, and then he began to stammer through the saga of the man crawling in the mud who meets another man, the man he instinctively torments, the situation always the same, repeating itself to infinity, down in the dark, the mud, listening there for "a voice which is no voice, trying to speak," and he couldn't explain it but tried to explain, "I can't, I must," now the stammer not a stammer but the compulsion of how it is—"I can't. I can't. I can't. I can't."—and all of it a betrayal if it approaches the condition of speech. (Down there in the mud, he says, "writing is like breathing, a tube up to the air.") And what is he listening for? I ask, as he speaks of a point before the beginning where the torment also occurred. "It can go on forever," he says, "listening now and forever, to the process of aging, for the lethal rhythm of death."

If birth was the death of him, as we hear with variations, Beckett's writing about aging may have been, when he began, somewhat premature. But if we grow into our affinities, as he did, this one thickens for me, I am sorry to confess, by my own aversion to the no longer merely pending ("Old enough. Listen") humiliations of age, "Waiting for the hag to put the pan in the bed." Which is a little more distasteful than the waiting for Godot. While the aesthetic of Beckett would seem, as with the narrator of *First Love,* to form itself around death ("And my father's face, on his death-bolster, had seemed to hint at some form of aesthetics relevant to man"), there were, in the earliest declivities of his thought, with its graveyard sensibility, intimations of the loveliness evoked (to be sure, with sardonic longing) in the herring fleet, and with it a sense of transcendence ("Pfft occulted. Nothing having stirred"), as if from the mud, the burial ground, the desperate deep: "I admired in spite of the dark, in spite of the fluster, the way still or scarcely flowing water reaches up, as though athirst, to that falling from the sky." In any case, flowing up or bottoming out—or, as in *Texts for Nothing,* "down in the hole the centuries have dug"—when you get older, you think about death, which is what I say at the beginning of "Astride of a Grave; or, the State of the Art," written for a symposium on "Theaters of the Dead," for which the "charnel house" of Beckett, all the dead voices, speaking at once ("Where are all these corpses from?"), surely qualifies.

Recapitulating the period when we first encountered Beckett, "Notes from the Underground" is preceded in the collection by the two program notes, for *Godot* and *Endgame,* which may function here, memorially, as something like epigraphs. Whereas the drawing on the program for *Godot* showed the letters of the title dancing along with the two tramps in a sort of ebullient Irish jig, with the stain of a yellow moon on a white background—nothing particularly grim about it—the cover for *Endgame* showed the title and the rather cadaverous figure of Hamm, with a large chain necklace suspended from his shoulders, materializing through an abstractly lyrical haze of muddy cobalt blue. The note for *Endgame* was not as strategically lighthearted as that for *Godot;* yet, while we felt the play as more corrosive, ferociously realistic in a subcutaneous way, the despair was seen as ennobled, "haunting the limits of endurance," with a certain biblical amplitude in its implacable pessimism. "An elegy with the passion of the Old Testament prophets," I wrote, "the drama is almost unbearably humane"—anticipating, thus, what I said to Beckett about his cruelty.

If at this distance, the notes seem to me, with enduring fondness, maybe a little callow, they may still suggest—especially in the playfully cautionary tone of the one on *Godot*—how wary we had to be, how careful, in alerting audiences to what, at first, put off our actors, and to the kind of lapsed dramaturgy we were not quite sure of ourselves. While people complained and walked out or stayed (as the note invited them to) for after-curtain discussions to engage in diatribes, the production was, as I've said, enthusiastically received beyond anything we'd imagined. Certainly, we had nothing like the devastating experience of Alan Schneider, when he directed the American premiere at—speaking of the anomalous—the Coral Gables Playhouse in (then) paradisal Florida. Alan and I had our differences over more than the staging of Beckett, but when he directed *Godot* again some years later at the Alley Theater in Houston, he wrote (as others did) to ask if he could borrow that program note, which began with the hapless question nobody asks anymore, "Who is Godot?" and, through an echo of T. S. Eliot (an early influence on Beckett), inflects the drama's absence of action toward the metaphysical: "Do they also serve who only stand and wait?" If they argued about it in San Francisco, I'm not sure how it played in Texas. But when we did the revised staging of *Godot* in another one of our theaters—five years later, in 1962—we used the same program note. In that short period, it was possible to write, as I did in a brief statement explaining that it was the original one, "The performance changes, the avant-garde play becomes a classic, the dilemma remains."

The essays go from the idealistic discoveries of that period at the Workshop, when I was theorizing a future for the theater, to the period of poststructuralism and schizoanalysis, with its performative fiction of a perpetual present in a libidinal economy of gratuitous play, which was an ethos forever foreign to the sensibility of Beckett, for whom, in the play called *Play,* play is deadly. *Jouissance* was still in the air and deconstruction still lively in theory when I wrote "The Bloody Show and the Eye of Prey," which makes particular reference to Derrida's "Structure, Sign, and Play," which itself was an outcome of the sixties and its celebration of play as a refusal of power, as if it were picking up from Norman O. Brown's transfiguration of Freud and, as it entered the counterculture, through *Love's Body,* his notion of "polymorphous perversity," which turned up schizzy later in Deleuze's "desiring machines." By the end of Derrida's essay, however, there were among the signs an indication of the limits, if not burnout, of play in "the *seminal* adventure of the trace," which Freud might have predicted in the scene of writing itself, or as if—the adventure never ending, but love's body a fizzle or fart—Beckett were the exemplum.

We'll come back to love in a moment, the body as always bereft, but one of the last times I saw Beckett we talked about that in Freud, whom he had studied when he was in analysis, and particularly in *Beyond the Pleasure Principle,* which he didn't seem to know, though he knew the death wish as if it were reality principle. That is why, though he was very impressed with the story told by Jung—when he was taken to hear him by his analyst Bion—about the fifteen-year-old girl (was it Lucia Joyce?) who had never really been born, Beckett could never really be at ease with some of Jung's ideas. The birth that never took place, the birth that is no birth, he had no trouble accepting that, and it became a recurrent theme, but the implied continuum of the collective unconscious—"Can't believe in that, can you?" he said to me—it had the stink of redemption or "solution of continuity." And he readily agreed when I said that the dreams recorded by Jung seemed contrived to look symbolic, as compared to the real thing in Freud, whose dream accounts are more convincingly overdetermined (thus endlessly interpretable) and, even if fictive, more like the fiction of Kafka, in which play is deadly too.

We had moved somehow to the letters to Fleiss, when suddenly there was a glow on Beckett's face as he spoke of the heroism of Freud's dying. He asked me if I knew what Freud said about his cancer, then leaned forward, quoted it in German, and translated—in a tone quite different from what he had said to Pinter about the scream—"Highly undesirable." So it was with his own somatic miseries, such as psoriasis or boils or sebaceous cysts in the anus, when the physical mess seemed not only messier but more painful than the mental, though the notion of mess in the mind was, almost in principle, just about steady state until the day he died.

There are also, in the collection, several pieces written after Beckett's death, including an elegy, "The Less Said," mourning him in the fusion of voices suggested long ago, and the essay mentioned before, "Astride of a Grave," which actually reflects on what I had said at memorial ceremonies for the deaths of friends, a sort of memorial of memorials (whose ultimate subject, of course, was risking solipsism again), with afterthoughts on the

Beckett elegy at the beginning and the end. At the symposium for which the essay was written, amid much talk of other cultures and their myths of rebirth—in performance studies today, a sort of anthropological wish-fulfillment—my own aging consciousness turned with a certain dead reckoning back to Beckett, and to the reality principle, as formulated by Hamm in a rage, bedrock real, forget the "talking cure"—in a line that I tend to quote more than any other, though I won't do it again here.

With that principle still in mind, however, let me pick up a prior theme. In "Barthes and Beckett" I speak of that stigmatic intractability, "the irruption of love in the memory of the dead," not knowing when I wrote that the love might persist, with the memory doubled over, though as I look at the phrasing now, it almost prompts me to say, *who knows in what direction?* (But let it go at that, we're staying with the reality.) In that essay I refer to a passage in which Beckett—very young at the time—speaks of the dead in the heart of the survivor, whereupon he observes that, whatever the dead may have suffered in dying, they are exempt from "the despair of the spectator." And it is precisely this despair, introjected in the writings of Beckett, that recurs as the obsessive and painful consciousness of being observed as well as an equally powerful "disdain for the trust in observation which thinks," as I wrote, "like the lover gazing at the loved one, that if you look long enough and hard enough you will really *see*." Which suggests that the obligation I've spoken about before is not exactly a guarantee; but then, who can stop a lover from looking?

The last essay, largely about the shorter pieces, returns to the performative mode, again with an elision of voices. But at a time when identity is being thought of as a nomadic abstraction or a set of digital messages in the interstices of cyberspace, and the litany continues about there being no such entity as a self—the litany nowhere so perplexingly sustained as in the voice of Beckett, intricate and indelible, echoing from the grave—what comes across finally is its unmistakable singularity, to which I attest, in resounding short, through "The Right Aggregate, the Grand Apnoea, and the Accusative of Inexistence." There may be—among the materials here: essays, interviews, program notes, and this preface itself—no *solution* of continuity, but the continuities are there, and in the mode of rehearsal, certain repetitions, with years between them ideas rethought, as there is, for instance, about "the function of the gaze, its cross-eyed uncertainties," as examined in "The Babel of Beckett." That was picked up, actually, from "The Oversight of Ceaseless Eyes," while the notion "pick it up," that final exhortation from the Mouth of *Not I,* was appropriated in "The Bloody Show" as a sort of discursive imperative, on that occasion to the audience, but first of all to myself: finished, nearly finished, but never quite enough, despite his story with that title, so moving you could almost believe it, what was there not to believe? surely better to forget, what could ever be *enough?*

And to be as truthful as insufficiency can be—"What do I know of man's destiny? I could tell you more about radishes"—that was often true when I saw him, not because he wouldn't talk, or was holding too much back, he could be as voluble as he was generous, but the solitariness that was notorious was, if not existential fact, without nothing but mystery at the level of the drives. Or so it appeared to me once, crossing the street to meet him, as I saw him through a window, "Still shy, waiting, slope of indigence, alone at the Coupole. The streets sunny and jammed outside, tables full and vivacious. The American Bar was surprisingly empty, as if the environment was prepared for him." But let me continue somewhat through this not always legible entry from a journal (with slight interpolations) to suggest the sort of view of him that still remains when I'm reading his texts today, more or less inflecting the reading, as that in turn has inflected the remembrance of him here. "He slouched at the table, sipping a tumbler of Irish whiskey, looked up and saw me coming in. Furrows the same, not so hawkish, hair high, blue eyes clear (*not* piercing, but—he said later—cataracts cured, 'I can read any sized print'); shyness, the same, or from too much visitation, habitual weariness, so he asks about *you*," but also because he remembers, and often in some detail. After I told him, "with as much brevity as possible, my part [I won't go into it here] of our somewhat whimsically shared sad story, the same," he said, "'I'm a fumbler, I've always been a fumbler.' 'An exquisite fumbler,' I said. He seemed to like the word, the recognized elegance, amusing. The waiter took my order, 'Martini sec.' 'Avec gin?' 'Non.' He had another tumbler of whiskey, pressed a wad of bills against the waiter's chest, the waiter reluctant to take it, backing off with Beckett insisting, the bills floating to the floor. Nobody picked them up. 'He's Russian,' Beckett explained, 'here since before the war, an old friend.' The money was something new, he handled it as if it were a nuisance." We talked for a couple of hours, the bills still there on the floor.

"What had I been doing in Paris? I said I'd been to the Louvre several days running, to study the 18th and 19th century French, the differences—vast spaces—between Chardin and Fragonard. Chardin's *Raie,* in Beckett's mode; and then, in Chardin as in de la Tour, the uninscribed book, gray spaces instead of words: in de la Tour's St. Jerome and in Chardin's *Le Souffleur* [The Prompter]. Only gray spaces where the words should be. What is there, then, to be prompted? glass blowing? the form of air? So I prompted: why is it, after the stenographic, syntactically decomposed prose of *Ping,* the writing of *Compagnie?* He saddened, or acted so—is it, even his deepest sincerity, the posture, now, of this unpretentious man? fabled figure, trying to live it down. To live the living down, the modesty of it, the sense of ending, still, as it always was. The same. 'It always comes back to the same thing.' But *not* the same? No, it always comes back to the same. That was (meaning *Ping*) the illusion of 'the ellipsis.' (It was another word, *'temptation'?* then *'illusion,'* but nearly the same.) But there appears to be no way to condense it, the same, which demands the repeating and so the expansions, expansions of gray spaces, like the pauses of the plays—as if they were the words, logorrhea of abbreviation, rhetoric of the last words. 'Seul. [Alone.]' We invent second and third persons to alleviate what it comes to, but *seul* is something more, now, than the nothing that came before. 'For a fumbler,' I said, 'you have a terrible desire for coherence and continuity, through the ellipse.'" He nodded, and we talked about Ezra Pound ("always a difficult man, rude") and Giacometti (who knew all the whores in Montparnasse) and whether English (he had been using the word *fréquentation*) was really his natural language anymore ("French is a long shot, English is the close-up"). As usual, though I asked, he wouldn't talk much of Suzanne. It was dusk when we left, nobody else in the bar, the bills spread out on the floor.

I

Who Is Godot?

Never mind. We ain't talking. You sees the play and you takes your choice. But if you must have questions, there are better ones. Who am I? What am I doing here? "You do see me, don't you," cries one of Beckett's heroes to Godot's angelic messenger. "You're sure you saw me, you won't come and tell me tomorrow that you never saw me!"

Always there is something to give us the impression we exist; but habit is the great deadener. It takes a play like *Godot* to remind us that the little rituals of biology, the harmless obscenities of being, help keep us human, and conscious of our humanity. For Beckett, irrelevance is next to godliness. "My creatures," he writes on one of his novels, "what of them? Nothing. They are there, each as best he can, as best he can be somewhere." They mark time by child's play, and their neurotic games, like charades in Hollywood, are exhibitions of cultural hysteria. If they can't remember anything, it is the malady of the age: cosmic thoughtlessness, Pan sleeps, life on the knife-edge of the absurd, a grin to bear it. In the immense confusion, in the enormous buffoonery of the modern soul, one thing alone is clear, they are waiting for Godot to come.

With techniques borrowed from the circus, the pantomime, the music hall, Marcel Proust, burlesque, vaudeville, the daily newspaper, Kafka, the comic strip, and St. Thomas Aquinas, Godot acts out the project of being— just being. The two tramps are nothing but the concrete fact of their waiting. Sans history, sans memory, with nothing but a few carrots, radishes, and verbal scraps and tatters and grease spots from the rag and boneshop of the western tradition, they wait for "the hour when nothing more can happen and nobody more can come and all is ended but the waiting that knows itself in vain." Do they also serve who only stand and wait? Maybe. There are echoes of good classical discretion in this very avant-garde play: Teach us to care and not to care, teach us to sit still.

About some plays the less said the better; about others the more the merrier. About *Waiting for Godot* it is not yet certain whether more or less has been said than should be. After all, who is Godot? Beckett said if he knew who Godot was he would have said so. Was he kidding? That remains to be seen.

(Program note, The Actor's Workshop of San Francisco, 1957)

FIG. 1. An elegy with the passion of the Old Testament prophets, the drama is almost unbearably humane. (Program cover for *Endgame*, directed by Herbert Blau at The Actor's Workshop of San Francisco, 1959; cover design by Robert LaVigne)

2

In Memoriam

It may seem paradoxical to celebrate the opening of a theater named The Encore with a play named *Endgame;* but those who saw *Waiting for Godot* might expect the despair of Samuel Beckett to be more ennobled, and salutary, than the politer optimism of lesser men. An elegy with the passion of the Old Testament prophets, the drama is almost unbearably humane.

Even more than *Godot, Endgame* is a play with magnitude, achieved through the most excruciating constraint. The action haunts the limits of endurance, finding grandeur amidst the trash, trivia, and excrement of living. With an enormous sense of loss and remorseless memory, it sees through the failure of a culture back to its most splendid figures: Hamlet, Lear, Oedipus at Colonus, the enslaved Samson, eyeless at Gaza.

Few characters are more savagely solitary and dreadfully engaged than those Beckett has created for this play. Old endgame, lost of old, every move a crisis—the term taken from chess, the emotions from the world of Buchenwald and Lidice and Hiroshima; extinction a datum, its possibility a commonplace, something we learn to live with. Absurd. With laughter to boot.

When and where is the play set? After an atomic war? Now? Here? Beckett is a writer of whom it is impossible to say just what he means, though we know he means beyond question what he says. And what he says is all there, upon the stage, an immaculate concentration of nerve and mind. He is beyond paraphrase but not beyond sense. This is what exasperates us and forces us back again and again for meanings, for cues and hints, puns, echoes, and ambiguities.

In *Godot* the characters, having forgotten their history, live moment by moment improvising, as though time didn't exist, astonishingly active in a static scene. In *Endgame,* time is the measure and the plague—every action seems the consequence of something prepared moment by moment mounting through unnumbered years. By reflex of the characters we move through an eternal patience, fevered and fierce, through stages of decantation, down corridors of hopeless end. And always, we rage, rage against the dying of the light.

(Program note, The Actor's Workshop of San Francisco, 1959)

3

Notes from the Underground

There is nothing so stimulating as nothing, at least now
and then.
   —Max Frisch, *Diary*

You could not be born at a better period than the present,
when we have lost everything.
   —Simone Weil, *Gravity and Grace*

HORATIO: Oh, day and night, but this is wondrous strange!
HAMLET: And therefore as a stranger give it welcome.

A woman once asked Chekhov: "What is the meaning of life?" He replied,
"You ask me, what is life? It is just as if you had said, what is a carrot? A
carrot is a carrot; that is all there is to it."

I have a feeling he really knew there was more to it than that, but a
goodly amount of art in our time has been created or talked about to put
off people who are always looking for meaning. That is why so much of it
has acquired the reputation of being without meaning. The artists encour-
age this. Eliot says he would tell us the meaning of *Sweeney Agonistes* if he
knew; Beckett says he would tell us who Godot is if he knew. In a discussion after our production of *Godot,* a chemist insisted it couldn't be a good
play because there was no meaning, no message. "I want to know the message," he said, pounding the table.

Well, all you can say to that is, if there is a message it's not glad tid-
ings. And when you're really aroused you may insist in return that an
empirical scientist ought to know better than that—that a carrot is a carrot
is a carrot, overstating the point.

Even so: after we satisfy our aesthetic egos and get rid of the boors by
saying the thing *is,* or "nothing happens, twice," we can settle down and
say a good deal about the meaning of *Waiting for Godot,* as we could
about the carrot if pressed to it. If, however, you work on the assumption
that "A carrot is a carrot; that is all there is to it"—nobody dramatizes the
idea better than Beckett.

As for the despair which is the "objective content" of Beckett's plays, he has given the best answer to that: if it were all dark, everything would be easy, but there is the light too. You might say Beckett begins where Chekhov leaves off. I remember a drawing by Robert Edmond Jones of the last moment in *The Cherry Orchard* as produced at the Moscow Art Theater: a brooding pointillist darkness; a sliver of light, like the vertical beam of the Cross (which you complete in your mind), the slumped figure of old Firs crawling toward the couch to die. Look again: it might be the opening of *Endgame*. Adjust your eyes to the darkness. Now you see the closed shutters, the covered furniture, the spaces on the walls where the pictures had been. The decrepit motion of the servant is the last residue of pure behavior. It is the gravitational field where Beckett works. If you stay with it, it may even become lively. I recall a speech by an official of the Peace Corps, who said that people today *do* want to act. He quoted Confucius: "Better to light a single candle than to curse the darkness." A Beckett play lights a candle *and* curses the darkness.

For a man who has *chosen* loneliness, there is something unreal about the theater, a betrayal: the public premises, the assumption of a contained space, actors, others, an audience. As though in penance, the drama contracts to a needle's eye. The action crawls through the eye out of time, "in the dark, in the dark mud, and a sack—that's all"; or there is "a voice which is no voice, trying to speak" (I am writing from his conversation), then the crawling, the mud, "the form of weakness." When you try to imagine the play before it comes off the printed page, you may think of Beckett's favorite sculptor, Giacometti, whose figures yield, in metal, as much to the air as the air needs to surround them.

The true rhythm of Beckett's plays: "I can't, I must." When the voice rises it can be apocalyptic: "Mene, mene? Naked bodies. . . . Your light dying! Listen to that! Well, it can die just as well here, *your* light."

One might say about Beckett in the theater what Walton said about Donne, who slept in his winding sheet but appeared to preach in Saint Paul's when he should have been on his deathbed: "And, when to the amazement of some beholders he appeared in the Pulpit, many of them thought he presented himself not to preach mortification by a living voice: but, mortality by a decayed body and a dying face." Donne, like Beckett, was a man of great erudition. His most searching devotions were born of the Plague. So in *Godot*, the tramps look over the rubble of the audience and say, "A charnel house! A charnel house!" In one little diabolic canter we have the decay of Western civilization and Beckett's opinion of the modern theater. If, however, the cultural diagnosis seems merely misanthropic, let us go back a few years before *Godot* to another voice, renowned for grandeur and hope: "What is Europe now? It is a rubble-heap, a charnel house, a breeding-ground of pestilence and hate." It is the atmosphere out of which *Godot* was born—the despair, hunger, and disease of postwar Europe—being defined by Winston Churchill.

As Beckett didn't invent despair, neither does he rest in it. Salvation is a fifty-fifty chance ("it's a reasonable percentage"); his favorite parable: the two thieves, one of whom was saved. Because Chance leads Power in the end—Pozzo tied to Lucky—the protective device, the living end, is laughter, "down the snout—How!—so. It is the laugh of laughs, the *risus purus,* the laugh laughing at the laugh, the beholding, saluting of the highest joke, in a word the laugh that laughs—silence please, at that which is unhappy." So Nell: "Nothing is funnier than unhappiness, I grant you that. But. . . ." The laughter dies like the funny story told too often. The trick, perhaps, is to find another way of telling it. Technique again, to baffle the fates, and Time. But when technique fails—as it must—more rage. So Hamm: "Use your head, can't you, use your head, you're on earth, there's no cure for that! (*Pause.*) Get out of here and love one another! Lick your neighbor as yourself!"

The message is clear—but the message is not the meaning. As we wade through the boots, the gaffs, the bicycle wheels, the ubiquitous pipes and spoools, the circular dogs, the colossal trivia and permutations of loss, the spiritual mathematics of his withered heroes and amputated clowns, you may be bewildered. But then you accept them as a matter of fact: fact—each world to its own protocol. For instance: a man needs a hat to think. "How describe this hat? And why? When my head had attained I shall not say its definitive but its maximum dimensions, my father said to me, Come, son, we are going to buy your hat, as though it has pre-existed from time immemorial in a pre-established place." Where did Lucky's second hat come from? It was just there. In our second production of *Godot,* when Didi and Gogo were terrified by the invaders who never came, Gogo hid behind the tree and Didi jumped into a hole we had cut into the front of the stage. Then, using a technique borrowed from the cowboy movies, he tossed his hat in the air to test the enemy. No shot, all clear. One picks up his hat and proceeds. On opening night Didi threw his hat into the air. No shot. But nothing came down. It was perfect. One picks up Lucky's old hat and proceeds.

For those willing to play the game, the acrostics are alluring, the virtuosities entrance. But at the end of the wild-goose chase we are entangled in the net of inexhaustibility. That, rather than exhaustion, is Beckett's real subject. "You're right," says Didi, "we're inexhaustible." That, too, is terrifying. It's funny, but then it's no longer funny. Lest we think the universe too inscrutable to bear: the hat thrown up by Didi (Ray Fry) had stuck in the light pipe above. "So much the better, so much the better." It's the proceeding that counts.

One learns, in doing them, that the plays—with their whoroscopic revelations and buried performances—are always looking in on themselves, throwing up readings, telling you how to do them. If any dramatist has the right to speak of drama as an ado about nothing, it is Beckett. And he means what is *there*. The picture waits to be turned. The window asks to be looked out of. The tree is meant to be done. The empty landscape waits to be recognized. The boots wait to be worn. Beckett may say (at a café in Paris), "that cup, that table, those people—all the same." And yet which of the New Wave—hovering over images with the camera's mind—can invest man-as-object with so much humanity? Why, tree, boot, bowler, and black radish seem more human than the people in other plays.

As for uncertainty of meaning, just perform what he tells you to perform, and you will feel—as if by some equation between doing and feeling—exactly what you need to feel, and in the bones. Climb up the ladder like Clov, backing down the rungs as he must, and you will know why he walks as he does. Speak the speech of Lucky trippingly on the tongue, clutching through all the eschatological gibberish at the loose ends of Western philosophy, and you will know—if you follow the rhythm—the full, definitive exhaustion of thought. Let the tramps and Pozzo pummel you at the same time, and you will know what it is to be "finished!" Try keeping Hamm's chair exactly in the center of the stage, and you will know what a tortuous thing it is to wait on him. Try to hang yourself upon the tree—go ahead, try it—and you will see, decidedly, the degree to which the tree is useless. Eat Gogo's carrot and try to carry on a conversation, and you will know quite materially that a carrot is a carrot.

On the physical level the inexhaustibility of the plays is just plain exhausting. Even thinking is a physical task, not only for Lucky. Look at Didi's face agonized with the effort to use his intelligence. Our actors discovered the physical investment demanded of them in this apparently intellectual play, as they discovered a new conception of character-in-action. Indeed, Beckett has fulfilled onstage the idea of character advanced by Lawrence in his famous letter to Edward Garnett. Not character defined by "a certain moral scheme," but character as a "physiology of matter, . . . the same as the binding of the molecules of steel or their action in heat." Not what the character *feels,* for "that presumes an *ego* to feel with," but what the character "is—inhumanly, physiologically, materially." Lawrence speaks of another ego with allotropic states, in which the individual goes through transformations "of the same radically unchanged element. (Like as diamond and coal are the same pure element of carbon. The ordinary novel would trace the history of diamond—but I say, 'Diamond, what! This is carbon!')"

Like Lawrence, Beckett is out to recover *wonder,* the mysterious harmony of man-in-nature, man-as-nature. But characteristically, like chipping a hairline in marble with a nib, he does this in the form that puts character—in all its flux and transformation—in *separate bodies* before you. By an act of histrionic juggling in which they perform no-action, the two tramps convince us they live one-life. Between them—urinating, eating carrots, putting on boots, scratching the head, playing charades—they compose an identity. While habit may be the great deadener, bare necessity gives energy. The rhythm is a continuum of crossed purposes and lapsed memory. How did they get that way? As Gogo says, unable to recall what happened the shortest time before: "I'm not a historian." For the actors, identity has to be rehearsed into being. As there is no biography, there is no other way.

Nevertheless, instead of demeaning men by reducing them to tramps in an inscrutable dependency, *Godot* restores the idea of heroism by making the universe their slave. They are, as Simone Weil says of Being (in a book with a title that describes the play, *Gravity and Grace*), "rooted in the absence of a place." What would it be without them? "To see a landscape as it is when I am not there," she muses. Unimaginable. "When I am in any place, I disturb the silence of heaven and earth by my breathing and the breathing of my heart."

Because the waiting, for all its avowed purpose, is purely gratuitous, it is bound to look comic—especially when, as with Pozzo, the heart seems to stop. If, like Chaplin, the tramps are victims too, there is a comparable sweetness in the terror. And unconscious power: Godot is concealed in their names.

The movement is circular, like a worn-out wheel of fortune at a deserted fairground, mysteriously turning. Having come out of history like shadows, the tramps are nothing but, and something more than, the concrete fact of the time they pass. And the question of Time in the theater is limned in their every gesture. Time-in-space. If the landscape needs one of them, the one needs the other. And, as we sit superior to their impotence, our whole past vibrates in their ready presence. Patience. The future stirs in the magic circle, wheels within wheels within wheels.

Do they also serve who only stand and wait? There is an exemplum in the stasis. To a country always in danger of floundering in its industry, *Godot* is a marvelous caution.

And with all its pretended anti-drama, we know it is brazenly theatrical—an occasion for Talent: the Noh, the pantomime, the music hall, the circus, the Greek messenger and the medieval angel; the play is a history of dramatic art. There is even the Secret of the well-made play, Sardoodledom's ultimate question: Who is Godot? Will he come? But above all, there is Racine, the great dramatist of the closed system and the moral vacuum, salvaging exhausted *données,* illuminating what was at the beginning almost entirely known.

Someone cries, another weeps—by the sorcery of form Beckett defies the Second Law of Thermodynamics. Energy is pumped back into the dead system by having it come back from the other side of the stage, crippled and much the worse for wear, crying pitiably for help and then behaving like an Ancient Hero, wisdom come from suffering: "Have you not done tormenting me with your accursed time! It's abominable! When! When! One day, is that not enough for you, one day he went dumb, one day I went blind, one day we'll go deaf, one day we were born, one day we shall die, the same day, the same second, is that not enough for you? (*Calmer.*) They give birth astride of a grave, the light gleams for an instant, then it's night once more. (*He jerks the rope.*) On!" In the great mystique of modern helplessness, Beckett's strange achievement is to provide us, exploring the rubble, with the most compelling theatrical image of the courage-to-be.

As character grows fabulous, so does nature—with the same paucity of means. The tree grows leaves, the moon appears in an instant. In this effect and in the knockabout farce, there are similarities to Brecht, who admired the play and wanted to write an answer. The difference: Brecht's moon is hung on a chain; Beckett's "bleeds" out of the sky. If Alienation means to be made strange, coercing you to look again at the familiar, salvaging it from history, Beckett is the most conspicuous dramatist of Alienation. It is another way of describing his subject.

In discovering a style, the effort was to extend the natural into the unnatural, to create the reality of illusion *and* the illusion of reality, to make the theatrical real and the real theatrical, to test the very limits of style and stage. Thus, the actors, who might be going through the routine motions of anxiety, as natural as possible, would move, almost without transition, into the shoulder-to-shoulder, face-front attitude of burlesque comedians. Or Gogo, wandering about the stage in irritation, would suddenly strike the proscenium and cry: "I'm hungry!" The motive was personal, the extension

FIG. 2. Having come out of history like shadows, the tramps are nothing but, and something more than, the concrete fact of the time they pass. . . . (Robert Symonds as Gogo, Eugene Roche as Didi, in *Waiting for Godot,* directed by Herbert Blau at The Actor's Workshop of San Francisco, 1957)

theatrical, the biological urge becoming the aesthetic question. The proscenium had, in our production, no "real" place in the "environment" presumably established by the scenery, but it was an immovable fact in the topography of the stage. It was part of the theatrical environment as a painter's studio is an environment for his painting. Our task in performance was to make such gestures believable moments of action, to reassert the oldest criterion of dramatic truth, to make the improbable probable. Gogo's strike was a criticism, encapsulating years of protest, as if he'd be less hungry if the proscenium didn't exist. The character's problem, the actor's problem, the theater's problem, the philosophical problem, were rolled into his fist.

Needless to say, the proscenium didn't fall.

When we played in New York, an actor who had studied truth objected to another extended gesture by saying, "People don't do it that way." What beguiled us—aside from his certainty about how people do what they do, the different conceptions of reality and style involved—was that he thought we didn't know it.

Godot, indeed, gives the definitive turn to the idea of Alienation. A subterranean drama, appearing to care for nothing but its interior life, it searches the audience like a Geiger counter. No modern drama is more sensitively aware of the presence of an audience, or its absence. There is this consciousness in its most delicate dying fall, when the actors are most intensely self-absorbed. Empathy is controlled with diabolic precision. The Chekhovian silences, the residue of aimless doing, are measured as carefully as in Webern. It is then, in silence, that the whole emotive tapestry of the theatrical event can be *heard.* The music is the most artful polyphony. Listen to the awakened boredom, the very heartbeat of the audience in this superb threnody on desire, mortality, and Time:

> All the dead voices.
> They make a noise like wings.
> Like leaves.
> Like sand.
> Like leaves.
>   *(Silence.)*
> They all speak at once.
> Each one to itself.
>   *(Silence.)*
> Rather they whisper.
> They rustle.
> They murmur.
> They rustle.
>   *(Silence.)*
> What do they say?
> They talk about their lives.
> To have lived is not enough for them.
> They have to talk about it.
> To be dead is not enough for them.
> It is not sufficient.
>   *(Silence.)*
> They make a noise like feathers.
> Like leaves.
> Like ashes.
> Like leaves.

I am talking of *action-to-be-played*. Gogo and Didi are like dully
dressed bowerbirds in what the ornithologists call a "tight arena,"
absolutely attuned to each other but waiting for someone else. Here they
are actually engaged in a competition of sound and image, two *performers*
trying to top each other, while character disappears in the metabolism. If
nobody comes, together they are (the word was said with a beautifully syl-
labified sibilance) *sufficient*, constituting a rhythm. The rhythm is their

FIG. 3. In the great mystique of modern helplessness, . . . the motive
was personal, the extension theatrical, the biological urge becoming
the aesthetic question. (Robert Symonds as Gogo, in *Waiting for
Godot*, at The Actor's Workshop of San Francisco, 1957; stage design
by Robin Wagner)

bower. And as they sit side by side, staring out into the dark auditorium, listening to nothing, who can avoid hearing more of himself and thus becoming a participant in the drama?

"The air is full of our cries," loudest in silence. To live is to be dubious, the acting is a revelation, we are all exposed: "At me too someone is looking, of me too someone is saying. . . ." The play-within-the-play was never so poignant, so particular, in its quiet dignity.

For our company, in the midst of the Silent Generation, Beckett's silence was a considerable shock. And the actor, associating through his own anxieties, had to submit to the rhythm. If *Waiting for Godot* was another testament to the decay of language, it was no mere pantomime of impoverished rhetoric, a mere autotelic gabble of words, words, words. Beckett worked like an engraver or a diamond cutter. And in the best classical French tradition he was purifying the language of the tribe, by referring words back to things, by making things of words. Despairing of communication, some of us were getting our kicks from silence. Thus catatonic jazz, thus dope, thus Zen. I don't mean to simplify these phenomena of the period, but Beckett knows well how deceitful, and lazy, they can be. His personal addiction is to the hardest task. "It is all very well to keep silence, but one has also to consider the kind of silence one keeps." As Roger Blin has pointed out, Beckett is not only prudish, but "In daily life we are confronted with a positive personality; a man who has fought indignities."

If *Godot* was the most authentic revelation in our theater's history, it was some time before we could get to do it. By then it had become a cause célèbre in New York, when Michael Meyerberg asked the support of eighty thousand intellectuals to keep his production going. In San Francisco we could parlay the notoriety into something of an event, but it was more than likely to be a hapless one. Even the actors were wary of the play. Others were revolted. Several weeks before it opened, a sense of disaster circulated around the company. Irving asked me whether I wanted to go ahead. This had nothing to do with rehearsals, where the rarity of the play mostly prevailed. The meaning was becoming plain below the level of meaning. If the play seemed at first sight appalling or remote (and we forget how remote it was a short time ago), it soon acquired the queer presence of the utterly familiar, the beauty of a manipulable thumb trying to undo a shoelace under water.

Some of us became so engaged with the play that when one of the actors baited me at a company meeting until I dropped him from the cast, another one ran down the hall after him, pinned him to the wall, and shouted, "You bastard! it's like running a knife through a painting. You hear, it's a desecration!" We made a replacement, and in about a week I talked him through the play like a catechism, directing by hypnopaedic suggestion. He is a Catholic and was suspicious of the play's despair, but no movie director ever had an actor who succumbed with such simple faith.

"On this soil of Europe, yes or no," André Malraux once put the question quite bluntly, "is man dead?" "No," Beckett answered in his novel *Watt,* "but very nearly so." If we were exempt from that question, *Godot* nevertheless broke through the hostility of our company and our audience. And there was a time when I was almost convinced that this very European play, written in French and translated into English by an expatriate Irishman, was by some miracle of cultural diffusion meant expressly for Americans. As a keynote to his book on *The Theater of the Absurd,* Martin Esslin

FIG. 4. If the play seemed at first sight appalling or remote (and we forget how remote it was . . .), it soon acquired the queer presence of the utterly familiar. . . . (Jules Irving as Lucky, with Eugene Roche as Didi, Robert Symonds as Gogo, in *Waiting for Godot,* at The Actor's Workshop of San Francisco, 1957)

has already described our experience with the production at San Quentin, where fashion could hardly have been the reason for the play's success. The word *Godot* has since become a clinical term at the prison, where a good portion of the inmates had, before our production, never seen a play of any kind. They knew nothing of the play's notoriety. Nor did it appeal only to their sense of confinement. As a teacher at the prison remarked: "They know what is meant by waiting . . . and they knew if Godot finally came, he would only be a disappointment."[1] *Godot* was the very subtext of an "International Style."

Though the San Quentin experience was, in the performance, almost surrealistic (I sat among the inmates, who tossed matches in the air) and in the response, one of the purest we have ever had, it was a while later that I had occasion to define our own relationship to the play. In 1958 we were invited to represent the United States regional theater at the Brussels World's Fair, and we chose to play *Godot*. Prior to the trip abroad, we were to play six weeks in New York. I went there with the cast but returned to San Francisco after two weeks to start on another production. At the conclusion of the run the cast was to go on to Brussels without me.

Unlike the performance at San Quentin, the opening in New York was a terrible disappointment. To begin with, there were murmurs before our arrival about letting this pessimistic foreign play be performed as an American offering at the fair. The New York representatives of the State Department's Performing Arts Program, possibly rattled by newspaper criticism of our selection (adverse publicity makes everybody quaver in New York), didn't even show the courtesy of greeting us before we went abroad. Heat and humidity were high that summer; we felt the coolness. As for the performance, it began (I thought) with all the verve and precision that had been so triumphant in San Francisco and on other tours, but the audience seemed frozen too. Through the whole first act there was hardly an audible reaction to any one of the reliable lines or pieces of business that had enjoyed more than a year and a half of success in our own theater. Could San Francisco be that provincial? The actors nearly panicked, but by sheer doggedness they aroused some response in the second act. When I had gone backstage at intermission, one of them said, "We'll show the sons of bitches!"

The reviews were mixed, the talent of the actors couldn't be denied, and the houses were as good during those six weeks as anybody expected. But during my stay in New York no suggestions I could make, no dressing-room critique could restore full confidence and spirit. Maybe we had been playing it too long. In any case, the actors were going through the motions, showing mainly technical skill, and I left New York with misgivings about the appearance in Brussels, wondering too whether in our previous revivals and in rehearsals before the trip there hadn't been a mechanical set that I had hoped would disappear in the excitement and purpose of the tour.

About a week before their departure for Brussels, after they had been plagued by the snub and the heat, and then a State Department ban on our stage manager for unspecified reasons, I decided to write the actors a letter, in an effort to review the basic impulses of the production. The affair with the State Department had made the Brussels trip all the more meaningful, because we were now going under protest. After he was first informed of the ban, Irving (who was playing Lucky) and I exchanged long-distance calls and decided, after much legal counsel and because the choice of *Godot* was already an issue, that the strongest action we could take was not to refuse to go—we had the impression they would just as well have been rid of the play—but to go to the Fair and make the production work and to publish widely a denunciation of the ban. When the State Department—to which we showed the protest in advance, hoping they would change their minds—tried to persuade us against publishing it, saying it would be embarrassing to the Performing Arts Program at the fair, we said that, if America wanted a good reputation abroad it ought to learn how to behave at home. To which we added: "We have no political character, except that we cannot abide political censorship of our work."

The protest was, indeed, picked up by the news services and the foreign papers, and when the company arrived in Brussels, there was a great deal of extra-aesthetic attention to the production. As for the eyebrow-lifting over the choice of *Godot,* we had contended before that the risk was worth taking, that Europeans would prefer it to *J.B.* or *Carousel* and soda fountains, that the play was one of the seminal dramas of the postwar era, that Europeans would not only be interested in seeing an American company perform it, but they would be impressed that Americans could have some sense of the peculiar anxiety and dread underlying the European recovery.

Our view was confirmed. The performances were wonderfully applauded. The interpretation occasioned much discussion by theater people, who remarked especially on the Chaplinesque comedy of it. Moreover, it outdrew everything—we were told by the State Department—except Harry Belafonte and the jazz concerts. As I do not believe the protest was responsible for that, let me not imply that my letter to the cast remade the performance. I quote from it at length now because neither my notes nor my production book will convey more immediately the directorial problem involved, the character of our work on the play, and the ultimate motives behind its original production. What the letter demonstrates (aside from the high-minded idealism that, in the atmosphere of the time, went into building a company) is the degree to which *Godot* had provided us with a vocabulary for our own condition:

"At this distance I can hardly pretend to be an authority still on your performances. But I am restive with intuitions and would like as usual to have the last word—this time before you take off to Brussels. These are my considered reflections and my blessings. If they range beyond *Godot* itself, they may by indirections flush directions out.

"I was, not to begin too solemnly, disappointed by our reception in NY and by our initial response to it. The response was natural enough; pride only makes me wish it could have been otherwise. Perhaps that was impossible under the circumstances of heat, hostility, and what seems to be a proprietary interest in Beckett or a naive contempt for him. But your disappointment had its fly open; it was profoundly on stage at most of the performances I saw, either in a sluggishness that verged on resignation, a caution unbecoming your talents, or a determination (admirable enough) that made you strain to show the bastards when you weren't saving yourselves. You never quite showed them what I have seen, and I suppose the most irritating result was not the intolerable comparisons . . . but the faint praise and blind phrases that hurt all the more because they were kind. You were not, we all agreed, so brilliantly received as in our richest fantasies. The fantasies were natural, too; something makes me wish they could have been otherwise.

"For I should like our work to be more pure, more selfless (hence deeper to the Self), less deluded, and more durable. I don't think we have reached the point yet in The Workshop where we are perfectly at home with this grand conception of our vocation. But I hold these truths to be self-evident, that neither fame nor fortune means as much as the personal integrity of art and that to lose faith in the face of disapproval of what you have believed to be good and true is not itself good and true. This happened, however briefly. You were stricken. So was I. I hope you have recovered, because you are not going to Brussels merely out of dedication to The Workshop or to prove anything to the world. . . . I should like to believe you are going to perform—as the word generically implies, to complete, to carry out to the finish, to perfect, the action you have begun. . . . You are committed, personally, each to yourselves. I should like us to reach that serenity in our collective work, someday, when we are proving nothing to anybody, even ourselves. Here we are. On the stage. We begin to act, for whoever happens to be looking, but more, for the sake of the action itself . . .

"I used to think of our production as a Noh, an accomplishment, with something ritualistic and devout about it. I don't mean to be sentimental; I think you have all felt something of this yourself—and our audiences too. . . . But there are dangers to devotion; you close your eyes. I think we have, through negligence and necessity, and through intimacy, come to take the play for granted and moved away from its nature.

"Let me clarify this. Remember in our first discussion of the play a drawing by Paul Klee that I showed you, of an Egyptiac-Negroid woman with a rat growing out of her hair? The effect was grotesque and funny at once. I said then that unless you grasp the play's morbidity (seriousness is not the same thing), you'll never gain its humor. Intimacy has made the play less strange and less repulsive, and whatever gain that may be in catholicity of taste, it may be necessary to recall your first experience of it to perform it again with maximum force. The performance needs a sense of wonder. You have to be alive to the landscape of the play and its many marvels, for it is an Odyssey of a kind, though it stands still. Its action is a beautiful tension of buffoonery and gathering darkness, inevitable refrains and seizures of truth, asceticism and acerbity, and a ruefully inadequate humanity. I remember Gene [Roche] telling me before we left SF that someone had told him that the play was not, when he saw it, serious enough, and Gene defended it by saying that we saw the comedy in the play. We did. But we saw much more. Only I think that Gene, with his alert and vivid sense of humor, slights, as we all have, the remorseless pessimism of Beckett. The drama, take it or leave it, offers very little in the way of salvation and you must, for the duration, live with the pittance it offers. Without accepting the next-to-nothingness that Beckett gives, you will never achieve the proper intensity of desperation. Didi and Gogo are incurable patients locked in an eternal Patience, sad, lonely, dreadful, without avail, two hands clasped in numbed fear and trembling:

> We are the hollow men
> We are the stuffed men
> Leaning together
> Headpiece filled with straw. Alas!
> Our dried voices, when
> We whisper together
> Are quiet and meaningless
> As wind in dry grass

Or rats' feet over broken glass
In our dry cellar
Shape without form, shade without colour,
Paralyzed force, gesture without motion. . . .

"Pozzo and Lucky are gesture with motion, motionless. Beckett's sense of the human condition, what makes it ironic and universal, is not that they are trapped or condemned, but they are condemned to be free. Any way you look at it *condemned* sounds like *damned,* and you have a world with all the symptoms of original sin and neither cause nor recourse.

"The rhythm and the meaning, the power and the glory, are in total surrender to this state of being; one's own optimism, negligence, or cosmic indifference cannot be imposed upon the plaintive and static anxiety of the play. And since the play was created so obviously with piety, like a stylistic prayer, you betray it by carelessness. And betray yourselves. In literature of this sort, precision is next to godliness. . . .

"I think you've had your fill of NY, but be sure you've had your fill on aesthetic grounds too. Ask yourself what you might have thought of your stay if you had been much better received. I am as much concerned about your return here as your stay in Brussels; each time I go back to NY I am more than ever convinced that with all our frustration and floundering, we know better what we are about, and that a theater worth the effort of decent artists cannot be built without vision. . . .

"At the risk of wandering, the trouble with the NY theater is not merely that everybody acts alike, as they do. The more serious trouble is that they act alike because, minor reservations aside, they see alike. At Stratford, there is in my opinion no grasp of Shakespeare not because American actors have not been taught to gesture gracefully or tell a pike from a halberd, but because the American theater, even when it speaks trippingly on the tongue, gives only lip service to the Shakespearean reality, which includes an allegiance of spirit to the absurd, the destructive, and the demonic, that is at the heart of *Godot,* and that is systematically expunged from the Broadway theater as we mostly know it. Broadway has ejected the Devil; it had made fashionable peace with evil by labeling it. *Godot* has the real devil, the good old-fashioned Devil that floats on the face of the deep and grins like a blessed idiot. Its sympathies are not with the party in power, with the belongers, even when they are social liberals; but with the outsider, the way, way outsider. Broadway . . . pretends to love the outsider . . . but really patronizes and insults him. We are a culture given to delusive togetherness and the most frightfully egocentric group therapy; we are a culture playing it safe because we know no other way to play it. But we are not safe. Like it or not, we are on the edge of the absurd and . . . the direst problem of our time, in a labyrinth of power politics and infinite bureaucracy, is to make yourself known, to be felt, to let somebody know you are here. 'You do see me, don't you?' That, in a country given to knowing people by statistics and cocktails, is the heart of the matter. The problem, I know I am repeating myself, is not who is Godot, but who am I? And I do mean you. And as you assess your stay in NY and your purpose in Brussels, your purposes indeed as actors in the American theater, the foremost question in your minds should always be: Who, really, am I? What, really, do I want? What am I doing here? . . .

"True, by all popular and conventional American standards, Beckett is on the Devil's side. But remember, as the Reverend Hale said [in *The Crucible*], an instant before the Devil fell God thought him beautiful in heaven. I am twisting the point as the devil's advocate, and maybe obscuring it too. Simply this: as regards *Godot,* we have made our choice, let's live with it, beautifully. And whether they like you or not in Brussels, if you have done what you have done with courage and conviction, 'Be secret and exult, / Because of all things known / That is the most difficult.' "

I would eventually be qualifying my position as the devil's advocate, but it was that spirit of secret exultation that was even more wondrous in *Endgame*—in my opinion the most profound drama in the modern theater. It was also probably the most perfect production we have ever done at The Workshop.

Endgame is a play with a tenacious memory. One may understand more about it by contrasting it with Godot. For some the difference may be marginal, but in Beckett, a dramatist of the selvedge and salvage, the margins are immense. If the characters in Godot suffer from lapses of memory, that has certain disadvantages for behavior trying to place itself. Rational discourse depends on propositions that have gone before; you have to have something to refer to in order to proceed. All consecutive argument depends on memory and when, exasperated by an empty stomach, you refuse to be a historian, that's the end of consecutive argument.

Still, not being a historian has compensating advantages for behavior, which also likes to take its head. The lapses of memory are liberating. Unimpeded by custom, form, tradition, ceremony, canon, and code, all the restrictive appurtenances of the past, behavior becomes vital, improvisational, with a childlike sense of wonder, a thing unto itself. It is. A pebble in a shoe is a catastrophe, that carrot is really a carrot, never to be forgotten. Or so one thinks. Whatever one thinks, *Endgame* puts it to the test. The title taken from chess—the crucial, deadly terminus of the game—one has a sense of looking back through thousands of years of cultural history at almost every instant. One feels inside those gray walls, as amid the odalisque splendors of Stevens's *Sunday Morning*, the dark encroachment of old catastrophe. History dank and stagnant, ineliminable, the characters forget nothing. Thus, we have an intensification of the Hamletic condition, the maximum impediment of what Coleridge described as a "ratiocinative meditativeness." All motives present at once, moved equally in opposite directions, Clov can barely act. (There were times in rehearsals when Tom Rosqui, playing the role, nearly passed out by concentration to brain fever.) The choices are marginal; the stance is indifference; the effect is excruciating. We are in Artaud's Theater of Cruelty, at the dark root of the scream, unbearably humane. What is amazing about the play is its magnitude. Haunting the limits of endurance, it finds grandeur amid the trash, trivia, and excrement of living. More than any modern drama I know it creates explicitly that place where Yeats said Love has pitched its mansion. And it does this by converting an enormous sense of loss into a retrospective vision, reaching back through the failure of a culture to its most splendid figures: Hamlet, Lear, Oedipus at Colonus, the enslaved Samson, eyeless at Gaza. This vision turns up in the acting out, affecting style. The characters are savagely solitary and dreadfully engaged, the engagement impacted by paralysis. In comparison, Didi and Gogo—having forgotten their history—live moment by moment improvising, as though Time didn't exist, astonishingly active in a static scene. In *Endgame,* Time is the measure and the Plague. Every action seems the consequence of immaculate preparations mounting moment by moment through unnumbered years. Again Patience, but fevered and fierce, moving by delayed reflex of the characters through stages of decantation, down corridors of hopeless end. And there is rage, rage, against the dying of the light.

At our first rehearsals I kept emphasizing the savage dignity of the play and the great figures in the background. But in looking back through the grotesque image of the master Hamm, whom Clov attends with his rage for order, I had forgotten to mention another character, of whom I was reminded in the foyer of the Comédie Française. There, encased in glass, is a large chair, its leather long worn—the chair in which Molière was supposed to have died while playing *The Imaginary Invalid*. (Biographers tell us he died after the performance, but the other is the kind of story that, if not entirely true, should be.) Now, if in some way the mind creates its world (nothing either good or bad but thinking makes it so), you can become sick

FIG. 5. . . . the dark encroachment of old catastrophe . . . . Every action seems the consequence of immaculate preparations moment by moment through unnumbered years. (Tom Rosqui as Clov in *Endgame*, directed by Herbert Blau at The Actor's Workshop of San Francisco, 1959; designed by Robert LaVigne)

by playing sick long enough. Blind and paralyzed in fact, Hamm is in this
sense an Imaginary Invalid. He is given to an excess of that self-dramatiza-
tion which mars and aggrandizes the Shakespearean hero; like Othello or
Lear, he savors his grief and his role.

After the dread pertinacity of Clov's opening mime and the mournful
cadence of his first lines, Hamm stirs and yawns under the bloody handkerchief which covers his face. In the production we decided to meet head-
on the problem of stasis in relation to Time: the opening mime, before the
ritual unveiling of Hamm, took anywhere from twelve to fifteen minutes
without a word being spoken, with hardly a sound in fact. When Clov,
after about ten minutes, opened the curtains of the small windows with a
sudden jerk, the scraping of the curtain rings on a brass rod was a major
"event." That one action was prepared by improvisations in which, at
times, he took several minutes to pull the curtains apart. The single gesture
was an expressive condensation of all the remembered effort. Since there
was as much reason for not pulling as for pulling, by the logic of the play
the action might have taken an eternity.

In this context the stirring of Hamm was a "miracle"—and it was
waited on as such. If Clov revealed the ashcans by some untraceable canon
law, lifting the sheet like the cloth from a chalice, he folded Hamm's sheet
with devotional care, painstakingly each fold, and the actual unveiling
before that had all the grace of a matador in his moment of truth—the
physical feat was to remove the cloth in one swift gesture, without disturbing by more than a dove's breath the handkerchief on Hamm's face. It was
grueling for Clov. It seemed to be, for no reason, his duty. But the privilege
of lifting the handkerchief itself—always a temptation to Clov—that was
Hamm's own.

"*Very red face. Black glasses.*" Under the glasses, the blank eyes
("they've gone all white") like the hollow sockets of a pagan statue; the face
red from congested blood, suppressed rage, and the intensest narcissism:
"There's something dripping in my head. (*Pause.*) A heart, a heart in my
head." If Didi and Gogo listen to the atmosphere and hear the pulse of the
audience, Hamm bursts out at the audience and loses himself in his pulse.
The actor takes his cues from the throb of his temple. Action: listen to your
life, damn you! The issue of subjectivity in the art of the actor comes to its
dead end, vitally. He is his own object. (Or so he says, thinks):

Me—
(*he yawns*)
—to play.

(*He holds the handkerchief spread out before him.*)

Old stancher!

(*He takes off his glasses, wipes his eyes, his face, the glasses, puts
them on again, folds the handkerchief and puts it back neatly in
the breastpocket of his dressing-gown. He clears his throat, joins
the tips of his fingers.*)

Can there be misery—

(*he yawns*)

—loftier than mine? No doubt. Formerly. But now? (*Pause.*)

My father?

(*Pause.*)

My mother?

(*Pause.*)

My . . . dog?

(*Pause.*)

Oh I am willing to believe they suffer as much as such creatures can
suffer.

But does that mean their sufferings equal mine? No doubt.

(*Pause.*)

No, all is a—

(*he yawns*)

—bsolute . . . .

And with that yawn, indifferent and cosmic, Hamm fractures the
absolute. There is a sough of history in that joke, the crossbreeding of
satanic laugh and sonic boom. It is the somnolent zero of the Cartesian
abyss, the penultimate sigh of romantic irony. Can things be that bad? It is
to laugh, as they say. Beckett—and to a large extent Hamm—is precisely
aware of the possibility that the world may turn into his own worst fears, if
it is not that already.

In exploring the beauty, let us not minimize the gloom, the antarctic
frost of vast emotion. There is reason for withdrawing, and as our production gathered devotees, I felt like Hamm, enraged by the ritual performance
of those who came to it for negative kicks, without the discipline of Clov,
who would not pull back the lids and look at the eyes while Hamm was
sleeping. The play is indeed forlorn, taking place as it does—water out one
window, land out the other—on the cracked landscape of extinction. "Finished, it's finished, nearly finished, it must be nearly finished." Dread and
desire, in contemplation of the imminent "little heap, the impossible heap."
(How does Clov read the phrase "must be nearly finished"? Speculation or

aspiration? There are countless choices like that to be made. The actor may stress the first and think the second.)

Endgame deals with "abstractions" of character (allotropic forms), but abstractions attached to our nerve ends. Once again we are dealing with man without a local habitation and a name, dispossessed and deracinated, apart from the propriety, promise, and facile redemptions of region, home, family, custom—which are not absent, but cut down to their stumps. Its memories of the past are, however laughable, full of regret for its passing; and it reminds us of a heritage, worthy, but next to impossible to sustain. The actor must be very aware of these resonances, they must come to mean something to him.

In one facet of its being a play like *Endgame* is so appalled at the human condition, it can hardly speak. The compulsive talk, when it occurs, is the distress signal of silence. The language of excommunication. Its view of the future is the whisper of the faintest perhaps. In this respect, it is the consummation of other dramatic visions of our century, from disparate sources: the final words of Mr. Kurtz in Conrad's *The Heart of Darkness,* "the horror, the horror"; the desperation of Willie Loman's "I've got no seeds in the ground"; the image of Mother Courage careening through the void of the empty stage, with its attendant feeling that "the world is dying out"; and the more genial despair of the early O'Casey, "the whole worl's . . . in a terr . . . ible state o' . . . chassis!" The parallels are endless, going back in nineteenth-century drama to, say, the old wives' tale of such a schizoid play as Buechner's *Wozzeck,* where the universe is like an empty pot, and "everyone was dead and there was no one left in the whole world."

It's an old Story, no less truthful for its repetition but encouraged by its repetition (thinking makes it so). It's funny, but then it's no longer funny. Ubu mourns and becomes Clov. The laughter turns elegiac, fading through the twilight of the gods. A friend of mine once objected to *Endgame* because "You can't call the characters on the telephone." True. But if you could, you'd only be talking to yourself. *Endgame* is the crisis of exhaustion playing itself out in the suburbs of hell. It has the eloquence of blood beneath the eyelids of the nearly dead. It comes out of the world of men and affairs like a scarcely audible bell out of the enshrouding fog—no less alarming for its remoteness. It is just such a story as Horatio might tell if he tried to fulfill the impossible burden placed on him by Hamlet in those exquisite dying lines: "Absent thee from felicity a while, / And in this harsh world draw thy breath in pain / To tell my story." How tell it? Where that story really took place, Horatio never was. To tell it, he'd have to reenact the play, he'd have to become Hamlet. But wasn't it he who said, " 'Twere

FIG. 6. . . . the crisis of exhaustion playing itself out in the suburbs of hell. It has the eloquence of blood beneath the eyelids of the nearly dead. (Robert Symonds as Hamm, Tom Rosqui as Clov, in *Endgame*, at The Actor's Workshop of San Francisco, 1959)

to consider too curiously to consider so." Failing to tell the story, he'd become Hamm.

In such a play, rehearsing visions of greatness around "the insane root," the magic is blacker than we might like; but you can't run away because where in the world would you go? No modern drama comes closer to making you feel what Socrates meant when he spoke of "a doctrine whispered in secret that man has no right to open the door and run away." There is no more poignant moment in our theater than when Clov, responding to Hamm's request for a kiss, says no; there is no braver moment than when Hamm discards his properties, his dog and his whistle, retaining only his stancher to support his Self in defiance of Nothingness. Yet, choosing estrangement, he is dependent in bristle and bone—and the play's black art awakens our will to survival by cutting us to the quick.

There was nothing more regenerative in our repertoire.

And this was also true of Style. If *Godot* made us significantly aware of barriers to cross, with *Endgame* we made a decided leap. I am talking of the whole visceral life of performance, which was to a large extent prompted by the scenic idea. For it was with *Endgame* that the eye-opening blitz of modern art came most subtly and vividly into our theater.

We did a second production of *Godot* after we did *Endgame*. The first, designed by Robin Wagner, was enchantingly "seen," but it was more deliberately "symbolic," with the clean Gothic line of a romantic ballet. There was a huge black backdrop with raggedly etched streaks of white and gray cloud. It was somber but very handsome. There was even a certain luxury in the bare tree, bent like a willow (or a question mark), two low branches twisted into the shape of Rosicrucian crosses; or, since there was nothing exactly to be read, a pair of crossed fingers. Above two molded levels there was a hint of barbed wire strung from three stakes. They might have been telephone poles on an abandoned road; the perimeter of a junk yard; or a concentration camp; even, vaguely, a circus. The action, suited to the impeccable bleakness of the open spaces, broke out of deepest melancholy into dance: a gavotte of musing. If nothing were to be done, it could be done with the most meticulously orchestrated activity. *Endgame* was similarly orchestrated, but every move was made at great cost—and the reason could be read in the nonobjective surfaces of the walls. How they came to be the way they were is worth looking into, in view of all the current urgings for our theater to catch up with the discoveries of painting and sculpture. For there are dangers, particularly as the "anti-form" of Beckett develops into a new Ashcan School, with ragtags of cadence and attitudes that are gratuitously worn, as though carrying by some willful assumption of feeling the burden of thousands of years of culture. With Beckett every discard is deeply felt. (I remember Roger Blin saying, after he dropped out of the role of Krapp, that he was tired of the Absurd. Coming from him, the most relentlessly disaffiliated *régisseur* in the French theater, that was quite an admission. Beckett had worn him down. When I returned from France,[2] I asked Bob Symonds—who had been playing constantly in *Endgame*— how he felt. He said: "I feel terribly old.") Innocence having ended, however, some of our young artists try to sound as if they were born to a dying fall, prematurely ancient.

Axiom for Absurdists: in art, even decay has to be earned.

About the time of *Endgame* I had been rereading Mann and thinking much about modern painting. Ruminating on Beckett, I thought of Cézanne. There were other places from which to look, but you could see the Magic Mountain from Aix. As I mused over Sainte-Victoire, I could see Hans Castorp aloft with his *petite tache* and Cézanne below with his *petite sensation*—the Wound and the Suture, the one a symptom of cultural disease, the other of the technique that, pat by inexorable pat of pigment, tried to seal it off against itself. (They came together in Hamm's stancher.) Rilke describes how Cézanne, aging, went about his little town between furious labors, guessing at the horrors without from the slightest deterioration within: "Ça va mal . . . C'est effrayant, la vie." For some, it was better not to look. The nineteenth century, with its passion for analysis, had looked too much. But if looking could take away, seeing could restore. It was a more stringent optical analysis—the oscillant contours and the facet-planes, the packed mosaic of the incorruptible gaze—that salvaged the reality of the apple from the wear and tear of history.

Not only life but the technique had something hermetic about it. The risk was tyranny. Cézanne's was one of those astonishing efforts of modern art to avert the time-serving disaster of experience by bringing form to its knees. At its most harrowing, there was a strange airless beauty about it, like James's Millie Theale, "heiress of all ages," who was also the "survivor of a general wreck." Like Proust (whom Beckett studied). A little grace goes a long way, and for all his doggedness and insularity, Cézanne opened vistas for the Cubists and others. Yet, through no conscious fault of his own, there seemed to be a dead end in the middle distance. The record is there, and I am no authority. But despite the ferment of all the *isms*, after two wars it no longer remained a question for some artists of redeeming the apple but, rather, what do you do with the funeral baked meats?

Cézanne tried to see things into being; now we can hardly believe our eyes. Max Ernst said "the object sees itself in me"; now the object, whatever it may be, may have reasonable doubt that we exist.

Thus: a good deal of our visual art is Lidicean, dreaming on vacancy. Born of relativity, rapes, and incinerators, it studies lasers and talks of "breakthrough." It has the texture of fallout. Look at it: the abscessionist canvas, the collage, the combine painting, the whole Tachist and tacky assemblage of gouge, slice, muck, and slime. The best art, Louis Aragon once said, might be produced by placing a stick of dynamite under a cathedral. Our most advanced art is a connoisseur of the rubble; annihilating the past, it lets nothing go to the junkyard. The stove pipe, the gear boxes, the slime of glue, the fur-lined teacup, the prophylactic, the umbrella ribs, and the severed hands of dolls—everything has its history, inescapable. We have made a ceremony out of what Artaud calls "the revenge of *things*."

I am not being pejorative. Art has its own reasons. And its own defense policy. In its fierce sluice and savage thrust it may appear to contend with the social wound by doing injury to itself. But, by the perverse logic of the new logistics, self-abuse is a mode of deterrence. In its desperation to keep things alive, some of the art reminds us of the fertilizer marches of backward countries. I have talked of it before: salvation by excrement. (They say that in Communist China some of those who march with leavings in their hands refuse to wash as a badge of honor.) In its remedial aspect it is the art of proctological science. As *mythos*—and this is the dramatic image behind its hallucinated forms—it is the manger without the Magi, but maybe a couple of deadbeat clowns. It believes, by compensation, in Magic. And it has a sense of humor, because all the horrendous incongruities sink to the base court of comedy—which, the most artful of forms, thumbs its nose at art. Appearing improvident, it practices a frugal economy. "Thrift, thrift," said Hamlet about those funeral baked meats. Collage and combine, like Beckett's plays, are the lumpen-heirs of *Poor Richard's Almanac*: junk-wise, crap-happy, they save everything.

There are many sources of the new anti-drama, from *To Damascus* to Harpo Marx, but one of them is Duchamp drawing a mustache above the Giaconda smile. It has something in common, too, with the self-destroying creations (or is it self-creating destructions?) of Tinguely. It stands between the old Dada and the new "Happenings." Cézanne could make monuments of sensations; we make sensations of monuments. A student of mine—a sculptor in a playwriting class—wrote a drama in obeisance to Artaud's "No More Masterpieces": the chief scenic artifact, aptly conceived, was a huge anus up which at one climax went Michelangelo's David (in the orchestra pit was a summer camp for survivors of Auschwitz). Another student (now studying architecture) announced he was going down to the Palace of the Legion of Honour—with its resplendent view of the Golden Gate—and desecrate a painting. I understood the fertility rights involved. As Sweeney said of the woman drowned in Lysol, every man has to, needs to, wants to, once in a lifetime, do a painting in. I had talked of the ethics of outrage and the virtue of "the destructive element"—now by my green candle! I had thrust the unmentionable mop into the hand of Ubu.

The trouble with Ubu is he can also be a terrible bore. Yet, through all the clichés of "breakthrough," we prowl the new frontiers for signs of order. In the beginning was neither Word nor flesh, only the beginning. He who was there first looks classical. So Pollock: study the Blue Poles—they take a lot of heart out of a lot of Happenings. The miracle of motion, however, has become an icon of the Id; postlapsarian turbulence is brought to a godlike halt. *Ur-mensch* of breakthrough, Pollock is now an Idea of Order. Through which we try to break through. The drips and blobs become "draggings" and the great rough beast slouches to the scrap heap to be born.

When art turns itself loose on art, the result can be monstrous. And the predicament is curiously described in a news item from Dar-es-Salaam in Tanganyika, where natives are warned to be on the alert for the blood-thirsty lion-men of Singidia, who are taught by witch doctors, usually women, to walk on all fours from childhood. They wear lion skins and kill at night with their claws. All the efforts of the government to wipe them out have failed. Reported on the rampage again, they caused the regional commissioner of the African National Party to call for their extinction: "Those still posing as lions and walking on all fours and killing others must be routed out. We must bury the traditions of the past."

Serious as it is, the whirligig is laughable. Breakthrough, as always, breaks down in parody.

Parody is the gamble made by Robert La Vigne, the painter who designed *Endgame.* His own *Black Art,* a series of collages done after he had been with us for several years, owes a debt to assorted lions: Ubu, Beckett, Genet, and Cézanne. "I am the thief in the night," he wrote to me once with dark humor. "Beware my shifty voice." He meant it in a mantic way, but given the nature of the collage as an art form, there is a relation between prophecy and pillage. What you see depends on what you turn up, and the reverence you have for it. For all the desire of this neo-Dada art to take off like the Bird, La Vigne is an incurable stylist, even a collector. "Standing away from myself," he wrote, "what do I observe? Another 'curator.' But what painter today is not?"

Still, there are collections and collections; and the style he cares for is agape in the blood, the trill of wonder. Though he presses down on nature with the optical nerve, La Vigne has a longing to be surrealist—against, he feels, the grain of the American temperament and language. Like Blake, he tries to see "through the eye, not with it." The art, thus, is not analytical but alchemical, like the theater imagined by Artaud. It is a matter of leashing spirit until, as Artaud says, "it has passed through all the filters and foundations of existing matter."

Whatever La Vigne picks up in his wary passage through the night (during rehearsals of *Endgame* an amazing pile of junk accumulated in front of the stage), forage and style go—when he is in control—through the crucible of a fine sensibility. There is the liability of a lot of thrashing about, an impulse to desecrate, but La Vigne, with a French ancestry, has Taste. Painting, he says, "is an old man's art." La Vigne himself is still young but has an instinct for the ages. And that is why I remembered him when the idea struck me for the scenic image of *Endgame.*

Beckett's stage direction calls for a "*Bare interior. Grey light.*" Nevertheless, as in *Godot,* I wanted a landscape. We are beginning to realize that much abstract expressionism is fundamentally landscape painting, collage being its most urban manifestation. Beyond that, it attempts to put time into space. And I wanted a temporal landscape—a cultural geography, allusive, visual quotations from history, crepuscular, rhythmic, emblems of decay, bleedings, rot, scum, fragments shored up eloquently in the general ruin, blending into the nonobjective surfaces of gray walls. I took my cue from the Japanese Noh, which is a kind of dramatic collage, impacted with allusions remote beyond memory of its oldest connoisseurs—*Endgame* was of this nature. There was also Beckett's essay on Proust, in which he speaks of personality as a "retrospective hypothesis": "The individual is the seat of a constant process of decantation, decantation from the vessel containing the fluid of future time, sluggish, pale and monochrome, to the vessel containing the fluid of past time, agitated and multicoloured by the phenomena of its hours."

So the walls, washed by the hours: the color of epochs coming back to gray. That's all to begin with: gray walls, and hardly a real object in sight. Only shapes: Hamm's shape under a sheet; the shape of ashcans under a sheet; Clov's stooped shape in the rear, barely discernible even as a shape. Bulk. Undifferentiated mass. Then more light. Two rectangles in the rear (the windows); the door; a patch on the wall (the picture turned in, waiting to be turned). The sheets removed: Hamm's stancher like a Veronica; the flutings of the ashcans, sulfated, like stumps of Corinthian columns, but ashcans. Collage was not only the principle of the scenery; it was also in the costumes and makeup. Clov, for instance, was virtually sealed into leather, as if preserving himself from whatever air was left, his face swollen red by concentration of his rage for order.

For all the implication that the drama takes place in the brain, the walls were rigidly squared, for chess play and precise measurement, a graph in three dimensions—adjacent to a kitchen ten feet by ten feet by ten feet. Nevertheless: with a collage made of hundreds of nails, lace, paint, brocade, corrugations, glue, and grit, there was history for Hamm to look at (though he couldn't see) when Clov pushed him on his Oriental journey amid these walls (the walls of the brain, the eyes of the mind) to the end that was hollow, hollow. It was a diffused, indecipherable sort of history, not easily read but appropriate for such a journey (counterclockwise, like the movements of Krapp). When Clov finally brought him back to the dead center of the stage, gray light laving from above, one had the feeling they had gone through a rite of passage lasting untold years. It is near the end, as at the beginning. Something has taken its course. And it had a profound influence on the way we conceived our plays from that time on.

When, for instance, we revived *Godot* at our small theater, La Vigne did a new design. As we were discussing possibilities for the play, I happened to read an account of an underground nuclear test, in which the released megatons accelerated the process of mineral evolution, so that artificial jewels were imbedded in the ground. It was such a landscape I had

in mind for the new production. The audience would be in the cave (our little theater has a low ceiling); the stage would look as if it were blown away
from the end of the building by a blast. The whole landscape would be
man-made. Junk would either be impacted in the ground or look like it
were growing out of it, like vegetation. The mound was a "found object,"
a gas tank rigged on a curved pipe; it looked like a toadstool. The entire
floor (on which the audience looked down) was covered with foam rubber
painted with black latex, so that the ground, tarred and tactile, would
impede motion. The background was a collage of cloud forms and found
objects, and the hole we cut in the front of the stage served numerous functions, a hiding place or a trap in an obstacle course. The floor of the stage
was so inviting, like marrow, like mud, like pus, like the "bubos" that
Artaud celebrates and children explore with their fingers, the bubos that
appear "wherever the organism discharges either its internal rottenness or,
according to the case, its life."

The floor led to one sequence in which, after abusing the crippled
Pozzo and trying out the names Cain and Abel, the tramps lay down to
sleep, and all four actors became part of the total collage. Immobile. Time
erased. The waiting reduced to inertness. Pre-totemic. (*Silence.*) Geologic
birth. A setting for "the truthful precipitates of dreams. . . ." Then slowly
the collage comes to life, motion festering in the inorganic, ontogeny recapitulating phylogeny. In their movements the actors rehearse both the natal
cycle and the process of evolution: Didi crawling in and out of the hole, lux-
uriating in the landscape, a reptilian form; Pozzo twisting, flopping in
agony, like a wounded mammoth; Gogo rolling into a foetus; and Lucky
there, still, a fragile crustacean, his white hair like some sun-bleached fun-
gus in the Encantadas. A preverbal poetry born of the death instinct and the
Plague; carrion man restored. The conscious waiting resumed in a rebirth of
action marked by the completion of a game and the line: "Child's play."

It was in this production, too, that we did one of our first experiments
with front curtains, in warfare with the proscenium (another Totem, with
its own Double). Again the cue was taken from abstract expressionism,
where the painter's desire to escape the constricting boundaries of the frame
is equivalent to the director's desire to escape from the proscenium stage.
The painter "solved" his problem by widening the canvas so that the verti-
cals and horizontals of the edges were out of his ken in the act of composition. He could work toward them, but they were, if he battled close in, no
a priori imposition on his impulses—they were a periphery out of immediate sight. On the stage we were doing just that, working inside the box to
lose sight of its limits. But once the director moves out of the frame and sits
back in the auditorium, there is the Totem again. So, in our losing battle,

we tried to violate it with a floating nonobjective form, with apertures—and when the lights came up on Gogo on his mound, he became part of a sculpted image. When the play began, the curtain jerked up once; no rise; then again; no rise, and then slid indifferently to the floor—a failure, disgraced. "Nothing to be done."

This action and the blitzed landscape were prepared for by a score of *Sound Blocks* by Morton Subotnick, electronic music composed directly on tape. The audience walked into this barrier of sound, this ambiance, as they entered the auditorium. They could not adapt to it because of its atonality and the accidental occurrence of its sequences, until, like a disarticulated Pied Piper, it led them directly into the play. Or so was the intention. For, while I think this worked, and the revival was much applauded, there was, for me, a failure of harmony in the production. It lacked the "completion" of *Endgame*. One of the hazards of collage is its prodigality—the difficulty of resolve in the art of waste. In La Vigne, while it releases fantasy (loot and lust making for restorations), it also encourages a natural equivocation. Though one never knows when a theatrical composition is finished, you can feel when it is unfinished (I do not mean under-rehearsed). And so far as the scenic investiture went, it suffered from a desire for total mastery that, in principle, doesn't give a damn—by which I mean the collage, however permanently built, is a tribute to impermanence. It isn't quite a Happening but doesn't know why it shouldn't be. In *Endgame* the possibilities were limited by the walls.

As for the acting and directing, it might have been submitted to a more ruthless scourge, in keeping with the landscape. The pocks should have secreted entirely new ghosts. I don't mean that it wasn't a compelling production, only it depended somewhat too much on findings from the first; and the balletic motion of the original sometimes stumbled on the more cluttered stage. At the same time some of the exploration induced by the new environment tortured some of the old rhythms out of shape. When we played at the Seattle Fair in the summer of 1962, we returned—because of the larger playhouse—to the old set, and the actors felt liberated by greater space. There may have been one additional factor: by the time of the revival we had become accommodated to Beckett, exhilarated, possessive, dilatory over the nuances. I was also intensely engaged in the effort to find our own hieroglyph—a theatrical style that would stretch every action to the limits of the credible. The mise en scène was becoming a more powerful motive force in my own work; and I was talking then—conditioned by our production of *Lear*—about "risking the baroque."

(1964)

4
_____

On Directing Beckett
An Interview

(What I'm saying here about Beckett, and the circumstances in which I first directed his plays, was extracted by Lois Oppen-heim from a longer interview in my Paris apartment, in July 1992. The questions she posed were not included but are implied by the section titles.)

The Actor's Workshop of San Francisco (1952–1965)

How did it start? There were a lot of little theaters in those days. The little theater tradition had come out of the 1920s. The Bay area was polka-dotted with them—not much, however, that was very memorable in the quality of performance. Actually, there was some adventurous or experimental work (e.g., the Hillbarn Theater in San Mateo or the Interplayers in San Francisco) but, overall, the actors were not very good. Jules Irving and I—Jules, my former partner, now dead—knew a group of actors in San Francisco, some with professional experience (including our wives), who were restive working in the local theaters, because of the acting level. They became the nucleus of The Actor's Workshop.

There was no great ethic in our beginning, except to provide good roles in a studio setting for each of the actors. Nothing like Beckett was on our agenda then. We started in a shabby loft above a judo academy on Divisadero Street, and in due time the Workshop became the major theater in San Francisco. We had at times three or more theaters playing simultaneously—at one dizzy moment there were five productions going on at various sites around the city.

The Workshop became known for several things over the years. First of all, its durability, if always on the edge of bankruptcy. It was one of the early, exemplary "regional theaters"—exemplary in its insistence on survival. A few such theaters were spread over the continent, but without much contact at first and without being acknowledged as a movement until the pump-priming advent of the Ford Foundation, which showed up in a period when there were no such things as grants or subsidies of any kind. At the outset Ford sponsored four theaters as its "backfield": the Seattle Repertory Theater, the Arena in Washington, the Alley in Houston, and the Workshop. There was the old legacy of decentralization from the days of "Tributary Theater" (i.e., paying tribute to New York, which was also the "source" from which the tributaries flowed), but it's unlikely that the newer mode of regional theater would have been authenticated—nor the work that these theaters had been doing for some years—if *Sir* Tyrone Guthrie had not come to Stratford and then to Minneapolis. Just when American painting, say, was starting to dominate the world, taking over from Paris, the theater's inferiority complex had to be given a boost by English knighthood.

The Workshop was, from the perspective of the Ford program, the most bizarre or anomalous of these theaters, because, for one thing, Jules and I were still teaching at San Francisco State College, and we were by then doing avant-garde plays. We were more outspoken on social issues than the other theaters, gravitating toward questions of style, certainly more innovative in our play selection. We became known, too, for developing the concept of a company, with an emphasis on continuity. That was spurred on by my first experience in Europe, where I was very impressed with the state theaters in Germany, where the actors had a certain dignity in the guarantee of longevity—a guarantee that can, of course, wear out its benefits when the actors age into predictability. At the time, however, given the humiliating circumstances of the American actor, the continuity of European theaters seemed like a utopian blessing. Then there was also the prevailing notion—to which even famous actors, like Gérard Philipe, were committed—of *théâtre populaire*. This was the period of Jean Vilar and the exhilarating years of the Festival at Avignon.

The man who was sort of my patron when I first came to France was one of the legendary figures behind this tradition: Michel Saint-Denis, Copeau's nephew, and founder of the Compagnie de Quinze. During the occupation he was head of the Old Vic Theater School in England. Michel had come to the United States when he was consultant to the prospective theater program at Juilliard. He visited San Francisco and saw our work just about the time we were doing *Waiting for Godot*. It was through him that I came to know most of the major theater people in France—particularly those involved in the popular theater movement—ranging from Vilar to Roger Planchon and Jean Dasté, and including Roland Barthes, who was writing then for *Théâtre Populaire,* the journal titled after the movement.

Actually, I had been put on to Barthes by Eric Bentley before I left the United States. I had directed (in 1957) the first production of Brecht's *Mother Courage* in America, and Eric—who was the source of most of what we knew about Brecht then—told me to look up this young, bright critic in Paris, who, at the time, was also Brechtian. This was the earlier semiological Barthes, who was dazzled by the appearance of the Berliner Ensemble in Paris. It was then that he wrote those short but still insightful essays on Brecht. I met Barthes the same week I met Beckett, who knew by then of the production of *Godot* we'd taken to San Quentin and (in 1958) to the Brussels World's Fair. I had also corresponded with him when we were doing *Endgame.*

But back to the Workshop: first there was the company concept, which was infused when I returned from Europe with the ideas developed from seeing the work of Vilar and Planchon, Littlewood in England, and Strehler at the Piccolo Teatro in Milano, as well as the Berliner Ensemble. I'd been invited to East Berlin by Helene Weigel, Brecht's wife, because of the production of *Mother Courage,* which was done at a time when Brecht was still pretty much on the canonical margins in America, relatively unknown, except perhaps as the lyricist for "Mack the Knife." The utopian ideal of popular theater was to be doing plays of high intelligence, from the modern and classical repertoires, for an audience of workers, students, intellectuals: in short, the great dream of the century, with a desire at its extremity for a fusion of socialism and surrealism—a notion revived in May 1968 at the barricades in Paris.

This had nothing to do, quite obviously, with the pre-therapeutical psychological drama then in the mainstream of the American theater. As for our own politics, after a series of plays from Brecht, Arthur Miller, and Sean O'Casey, we had developed something of a leftist following in San Francisco, some of whom felt betrayed when we turned toward the Absurd. About Beckett there was scorn and ambivalence. Left, right, or center, there was always contention over our repertoire. I had no real interest in what were the dominant American plays of that period. Our gestures in that direction—partly to keep the riskier work afloat—consisted of Miller and Tennessee Williams. They paid the bills. What we became known for, however, was our devotion to what are now canonical avant-garde plays, including some of the earliest productions of Beckett; aside from *Godot* and *Endgame,* we did *Happy Days, Krapp's Last Tape,* and various workshops of other pieces. We did the first production of Pinter in America (*The Birth-*

day Party), along with Genet, Duerrenmatt, Frisch, Ionesco, etc., and a pre-cursor to Pinter, the remarkable playwright, John Whiting.

Jules and I were the principal directors, then Bob Symonds, from the older generation of actors. But as the Workshop developed, it attracted various younger people from around the country, who have since established reputations for their own seminal work. Among my assistant directors were Lee Breuer, Ronnie Davis (the San Francisco Mime Troupe was founded by Ronnie on the perimeter of the Workshop), André Gregory, Ken Dewey (who became known later on for his action events, or happenings, in one of which he died in a plane crash). Ronnie was my assistant on *Endgame,* but since he was very much on the Brechtian side of the dialectic, with mixed feelings about Beckett, there was to him something suspicious in the obscurantism. André later did a production of *Endgame* when he was for a while head of a theater in Philadelphia, and, of course, the repertoire of the Mabou Mines (aside from Lee, Ruth Maleczech, Bill Raymond, and JoAnne Akalaitis were also with the Workshop) pivoted around Beckett. The Workshop was for such younger people—in the late 1950s and early 1960s, before things took an experimental turn off-Broadway—a kind of beacon or last outpost. They came there instead of dropping out of the theater entirely, since there was not much else around that they could believe in.

Some were not to begin with theater people but were drawn over from the other arts, as the other arts were theatricalized during the 1960s and 1970s. The performances of Beckett at the Workshop not only attracted artists—painters, sculptors, filmmakers, the new developing hybrid types—who had no previous interest in the theater but also served as models for the alternative modes of theatricality eventually known, through the era of happenings and multimedia events, as performance art. Along with these developments we were doing productions that involved direct collaboration with visual artists and musicians, with a scale pretty much unprecedented in the American theater and not much like it even today. Beckett was also determinative in some of this, not only in an altered sense of dramaturgy but visual style as well. If you had seen our production of *King Lear* in the early 1960s, you would have sensed, whatever you thought of it, that it couldn't have existed without our production of *Endgame,* if you'd seen that at the end of the 1950s. There was a conceptual and stylistic continuity between the two, evolved on our own premises, though the connection between Beckett and Shakespeare was, it seemed, part of the Zeitgeist, crossing continents. There was, you recall, the Beckettianism of Jan Kott's book and its impact on the *Lear* of Peter Brook.

Approaching Beckett

I knew of Beckett's work shortly after the war—that is, World War II—but we couldn't get the rights to it until after the Michael Myerberg production of *Godot* in New York, following upon the disaster in, was it? Coral Gables. By the time we came to *Godot* we had already done some reasonably way-out work in our theater. But *Waiting for Godot* was something else again, though it may seem now like second nature.

We gathered to read the play for the first time in my house just above Haight-Ashbury in San Francisco, after which two of the older, more experienced people dropped out of the cast. They simply refused to be in it. They had always been suspicious of my experimental tendencies (naturally "gratuitous"), but with *Godot* they thought I was crazier than usual. When they read through the play they simply didn't know what was going on, which didn't seem to be much, and much of that they didn't like. And these were quite intelligent people. There was a lot of skepticism about the play around the Workshop even when we replaced the actors and moved into rehearsals. When we finally decided to present the play, Jules and others were wary of doing it as a full-scale production at our theater downtown, so we compromised and played it, at first, only on Thursday nights. Suddenly, unpredictably, it became a kind of cult phenomenon. There was something in the air, it received a lot of attention, the audiences grew, and we multiplied the number of performances.

I think the hardest thing to reconstruct, now that Beckett has been deified among American theater people, particularly academics, is just how startling those plays were.

How did we work on the play? First of all, it was really a matter of *explication du texte*. Beyond that we talked about it in diverse ways, from the psychopathology of its dubious "characters" to its elegiac tone, a sort of drama of lamentations on civilization and its discontents. I tried to situate it historically. "On this soil of Europe, yes or no," Beckett has asked, "is man dead?" The very atmosphere of the play seemed pretty un-American. So we talked out the transition, from a European context to our own. Then there were the formalistic aspects of the play—its repertoire of subverted conventions. This was before the ubiquitous postmodern consciousness of self-reflexive forms, but it was soon apparent that the play within the play was a kind of discourse on the theater itself. You could take almost any theatrical convention and point to ways in which the (anti)drama, in some sense, reflected on the convention. We were conscious of these reflections, deviations, inversions, during the course of rehearsal. Eventually, you have to do it, sure, but the talking here was a precondition for insuring that the actors would want to do it (the "nothing") as it could be done—understanding, in a sense, that there was no way *not* to do it. I mentioned the resistance in our cast, but once *Godot* came to be a sensation, and even the newspapers approved, every actor in the company was ready, when we came to it, to jump into the ashcans of *Endgame.*

As regards the acting—and I have always felt this about Beckett's drama—the substance of it is realism in extremis. Which is to say that the realistic vision, its methodology, is taken about as far inside as it can go, interiorized so intensely that it seems to occur at the nerve ends. In the late 1950s actors were, reflexively, still inclined to think of themselves as interior actors. If they had any training, it was in that tradition. But there was something about the surface tension of Beckett's dramaturgy that seemed, paradoxically, to double up on interiority. At the same time there was a movement of thought through the phenomenology of the play—its things to be done, beginning with the opening "nothing"—around the dubiousness of the distinction between inside and outside.

San Quentin

We were invited to San Quentin through a series of circumstances, though I can't quite remember exactly how the invitation came. A lot of work has been done over the last generation in prisons, factories, Indian reservations, wherever, but there was no such active tradition at the time, and the production of *Godot* at San Quentin became a prototype. In any case, when the contact was first made we proposed a play that I had written. But that didn't go because there were women in the cast, a taboo at the prison (which, by the way, had never had a theater performance, unless—if rumor is correct—Sarah Bernhardt did appear there on her tour of America at the turn of the century). Our presentation of *Godot* was, so far as we knew, the first in a maximum-security prison in this country. When we proposed to substitute Beckett's play for my play, however, there was trouble: an argument at the prison, with the prison psychiatrist. He was put off by the "depressing" material of *Godot,* felt it would be too obscure, even traumatic, for the inmates. There was a confrontation before Warden Duffy— who looked like a southern redneck—and we weren't counting on his approval. But he heard us out, seemed to like me, and said simply: "That's it, let them do it."

We had a sensational response. It had such an impact on the prison

Vol. XVII, No. 24 — SAN QUENTIN, CALIFORNIA — Thursday, November 28, 1957

Workshop Players Score Hit Here

The Warden's Column

San Francisco Group Leaves S.Q.
Audience Waiting For Godot

Trade Training In Bastille Bakery
Prepares Students For Placement

Local Instructor Teaches Modern Production Methods In Fully Equipped Bake Shop

Cotton Textile Mill

SAN QUENTIN, Nov. 19 — For the first time within memory, live drama graced the boards of the San Quentin stage tonight; the more than one thousand in attendance enthusiastically captivated by the San Francisco Actor's Workshop's presentation of the surrealistic and symbolic drama, "Waiting For Godot."

Open Air Session
Swings For Big Yard Fans

New Year's Show

North Honor Block Now Open To Medium-A Inmates

Prison Made Film Debuts At Esque Theater—Finally

Christmas Cards

Christmas Draw

that the language of the play, the names of the characters—a Gogo, a Didi, a Pozzo—became part of the therapeutic vocabulary at San Quentin. It may be so to this day. Afterward we helped the inmates set up a drama group of their own. That performance had a major impact on the lives of some who were there, most notably Rick Cluchey, who was in for armed robbery and attempted murder. As a result of his work in the drama group, Rick was paroled, was introduced to Beckett (by which of us, I forget—maybe Ruby Cohn?), named a child after him, and was directed by him in Berlin, to top it all off. But that story is now pretty well-known.

On Beckett as Director and Other Productions

Was I interested in Beckett as a director? I would have been interested in almost anything Beckett did, because I cared about him personally. But no, I was absolutely not influenced by his productions. First, for the obvious reason that he hadn't directed yet when I was doing his plays. When he did start to direct, I didn't see any of the productions for some time; when I did, the couple I saw were quite ordinary, pedestrian.

Of other productions I've seen the most remarkable was Lee Breuer's *The Lost Ones,* with the fastidious focus of its funneled specularity in that claustrophobic arena of foam rubber. (I've written about that, briefly, in *The Audience.*) I saw a production of *Waiting for Godot* here in Paris last year (at the Théâtre des Amandiers in Nanterre) that was, scenically, very evocative—a vast blitzed space, below a viaduct perhaps, the action receding into it occasionally but mostly confined laterally to the forestage. David Warrilow was in it (his French is very good), but the acting was nothing special and, in any case, outdone by the magnitude of visual image. But I found that image, its bleak audacious scale, more interesting in itself than many more dutiful transcriptions, literalizing every stage direction. I think the directions are, at their most minimal, vastly suggestive, like those of *Imagination Dead Imagine.* It's the quality of the imagining out of the datum of nothingness that compels me in performance. I'm not particularly interested in versions of the plays that you can see without half-trying by merely reading the texts.

From time to time, then, you may see something really unusual, but, as you know, that turned out to be a problem with Beckett himself, though he never went to see productions. I happened to be in Paris a few days after he had tried to stop JoAnne Akalaitis's *Endgame* at Brustein's theater in Cambridge. I was meeting with Beckett and, though I hadn't seen the production

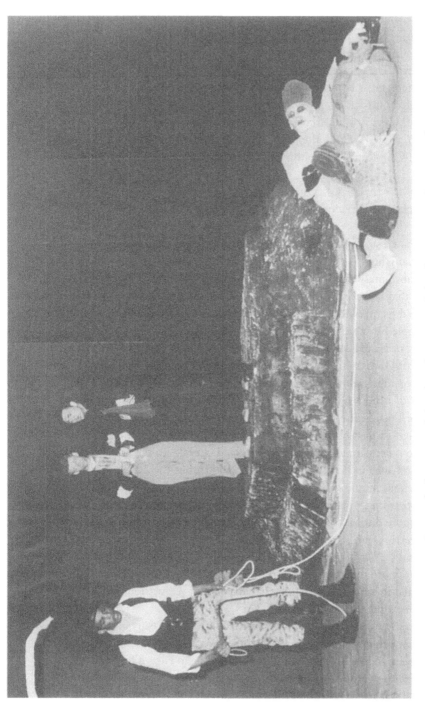

FIG. 8. . . . the language of the play, the names of the characters—a Gogo, a Didi, a Pozzo—became part of the therapeutic vocabulary at San Quentin. (The San Quentin Drama Group production of *Waiting for Godot*, at the prison, 1963; Manny Gonsalves as Pozzo, Carey Johanessen as Gogo, Rick Cluchey as Didi, Ken Whelan as Lucky; photograph courtesy of Rick Cluchey)

either, questioned his having tried to stop it. I reminded him that I'd known JoAnne since she was very young: "She grew up on your plays. People with the Mabou Mines were all deeply influenced by your work [as he knew], and they probably know it a good deal better, are engaged at deeper levels, than many who appear to be more faithful." I ventured that, even if she did something strange, it was with no less respect for the text, perhaps more. But whoever had gotten to him before this had done a good job: he was very upset, wouldn't listen. That had never happened between us before. Things were getting intense, so I made what I thought was a pretty good joke, something he'd have laughed at another time, about here we are in Paris, all that stuff about "the death of the author" . . . he was furious.

Nothing to be done. So, I said, "Maybe, after all, Alan [Schneider] was your best director." Alan was always very dutiful. He'd fly over to Paris to check out difficulties in the text and did, so to speak, what Beckett wanted. And he would do that, of course, with considerable skill. I never felt, however, that I had to see such a production. As I said, I'm simply not taken with productions of what, when you read a text, seems pretty much the way you'd do it if you did it straight. But I feel that about all productions, not only of Beckett. It's like in the teaching of dramatic literature—you hear people say the students have to go and see the plays; otherwise, they won't understand the drama. Maybe so. Maybe better they don't go to see the play, because they have to constitute it then in their own minds, *see it there,* finding their own image, no readymade standing between.

Particularly if it's a good production with famous actors. That gets in the way. If that's the only image they have of it, they're very likely to think that's what it's supposed to be. Oh, I'm not saying they won't gain something from seeing a performance, but there has always been an alternative tradition in dramatic theory that thinks of the casting and staging of a play of any stature as necessarily reductive, canceling out the prospects of one's own imagining. Of course, that tradition also intersected the antitheatrical prejudice, the notion that representation itself was bound to be misrepresentation.

Beckett understood this, I think, from the beginning and shared the antitheatrical prejudice as well: years ago, when I asked him why he'd turned to the theater, he said it provided some relief from the novel, because the theater is a contained space. But if it is in some way manageable, it is also a violation. As for the audience, what audience? He always knew that he was "writing into a void" or, worse, as with the tramps in *Godot,* gaping over the forestage: "a charnel house, a charnel house." Where does the play really take place? "There's something dripping in my head," as Hamm says. It's the dripping in the head from whence the drama comes, its deep structure. So, in a very real sense what's happening up here, the dripping at the temple, the throb in the fontanelles, is the source and realization of what's happening out there.

We weren't talking on that level when we argued that day. Which is why I said that maybe Alan, after all, was the most appropriate director. As for myself, Beckett had more than once wondered, other times, why I had stopped directing, and even tried to persuade me to start directing again. But if I had, I could simply never have assured him that I'd do what he wanted or strictly follow the manifest text. As for his knowing what he wanted, well, that's up in the air these days, if there's any truth to French theory and psychoanalytical thought—the degree to which the author's authority or the authority of the text has been, if not legitimately, provocatively questioned, as it has been with the canonical drama in revisionist performance. Despite all theory, a lot of people still have this reflexive investment in the Master's voice. This Master has given us, however, the conceptual ground for doing precisely what he didn't want us to do. I put the emphasis on the precision, which, as I've written before, is next to godliness in Beckett.

There was, by the way, a development at San Quentin many years before that reflects on this issue and any claim of infallibility for the Beckettian text. Some years after we did *Waiting for Godot* at San Quentin, the drama group there did its own version. We were all invited from the Workshop, but I couldn't go myself because I was rehearsing that night. But others from the company went, including Robert Symonds, who had been in the production we'd brought there years before. He described to me afterward what appeared to be one radical change in the course of things onstage: as I recall it, when Pozzo and Lucky came on, they stayed for about a minute, then went off for a while and then came on again. Or something like that. Bob watched this somewhere between astonishment and bemusement, and at the end of the performance he questioned the actors about the sequence and somehow came to ask about the text. What happened was that when *Godot* was first published in the United States it was done by *Theater Arts,* not the old yellow-covered journal but the later glossier one that published Broadway plays (Meyerberg's production having qualified *Godot*). When the play appeared it was with ten or more pages out of place! The inmates had used that text, and it seemed perfectly suitable. They hadn't remembered what had happened exactly in our production. And so far as the "true text" is concerned, they apparently didn't know the difference. I assure you that's not because those inmates were uneducated or naive.

That characterizes the theoretical problem itself. Beckett, after all, gave us the paratactical model of postmodern thought: dramaturgy as combinatory sets, repetitive, additive, recursive with permutations. With no old-fashioned causality at work, you could switch this here, put that there. The connectivity is musical. That's not wholly true, I know, but true enough.

I don't have any problem with people adapting Beckett's prose texts for the stage. Nor did Beckett eventually, though he objected to that strenuously at first. But he finally gave up, resigned himself. He couldn't keep up with it, though he remained vigilant, once he started to direct, about other productions. Or others were vigilant for him, to his detriment, I think. The vehemence of his objections, given his usual grace, didn't become him. And in a way it made no sense, for he had given us, as I said, the intellectual, theoretical, and ideological grounds on which any text becomes liable to dispersion, with the disarming authority of an open field. If you really understand what is going on in his texts, you don't need deconstruction, for that's the work in progress.

I realize some would say *that's* the point: Why do it when it's already done? It's not a matter of licensing any capricious reinvention, but who's to award the license in any case? As with Brecht, there's no law against turning his methods back upon Beckett, rethinking some aspect of the drama, or shifting the site of its occurrence. At any rate, Beckett taught us before theory that paratextuality is built into the language, and, as with the gospels derided by Didi and Gogo, no text is sacred. That people are inclined to do odd things with Beckett's own texts is, one might say, a matter of poetic justice.

A Beckett Sensibility

Did Bert Lahr have a Beckett sensibility? In some ways, yes. Did Buster Keaton have a Beckett sensibility? Though Beckett was looking forward to working with him on *Film,* the two of them didn't really get on together, which didn't preclude his doing what needed to be done. We know that Beckett was interested in these vaudeville types, though I do have some objections to what, in various productions of his plays, passes for comedy, the kidding around that I've seen. The substance of it wears pretty thin. The Beckettian theme—it's funny, then it's no longer funny—is okay, so long as you know that the datum, the bleak landscape of Beckettian thought, wasn't all that funny to begin with, as Didi said, funnily, "AP-PALLED!"

What's funny, as they say, is to have thought—that is, not only in the past tense but also in the sense of possession. To really think about it is to die laughing. Take it or leave it, that's an appalling thought, almost worse than Hamlet's there's nothing either good or bad but thinking makes it so.

There is, sure, a peculiar sort of optimism in Beckett (*On!*), but it's as stringently minimalist, as parsimonious, as the form. People try to make something positive of Beckett but somewhat more than the drama concedes. "They give birth astride of a grave, the light gleams an instant. . . ." There is something indefatigable, tragic, with an elegiac heroism that seems to be transcendent . . . well, okay, it's there, but minimally there, the light gleams an instant only, then it's gone, the large massive doses of bleakness also there. And the pain, the pain, it must be finished, nearly finished, because so painful, something dripping in the head . . .

An aspect of Beckett that seems to me of major consequence has to do with the pain of birth. Some time ago I was asked to write an essay on Beckett and deconstruction. It turned out to be about Beckett, Derrida, and the birth of my daughter. It's a very theoretical essay but also very performative, "The Bloody Show and the Eye of Prey." As it turned out, the morning I was about to start writing the essay, my wife—who was very pregnant—came down and said she was bleeding: the bloody show had begun. I couldn't help thinking about the subject of the essay as I watched my daughter being born. As I eventually wrote, "It's a little strange to watch a birth with Beckett on your mind. As a fetal monitor he leaves something to be desired." You can look up the rest if you want to, but the gist of it is the *pensum,* curled up worm in slime, at first suck the fiasco, and the monstrosity of it all—a little hard to take when your wife is having a baby, who should be a sign, a portent, rather than the first cruelly extorted deposit of a minimal quantity of being. This all has to do, if you want to be linguistic about it, with being born into the symbolic, the long interminable sentence of *The Unnamable,* the sentence of language, the sentence of punishment, language *as* punishment, the price of being born. If you don't have that right in performance, you can look for all the hope you want, but, sad to say, you don't have Beckett at all.

Theory and Theater

Theory has always been an issue with me in the theater, and all the more so after first encountering Beckett, who seemed to raise about the theater, in the deepest theoretical sense, all the most elemental questions. My own thinking went through a lot of changes before the formation, in the 1970s, of the KRAKEN group, where from my point of view it was like starting all over again—after more than twenty years in the theater—with those elemental questions. If Beckett had any sustained influence on me, it had to do with a certain obsessiveness about the theater in its most rudimentary form. What is it, ontologically, when you try to separate it out from whatever it is it is *not?* I've written a great deal since about that fine distinction, in a series of books starting with *Take Up the Bodies: Theater at the Vanishing Point,* to which disappearing point the work of KRAKEN was, in a sense, always directed. Those who saw that work know that it was physically adept and demanding, but it was also, to be sure, very heady stuff: something dripping in the head.

There may be a disarming playfulness in the distressing thought of Beckett, and he can even make a vaudeville turn of the excesses of lapsed consciousness—when the tramps put on their thinking hats, to "Think! Think! Think!" I find it all profoundly moving, but all the more so at the sticking point, as at the bitterest end of *Endgame,* where, if you're going to insist upon living at all, it's a desperate matter of thought: "Use your head, can't you! use your head! you're on earth, there's no cure for that." What I was always moved by in Beckett, through the woeful antics of the music hall routines, the slapstick comedy in the dying fall, was a certain manic fitfulness of mind, as in the iterations of *Footfalls:* "It all, it all." Where you could virtually bite your tongue over the painful indeterminacy of that (w)hole in *it.* It all, it all. What's the referent? I certainly didn't think of it, when I was first doing Beckett, in those theoretical terms, but he did. Read his little book on Proust, which sounds—and in its interlocutory, dense, elliptical prose—like poststructuralism *avant la lettre.*

So far as my own work with KRAKEN was concerned, what appealed to me in poststructuralist thought was that it seemed to be theorizing what we were doing, which was in the process theorizing itself. Which is why I say somewhere at the start of *Take Up the Bodies* that if the productions of KRAKEN that I describe in the book never existed, that if I were simply making them up on the page as I went along, the theory derived from them would be no less true.

On *Endgame*

I knew Beckett for about thirty years. I was not in touch with him when we did those early productions. I wrote to him afterward, commenting on what we did. Was he curious about them? Certainly. I don't believe I sent him pictures of the productions of *Godot* (we actually did two of them, quite different), but he did see pictures of our *Endgame* and seemed to admire them. Given, however, what he later came to feel about allegiance to his texts and stage directions, I'm surprised that he didn't take amiss some aspects of the design and costumes quite palpable in the pictures. I also described to him what we'd done with the opening sequence of *Endgame,* in which there were twelve to fifteen minutes of silent mime before the dialogue began. He didn't, as I recall, raise an eyebrow.

I even described to him the lengths we went to in rehearsal to let the resonances of the play sink in, before we extruded the dilatory excess, which was itself a reflection on the indeterminacy of the finish that must be but is never finished (*in*terminable in the Freudian sense). That was compacted in performance into the recursive enumeration of its almost diabolic resources of hilarious pain, so exquisitely painful that the laughter can't bear itself. (That's what Beckett called the *risus purus,* the laugh laughing at the laugh.) Sometimes this protracted endurance would take almost four hours in rehearsal, though the actual performance lasted about an hour and a half. That's not much more than par for the course ("something is taking its course"), though I've never seen a production that was as excruciating to begin with, in the almost paralytic lyricism of its opening moments, distended to the uncountable silent minutes of an eternity onstage. I don't think I've seen anything like it since.

If you'll forgive a further immodesty, I think the production of *Endgame,* entrusted to memory now, was probably one of the most richly conceived in the American theater. It was simply unusually seen. If the seeing of it was unusual, in the simpler sense of sight it was scenically extraordinary. Beckett calls for gray walls. What does that mean? Do you just paint the walls gray? Or what? What we did was to give him grayness, an abstraction of gray. The designer was Robert La Vigne, whose prodigious gifts included a capacity for mutilations and the grotesque in art that were nevertheless a function of exquisite taste. "First of all," I said to Bob, "let's think of those gray walls in this way: there's a structural relationship to the other gray objects as first perceived onstage." What materializes there, so far as the perceiver can tell at first, are inanimate objects: gray. You see a mass in the foreground (the ashcans), you see another mass center stage (Hamm enthroned), another form in the background, not yet perceptible as a human figure (Clov), and all of these gray, enclosed by gray. You see these things, and what you have, with nothing clearly discernible, is a kind of lumpish materiality of nonobjective forms: gray. Maybe Clov, depending on how he is lit, might be seen as incipiently human, but he too, ideally, would seem no more than a phenomenological object.

Then, later, they take this trip, the journey around the room. This, by the way, I did confirm later with Beckett, that is, the itinerary of it. "Shouldn't we go backward, counterclockwise?" I said. When Hamm makes that trip, wheeled by Clov, you have a decision to make as a director. Does he move erratically or in a clockwise or counterclockwise direction? Since it seems to me that the play has a certain recessive aspect to it, it should be something like the uroboric snake—the one that eats its own tail—turned back upon itself temporally. At any rate, we went to the wall, the hollow, counterclockwise, and in the process there was the subliminal appearance of a reversal of time.

It was gray, as you saw it, when the lights came dimly up. So far as one could tell, it was absolute gray. But I also suggested to Bob that there be inherent in the grayness a sort of history of Western culture moving backward, inscribed on the gray walls, so Hamm would have something to see on his journey; it wouldn't be totally boring: there, in the ground zero of grayness, the reversed processions of time. What Bob did over the weeks of rehearsal was to accumulate a mound of junk, tin, broken porcelain, rusty and fresh nails in front of the stage, and various fabrics, gauze, brocade, velour, lace. Out of all this he composed, as we rehearsed, an assemblage of gray that was precisely what I'd asked for, a cultural history in reverse, by no means literalized, but shadowy, suggestive, articulated by dispersion in the matrix of gray, mere hints and intimations of various historical periods in the abstract figurations of metal and fabrics, clusters of nails. The walls were in a sense encrusted with history but, unless you were alert to their visual nuances, nothing more than gray.

Those walls were just great. They were so beautiful that, after the production was stored, people ripped them off. Which was usually the case with whatever Bob designed; they were art objects. They were surreptitiously gorgeous walls; but they looked bleak.

Everything in sight was similarly designed. Hamm's hands, for instance (Robert Symonds played the role), were painted and furred; the sheet that covered Hamm was embroidered with a soiled elegance. As for the costumes, same thing: La Vigne had another pile of material around the stage, some of it onstage. I had spoken to him about Clov's rage for order, the anal intensity of it. So, as we rehearsed, Bob would be there, too, as in a dance, laying leather on Clov (Tom Rosqui) and then, wielding a razor blade, cut. Over a series of rehearsals, cut by cut, Clov was totally sewn into his costume, with a tight cowl of leather around his face, as if he had wanted nothing more than to be totally sealed in. This was also reflected in the acting, the spastic movement of Clov as well.

The relation between the materiality of the scenic elements and the acting was something Beckett's work encouraged as a matter of consciousness. I directed, after this work on *Endgame*, a second production of *Godot*. In the first production—the one we took to San Quentin—there was a large backdrop with faint streaks of white (painted) cloud and, like a fence or circus ring around the tree, an equally faint configuration of barbed wire on posts (which Beckett certainly didn't call for either). Yet there was a sense, nevertheless, of a very bare stage (which he did call for). The movement was, over a fairly large surface, more or less athletic or balletic, even in its incapacities. (The setting was by Robin Wagner, the first production he ever designed.) The second production was very different. It had a sort of see-through curtain that couldn't get (it) up. It would struggle to go up then plaintively fall down. The mound was made from an old rusted automobile radiator. It was quite drearily elegant too, didn't look like a radiator exactly but, rather, a mound or maybe a large toadstool. The floor of the stage was entirely foam rubber so that throughout the entire action—in a more intimate theater than the other—you couldn't hear a step. The actors would also sort of sink into the ground as they walked.

We did it in San Francisco at what was then (the theater still exists) called the Encore Theater. It was a long, narrow space with soffits at the sides, and to navigate the soffits, a specially rigged curtain, which when drawn raised away from the center in somewhat baroque scallops. When we did *Endgame* we didn't use the curtain. And that presented an interesting acting problem, because it meant that Hamm had to be in his seat before the audience came in, perhaps no great matter ordinarily, though it was with Hamm-as-object, not visible at first to the audience. He was actually there for something like thirty minutes or so before the start of the unveiling within the play. Since he has a sheet and a handkerchief over the black specs, that can be suffocating, claustrophobic. It would make him psychotic at times, which was exactly the condition in which we wanted him. Under the double veil he'd be hyperventilating. That was all conceived, to his silent sorrow.

When we were rehearsing, as I suggested, a run-through would sometimes take as much as four hours. If it took fifteen minutes to unveil him, as played, it sometimes took in rehearsal something like an eternity for Clov to open the window curtain. This was to get some sense into the metabolism of the actor of what it is to *not-want* to do it. It was excruciating to see

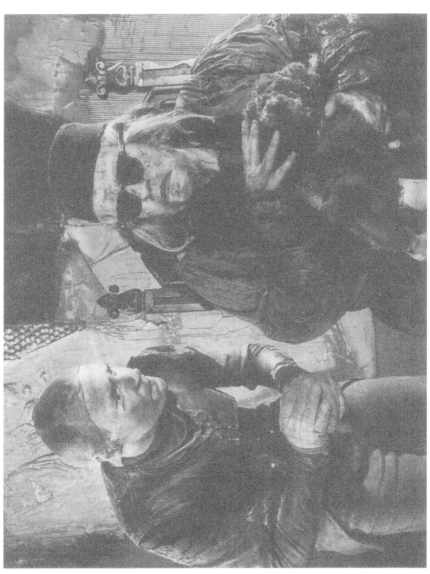

FIG. 9. . . . abstract figurations of metals and fabrics, clusters of nails. The walls were in a sense encrusted with history . . . . Everything in sight was similarly designed. (*Endgame* at The Actor's Workshop of San Francisco, 1959; with lights up to reveal texture of walls, detail of makeup and costume; design by Robert LaVigne)

him open that curtain millimeter by enduring millimeter, every ounce of resistance to the doing at every impossible moment. Why do it at all? What's out there, anyway? Zero. When Tom Rosqui opened it in the production he went like this: whoom! The slide of the curtain rings on a brass rod would make the audience jump. But that instantaneous movement had congealed in it each tormented instance of the hours of rehearsal, where he experienced the ignominy of having to do it at all. What made him do it? Well, what keeps them there? As the text says: the dialogue. The opening of that curtain was chilling in its compressed materiality.

One of the things that determined what we did with *Endgame* involved a structural contrast with *Godot,* not often talked about, if at all. Only Beckett is Beckett, but not all Beckett is the same, within the dramaturgical spectrum of universal grayness. There are improvisational appearances in all his texts, but not all improvisation is alike either, being a function of the psychic mechanisms at work. Let me put it in terms of the problem of memory: in *Waiting for Godot* not only can Didi and Gogo not remember what happened a million years ago, in the 90s [*those* 90s, not these], they can't even remember at times what happened a minute ago. Gogo, in particular ("I'm not a historian"), seems to be wanting in historical memory. They fall down with Pozzo, and, because they can't quite remember why, they just get up. Child's play! Without historical memory you can, like a child, be open and improvisational; there are no impediments in that regard to starting all over again, to enter again unthinkingly into the vicissitudes of play. In *Endgame,* however, the play is deadlier, if anything, more unendurable. And then there is this conceptual difference as regards the uses and abuses or liabilities of memory: let's suppose I take an object that can be turned on or off. In the moment that I am poised to shut it off I can think of every conceivable reason in the two thousand–year history of Western culture why I shouldn't and every reason why I should. Stalemate. That's exactly Clov. He functions like a kind of extension or exacerbation of the "ratiocinative meditativeness" that Coleridge attributed to Hamlet, an impacted figure (as a tooth is impacted) of the Hamletic condition. As when Hamlet finally kills the king, he does so out of maximum indecisiveness, as a reflex against the near-crippling inability to act. No wonder Clov lurches when he walks, as if he were impelled only by stasis itself.

That was a question raised by the actor in rehearsal: Why does Clov walk as he does? You might say, like Bert Lahr about picking up the pot, "It says pick up the pot, so you pick it up." I could have said, "Don't ask.

He just walks like that." It would never have passed muster with Tom. In any case, I think he walks against a resistance to walking at all. In other words, he'd rather not move at all. It is like some kind of competing reflex is built into his body, if not genetically programmed, as a function of history. Now, would Beckett have confirmed that? I wouldn't have cared if he confirmed it or not. The point is that it seemed to me inherent in what is going on. If something is taking its course, it is utterly anal. Clov is absolutely constipated. And when he moves he moves in such a way as to reflect that, the anality is almost metaphysical as well. There is also the immense pain in the body. That is also why he was sewn in, to seal him off as much as possible from the air, the world, the presence of others, who are the source of pain.

Things make sense, if you want to make sense, but they also have to have a performative sense. What does this mean in the way it looks? What does this mean in what he wears? What does this mean in the way he walks? That I had a good visual idea? I don't offhand think, despite my defense of possible relocations of the plays, that it's a particularly impressive idea to set *Endgame* in a subway. It depends, however, aside from the desire for relevance or updating, on the substance of the subway, what could be revealed there and not otherwise. That it is updated doesn't mean anything. But to think through the sense of metaphysical stalemate at the logical impasse of late capitalism, that is a different matter. This is not a question of delivering a message but, rather, of the thinking through itself, with precision about the complexities of the idea.

It's like when, in *King Lear*, Edgar leads Gloucester out to the edge of the cliffs of Dover, and the blinded father says to the disguised son, as Edgar is about to recreate the landscape, to give his father eyes: "Set me where you stand." I don't think he means that vaguely or approximately. Precision is next to godliness, or to the fairies and gods that are conjured up by Edgar for his father, after the leap into nothingness. Set me where you stand. Not here or there, but exactly where the other stands: the father in the son's footsteps. It is just like when Clov pushes Hamm back from the hollow in the wall after their vast journey around the room. "Am I right in the center?" Hamm asks. More or less, a push here, a push there. Am I in the center? An indifferent push. *In the center!* But we well know there is no center. We are talking deconstruction, no? There is no center, no origin. So, where do you put him? If you care about these things, if you care about thought . . . and if you don't, no matter, it's just a laugh. But that ain't Beckett. There may not be a center, but the desire for it—the source of his unerring poignancy amid the facile parody of the postmodern—determines the way the thing looks, and sounds, its *soundings,* the way the body moves, the way one thinks. Think!

Beckett has the virtue, it seems to me, of consolidating issues that way. That's the part of his idea of directing I admire, the intention of it, as he has spoken of it himself: the insistence in the soundings out upon an absolute music. Whether he saw what its absolute nature should be in material terms and could realize *it* onstage, that's another matter—it all, it all . . .

5

The Bloody Show and the Eye of Prey

> Of course, there is no need of a signifier to be a father, any
> more than to be dead, but without a signifier, no one
> would know anything about either state of being.
> —Lacan, "On the Possible Treatment of Psychosis"

I didn't propose the title of this session, "Beckett and Deconstruction," though fortune disposes in ways that might have been foreseen. For I became a father again as I started to work on this essay. I am not speaking, as they do in deconstruction, of the paternity of the text. The major obsession of poststructuralist thought is, to be sure, the question of *origins,* the allure and (re)lapse of beginnings, the illusory *subject* of the instituting trace. But peace to Derrida! The simple fact is that my wife gave birth to a baby. I'm sure it was she, that much at least, and I'm sure I was there, though Saussure and Lévi-Strauss and Lacan and Barthes have taught us to beware of pronouns.

The destined morning began with an image that might have been god-fathered by Beckett, who is agonized by pronouns—the unclotting preface to labor they call "the bloody show." And then, like the spastic phrases out of the Mouth of *Not I,* the contractions, and several hours before Thanksgiving, yes, "almost to the tick," the predicted day, "out . . . into this world . . . this world tiny little thing . . . before its time . . . in a godfor- . . . what? . . . girl: . . . yes . . . tiny little girl . . . into this . . . out into this . . . ."[1] But the passage—were I to continue through the recursive strips of its propulsive and aphasic thought—throws up problems, first of all about the echolocation of its "drifting" and labial subject—"what? . . . who? . . . no! . . . she!"—which/who, "if not exactly . . . insentient . . . insentient," nevertheless "came and went," not knowing "what position she was in . . . imagine! . . . what position she was in!" (*Not I* 15). But as you try to imagine you find yourself moving, not altogether voluntarily, into the "thin air" of conjecture between "this world" she came into and "this world"—the signifiers slipping in a site of becoming, *this* world or *her* world or, as the emerging subject is embraced and swaddled in perception, my world, perhaps, "without solution of continuity," as the stage directions say of the voices of *That Time* (*Ends and Odds* 28).

It's a little strange to watch a birth with Beckett on your mind. As a fetal monitor he leaves something to be desired. The ontological vigilance is accurate to a fault, true, a chastening asepsis. But once the tiny little thing is out—footprints taken as the assurance of an unexchangeable self—there is the problem of assenting to Beckett's vision, not only the pronominal shifts of an unstable identity, the metonymic corrosions and macerations "up to the mouth,"[2] by which the footprints seem erased, but the clawing and entropic bloody show itself: the running sores, the wounds, the risible mutilations, the excrementa, the paraplegics, the lactating abortions, the stumps, the stanchers, the skulls, the skulls, the leak in the fontanelles, "never but the one the first and last time curled tip worm in slime when they lugged you out and wiped you off" (*That Time* 31), the cruelly extorted *pensum* of a minimal quantum of being. Or even less, as in the purgatorial mathematics of *The Lost Ones,* the combinatory sets of annihilation, "in cold darkness motionless flesh,"[3] if not exactly insentient, still, the annals of rigor mortis.

"What I'd like now," said the narrator as far back as *Molloy,* the pages already accumulating in mortification, "is to speak the things that are left, say my good-byes, finish dying. They don't want that."[4] But since the Nobel Prize apparently they do. I remember that time when his plays were first performed and people who now swear by Beckett—including actors in my company who refused to be in *Godot*—were revolted by his vision. Were they right to begin with? "Nothing to be done"?[5] At the political impasse of postmodern thought, one can certainly understand the desire to go "Beyond Beckett"—but not, as in a recent conference, to those who, following after, are derivative and regressive, already passé. There is, however, the sort of feeling suggested by John Ashbery, who concedes with Beckett that there are no new stories and that, while he wants to believe there is "a lot of life to look forward to,"[6] the one who can look forward remains, like Didi and Gogo at the end of each act, or Clov at the ending or the beginning, motionless. Still, nothing to be done. For Ashbery it is the last humanistic scruple that is useless, the nostalgia, "the difference between now and other hard times [being] that now there was no comfort in remembering scenes of past unhappiness, indeed he was quite sure there had never been any, and was therefore quite content to remain as he had been, staring uncertainly into the fire as though looking for a sign, a portent, but in reality thinking of nothing at all" (*Three Poems* 47). Here we have a dispassionate postmodern permutation of Beckett—another is a facile postabsurdist parody passing as portent—with the rhythm somehow becalmed.

The difference is the *pensum,* curled-up worm in slime, with the penalty of remembrance ineluctably unnamable and maybe not-I, "but the brain still . . . still sufficiently . . . oh very much so!" (*Not I* 17). As for the earlier revulsion against Beckett, whether by thinking of nothing at all or thinking not at all, over the years the slime has dissolved in deference or reverence, and we've become far more accommodating to the crawling or catatonic humor of repetitively dystrophic flesh with its "fatuous little light" (*Lost Ones* 20). If "totalitarians like Lukács," according to Adorno, "hate in Beckett what they have betrayed,"[7] some of us may love in Beckett what, in that fatuous light, we cannot betray because we never deeply believed it, nor had "no notion who it was saying what you were saying whose skull you were clapped up in whose moan had you" (*That Time* 32). Even on the farthest Left, Beckett is almost universally admired now for the elegiac integrity of the inexhaustible gospel of the unexpurgated mess with its liturgy of humiliations. While it may now be taken for granted, often by a ready laughter that simply laughs it off, it is still an appalling vision—as Didi said, "AP-PALLED"—and not even the subsiding logorrhea and glyphic serenity of, say, . . . *but the clouds* . . . makes it easier to take to heart.

Especially not for the moment, betrayal be damned, with a baby in the crib, who by all rights should be a sign, a portent, though probably of nothing you intended and about whom you want to forget the "lesson" of *The Unnamable* which may be inseparable from the *pensum,* "too hastily proclaimed, too hastily denied" (31). Or, as Beckett puts it in *A Piece of Monologue,* rubbing the lesson in: "Birth. Birth was the death of him [who? . . . him . . . of her?]. Ghastly grinning ever since. Up at the lid to come. In cradle and crib. At such first fiasco,"[8] or even before.

It isn't that Beckett, who has suffered not only from the brain but from glaucoma, sees errantly with his "eye of flesh" (to which by the way—many years ago, before using the phrase in *The Lost Ones* (31)—he challenged me to "produce" my children (from a previous marriage) whom I kept promising he would sometime meet. It was almost as if he feared they might be a fiction or delusion, like the child out the window of *Endgame*). It is, rather, that he has an immaculate affinity for the inaugural fault, the child abuse of mere existence. Which is what makes the existentialism of Beckett, or his sense of the Absurd, not merely a passing fancy of which you can say it's time to go beyond. For the Absurd in Beckett, unlike Sartre or Camus, or Ionesco, is neither a dramatized doctrine nor formulaic with intention, but something to which meaning surrenders like the absence of meaning, as in the "breaking of the waters" into labor or the metabolic rhythms of his prose. What is canonical in Beckett, arising from the traumatizing image of the recurrency of birth, is the enfevered famished craving of what's to come, and come again, another kind of contraction, "all part of the same . . . keep an eye on that too . . . corner of the eye . . . all that together" (*Not I* 21), the diminuendo of gratification, not-I, lessness, as if abraded by the eye, the look of being looked at, for the "Sucklings who having no longer to suck huddle at gaze . . ." Or—another of what he calls "Picturesque detail," keep an eye on that too—"a mite who strains away," mechanically clasped at its mother's breast, "in an effort to turn its head and look behind" (*Lost Ones* 30), as if in some reflexive postnatal longing for what, empowering an impoverished future, remains in the womb of the past. This nesting stare of the scopic drive, the desire to see the dimly remembered, regressive as it is, may be itself the suggestive model, "the axis about which the sensation pivots," of "the model of duplication (*whose integral purity has been retained because it has been forgotten*)," as Beckett says in the essay on Proust.[9]

But, in the self-opposing annular rings of the "teeming precinct" of the lost, "such tiny ones are comparatively few." As for the lost one within us all, from biblical and romantic tradition, the tinier little thing within, asleep, who remembers what we forget: "None looks within himself where none can be" (*Lost Ones* 30). And the implication seems to be that, like the trace of origins itself, the wordless child—poorly duplicated, reproduced— is abandoned at birth to its drifting *appearance* in life, which is to say an economy of death, *always already* (to use the Derridean phrase) in arrears, overdraft, or default. "So true it is that when in the cylinder [birth canal? teeming brain? O world?] what little is possible is not so it is merely no longer so and in the least the less the all of nothing if this notion is maintained." Which notion appears to be the (other) recurrency that is born of death, dominion of *reproduction,* with its "devouring" and "unceasing eyes" (29, 33) which "suddenly start to search afresh as famished as the unthinkable first day until for no clear reason they as suddenly close again or the head falls" (32).

Even before this notion is maintained, one might have misgivings about reproduction in this world, which, like a breeder reactor whose core is toxic waste, has converted the ancient myth of pollution into ecological fact. One might also have second thoughts about what has become, since I last had a child, a new liturgy—in the books on pregnancy and the classes on reproduction—about the lovely experience of the joy of birth. As a very savvy, solicitous, and indefatigable nurse with something of the gaiety of

Winnie said when, with great labor of her own, the bearing down had bottomed out, "Let's face it, it's the pits." So, too, there was the appalling moment when the bloody head appeared and, instead of a starry *jouissance,* as in the discourse of desire, it seemed hideous and deformed. I took the skull for the placenta, as if the show had grown egregious and the appearance were reversed. I was not at all consoled for that terrifying instant by Derrida's exergue to "Writing before the Letter," in which we are told that the future "can only be proclaimed, *presented,* as a sort of monstrosity."[10] Nor by the conclusion of his essay "Structure, Sign, and Play," when he points to the irreducible difference between the "structuralist thematic of broken immediacy" with its sadness and guilt about loss, resembling Beckett's, and "the *seminal* adventure of the trace," in which Beckett is engaged, but "which is no longer turned toward the origin" as it maintains the notion of "full presence, the reassuring foundation, the origin and the end of play."[11]

Now that seems an attractive notion, the reassuring foundation, when you've just had a child, the very promise of play supplanting the bloody show that has been, through the entire history of our oedipal tradition, with its archives of power and domination, the remembered legacy of the aboriginal sacred drama. The notion of play has been hypostatized in postmodern thought, not only in deconstruction, as a refusal of power, a sort of new testament of polymorphous being, "outside time without extension," as Lucky says in his monstrous enunciation of the breakdown of Western metaphysics, the apathia athambia aphasia separated from the divine and the repetition of its redoubtable image. Play is recursive but unrepeated, *presented* not *re*-presented. "[As] a result of the labors left unfinished" (*Godot* 28) and the all-consuming recession of the phallogocentric source, there is the notion of a pregnancy *without birth,* and thus the end of reproduction, the *structure of repetition* which *is* the economy of death.

That other model of repetition, or duplication, whose internal purity has been retained because forgotten, is really the subject not of the postmodernist ethos but of *modernist* desire that may reappear, as for Proust, through involuntary memory. It overcomes as an epiphany "the poisonous ingenuity of Time in the science of affliction," which makes of life, through the initiation of birth, a "retrospective hypothesis." The ego that is deconstructed and *dis*-seminated through a seemingly perpetual present in the gratuitousness of play is, in this hypothesis, suspended in the fluency of its own desire, repressed, "the seat of a constant process of decantation, decantation from the vessel containing the fluid of past time, agitated and multicoloured by the phenomena of its hours" (*Proust* 4–5). If Beckett, despite himself, is still turned toward origins or the moment forgotten *as an appearance* in the fluid of future time, from things about to *disappear*—like the sails of the herring fleet or all that rising corn, the mordancy rising with the myth of rebirth, all that *corniness*—he turns away in time, like the painter or engraver: "Appalled."[12] So, within the very dispensation of play into which he has beguiled others, collapsing subject and object—"Me . . . to play" (*Endgame* 2)—he turns away from the simple-minded mythologizing of play, with its apparent relief from too much consciousness, disallowing play as a mode of salvation. Hamm: "Use your head, can't you, use your head, you're on earth, there's no cure for that!" (68). Though it's playful to remember, as Didi does, that one of the thieves was saved, a reasonable percentage, for Beckett, like Clov, the dominant percentage is *zero* and, finally, it is the obsessional play within the play that, actively forgetting, causes us to remember that play, agitated and multicoloured by the phenomena of *its* hours, is inevitably deadly.

So, too, in Derrida, try as he will, there's no relief in the play of mind from the impediment of the Logos, that history of being which desires to be completely history, *as being*. There is no escape from the movement of the sign, the mark of consciousness, the rustle, the murmur, the whisper, the tumult, "now this . . . this . . . quicker and quicker," as consciousness erupts metonymically from the Mouth of *Not I*, no escape from "the words . . . the brain . . . flickering away like mad . . . quick grab and on . . . nothing there" (22), except the being "produced as history only through the logos, and is nothing outside of it," as Derrida says; "all this clearly indicates that fundamentally nothing escapes the movement of the signifier and that, in the last instance, the difference between signified and signifier is *nothing*" (*Of Grammatology* 22–23).

The movement of deconstruction is, then, unavoidably through the remains of a metaphysics that *inhabits* our structures of thought, even when they think themselves exempt, "as the limitation of the sense of being within the field of presence . . . produced as the domination of a linguistic form" (23), even when they think themselves nonverbal. But, as with the waiting for Godot on the selvedge of speech, as if it were the circumference of silence, it is not just the inhabiting but *how* the inhabiting, inhabiting "*in a certain way*, because one always inhabits, and all the more when one does not suspect it" (24). That is what Paul de Man means, I suppose, by the blindness of insight which is, as with the Oedipus inhabited by an identity unknown, the insight of blindness.

The enterprise of deconstruction proceeds in a retrospective hypothesis, *against its own desire,* with such insight. It is forced to borrow—without any certainty about their "elements and atoms" (24)—the resources of subversion, strategic and economic (*borrowing structurally,* that is), *from what it inhabits,* and is inhabited *by,* the ontotheology of Western metaphysics. It thus falls prey to its own work, self-subverted, like the structure of Beckett's fiction, which might have been written at the eroding margins of self-observing thought, with afflicted eyes and the blood on Jocasta's brooch. For it is the incest taboo that, according to Derrida, following Freud (studied by Beckett), may be the source of all thought, that detour from the memory of gratification, "designed to leave in the domain of the unthinkable" the scandal that makes thought possible, "the *origin* of the prohibition of incest" (*Writing and Difference* 284; emphasis mine). Lest the scandal of thought congeal in the blood before it *is* thought, the *activity* of deconstruction requires, like Beckett's fiction, "the necessity of [a] *trick of writing*" (*Of Grammatology* 24) that is irreducible, fluent, yet hesitates, backtracks, erases its own thought, leaving the erasures there (*sous rature*), with a tremulously caustic indecisiveness. That irresolution is not incoherence. It is an inscription of what Derrida calls *undecidability.* It opens up the structure *to play,* that is, "the structurality of structure" (*Writing and Difference* 278) which, in order "to be thought radically," must play "without security" (292)—that first defensive instinct and last-ditch illusion of power.

So it is that, in Beckett and deconstruction, *powerlessness* is the disseminating proposition and impelling force of the seminal adventure of the trace. It works by *aporias,* as in *The Unnamable,* but always questioning whether it can be, as Beckett writes, "[by] aporias pure and simple? Or by affirmations and negations invalidated as uttered, or sooner or later? Generally speaking. There must be other shifts" (3) in the infinite play of signifiers which moves toward meanings that are always receding or vanishing and disremembers where it began. What we see in all of Beckett's writing is the trembling of perception at degree zero on the edge of its extinction. According to Derrida, the trembling is appropriate to all post-Hegelian thought, which, with the scopophilia of unceasing eyes, *speculating,* inevitably displaces itself and all it gazes upon. The quest of eyes begins, with suckling and mite (the power of a nonpower?) at the mother's breast, turning its head and looking as if, having no longer to suck, the suckling were proleptic and the future came from behind. It's as if the child were turning on a crack of the dialectic, the Hinge (*La Brisure*), which in the Derridean usage *articulates* difference, out of the imprint of a language that seems to be prior to speech, which is "originarily passive," but with an undeterrable passivity that is pointing to the past (*Of Grammatology* 65–66).

"*Where and how does it begin . . . ?*" asks Derrida. What is disturbing about the question of origin is that it carries with it a metaphysics of *presence,* the illusion of an absoluteness which is only the ubiquitous trace, always already subverted by the limitlessness of play (50). "The trace is not only the disappearance of origin—within the discourse that we sustain and according to the path that we follow [Beckett and Derrida] it means that the origin did not even disappear, that it was never constituted except reciprocally by a nonorigin, the trace, which thus becomes the origin of the origin" (60). In this self-enfolded and tautological path, curled-up worm in the history of Western thought, what undoes the fiction of metaphysical presence is *play,* swinging on the Hinge, "the *pure* movement which produces difference," whose "*(pure) trace*" is the (in)famous *différance* (62). Derived in part from the metapsychology of Freud, *différance* is an economic concept of the writing of the unconscious. It has the double meaning of difference and deferral, putting off closure or cathexis in the sensible plenitude of play, as in erotic play, *fore*play, that produces meaning which makes of play—seen in theatrical terms—not the captivated subject of the older bloody show, and the structure of power that goes with it, but the *condition* of a postoedipal plenitude. If, then, in Derrida's patricidal aversion to origins, it seems at times as though play itself—displacing the dead letter of the oedipal text with a dystopia of signs—has become a Law unto itself like the originary Word, the text in the beginning, quaquaquaqua, he invariably pulls back from that misconstruction with an erasure. Or in the trace, the slime, the sticking point of play, *equivocates.*

Between the dream of a playful plenitude—that reassuring foundation—and the desire for the unattainable presence of a disappearing origin, Derrida believes there really is no choice. It is, rather, a question of trying to work out some navigable common ground between absence and presence, the irreducible difference between the exile from origins and the affirmation of play in the odyssey of the trace. Which returns us—as if the Hinge were also a hymen—*to* the bloody show. For here "there is a kind of question, let us call it historical, whose *conception, formation, gestation, and labor* we are only catching a glimpse of today. I employ these words, I admit," says Derrida, "with a glance toward the operations of childbearing—but also with a glance toward those who, in a society from which I do not exclude myself, turn their eyes away when faced by the as yet unnamable which is proclaiming itself and which can do so, as is necessary when a birth is in the offing, only under the species of the nonspecies, in the formless, mute, infant, and terrifying form of monstrosity" (*Writing and Difference* 292).

Like the first impression of my child's emerging head. That was a case where apocalyptic metaphor yielded for me, against my usual instincts, to simpler medical prophylaxis. For when they grabbed the inverted slimy body and did wipe it off it was—whether or not this notion is maintained—quite another thing. It was, nevertheless, a sort of postmodern delivery. They gave me the scissors and I cut the umbilical cord. But even with that premature fulfillment of the doxology of desire, cutting it sooner than later, there was no guarantee of the disappearance remembered at the beginning of *Not I*. For, so far so good and so far as I can tell, the parents are known, *he* not vanished, that is, father still here, in the flesh, before you (I think), at least the Name of the Father (as the Lacanian feminists say), and the "speechless infant" is not unloved, not "spared that," but much loved (I think), for the time being, at least, appropriately for a tiny little thing born at Thanksgiving and no older than the Christmas season. Thus far, whatever the broken immediacy, the phallocratic order seems intact. And speaking of Lacan, the famous mirror phase, I can see by looking in her eyes the old oedipal reflection—although both Lacan and Beckett, reflecting this world in this world through the bloody show, locate the mirroring in the mother, a more enigmatic source.

"I am in my mother's room. It's I who live there now. I don't know how I got there" (*Molloy* 7). From the very beginning of *Molloy*, that exacerbation of a beginning—the mother "lived near the shambles" (28), but "It was the beginning, do you understand?" (8)—the rhythms of Beckett's perceptions are insidious. And with that deconstructive trick of writing, there is no chance of a beginning that is not a beginning again. What appears to be the mother is polysemously at the controls. The words fly up, the thought remains below, as in the operations of the unconscious which has no beginning or end: "the within, all that inner space one never sees, the brain and heart and other caverns where thought and feeling dance their sabbath, all that too quite differently disposed" (50). The insidiousness of perception, which then seems out of control—as when the Ghost appears in the Closet—affects not only what is being seen but *seen-as-being*, as if *to be* is only to *be seen*. But it's as if it can only happen in the reconstructed vicinity of the originary trace (thus the mother's Closet), as by the involuntary memory of the interpretation of a dream.

Beckett observes the valuelessness, for Proust, of voluntary memory as an instrument of evocation. It "provides an image," he says, "as far removed from the real as the myth of our imagination or the caricature furnished by direct perception" (*Proust* 4. This is what makes the assumed clarity of any congregation of spectators, huddled at gaze, a dubious proposition, a caricature of a caricature. The accuracy of an audience in a consensus of perception is to be counted on only if you assume that one error cancels another.) In the essay on Proust, Beckett writes that "our vulgar perception is not concerned with other than vulgar phenomena. Exemption from intrinsic flux in a given object does not change the fact that it is the correlative of a subject that does not enjoy such immunity. The observer infects the observed with his own mobility. Moreover, when it is a case of human intercourse, we are faced by the problem of an object whose mobility is not merely a function of the subject's, but independent and personal: two separate and immanent dynamisms related by no system of synchronisation" (6–7).

But they are synchronized, to that extent, in the contagiousness of the infection: there is always a wavering in the eye of flesh. If it makes the seeing indecisive, it also causes a waver. Doubled over in the contagion, it impairs the vision too. There is no immunity from the mobility even when, to begin with—before the declensions of the prospect—there is a promise in the air, the distance, "without solution of continuity," between the seer and the seen. "Nice fresh morning," Beckett writes in *From an Abandoned Work,* before the precipitation of rage, often sooner than later, in the increments of perception, "bright too early so often. Feeling really awful, very violent. The sky would darken and the rain fall and go on falling, all day, till evening. Then blue and sun again a second, then night." It is the brevity of the sun, the incessancy of the rain, night's plenitude, and the degree of violence, "feeling all this," that causes the narrator to stop and turn, looking with "bowed head" for "snail, slug or worm," the nearly immobile recursiveness of their slimy traces. There is great love in his heart too, he says, "for all things still and rooted." For there is a dread of motion, "all moving things," drawing us into perception with the cruelty of intrinsic flux, "no, no mercy."[13] Far from the shambles, it appears, it is still the mother who prefigures motion, the pain of indeterminacy, the very frailty of which is intimidating and seductive: "my mother white and so thin I could see past her (piercing sight I had then) into the dark of the room, and on all that full the not long risen sun, and all small because of distance, very pretty really the whole thing," which in its wholeness or seeming fullness endures for only a moment when perception—as it unmercifully does— fails.

"[If] only she could have been still and let me look at it all. No, for once wanted to stand and look at something I couldn't with her waving and fluttering and swaying in and out of the window as though she were doing exercises" (*Abandoned Work* 40). The word is somewhat unexpected, but the exercises are the gestural substance of the trick of writing in the perception of Beckett that is inhabited by and inhabits the activity of deconstruction: "one glimpse and vanished, endlessly, omit," as in *Imagination Dead Imagine*. The omission is an omen in the whiteness of the rotunda that encircles death and birth like "a ring as in the imagination the ring of bone" (*First Love* 63). There is a momentary ring of hardness in the image like the materials of the imagination that, dead, can only be imagined even when, as in the rotunda, it has the apparent exactitude of geometric form. The measures are a decoy like the allure of seeming symbols with which, as invariably as Kafka, Beckett teases us out of thought. He does so with the semblance of ontology or the stuff of subjectivity or the suckling of remembrance—"the white speck lost in whiteness" (66), like some truth in the mother's milk—or the hymeneal romance of nature glimpsed once and then omitted from the imagining of the ring of bone.

Between the disappearance of the "Islands, waters, azure, verdure" and "the light that makes all so white no visible source"; between the binaries thus conceived: nature/culture, light/dark, body/mind, spirit/matter, hot/cold, male/female, depth/surface, perceiver/perceived and, in that perceiving, the endless *gradients,* the rotunda, the illusory fabric of death/birth; between them, "No way in, go in, measure. . . . Go back out, move back, the little fabric vanishes, ascend, it vanishes, all white in whiteness [like the mother white and thin], descend, go back in" (63). What "experience shows" in its repetitions in the prose is that experience consists of this movement of perception at the meridian of apprehension, the membrane (brain?) in the pelvic ring of bone, where cerebral is (con)genital, derived from Ceres, goddess of grain, birth, verdure, all that rising corn: "Such variations of rise and fall, combining in countless rhythms. . . . The extremes alone are stable" (64), like the appearance of an object in a "temporary calm," always disrupted in the rotunda where things if not constructed are only as observed. Yet in the exhaustive enumeration of the appearances between, it is the appearance of an apparent stability at the extremes which, like the names we give to the binaries, "makes the world still proof against enduring tumult. Rediscovered miraculously after what absence in perfect voids it is no longer quite the same, from this point of view, but there is no other" (65).

The sighting of the little fabric, the membranous meridian between absence and presence—the hymen in the Hinge—remains "quite as much a matter of chance, its whiteness merging in the surrounding whiteness" (64), that is, the threshold of being/becoming or the origin of imagination in the trace of consciousness or the initiatory difference between memory and desire or—keeping those psychophysical exercises of the mother in mind— all that is *not* theater, the site of appearance in the ring of bone, and the waving and fluttering and swaying which *is,* the *incipience* of performance. It is this exercise of perception in the deconstruction of appearances that is the subject of expanding consciousness in the most abbreviated of Beckett's plays, which have always been about consciousness. Nor is there a moment in his fiction that is not subject to the tireless scrutiny—somewhere between theory/theater, the little fabric vanishing—of the eye of flesh. The gaze that begins when the suckling having no longer to suck turns to *speculation* is compulsive and unrelieved. What he says in *The Lost Ones* of the long period of reddening "in an ever widening glare" of the "eyes blue for preference" is true of his subtlest enticements to the activity of perception. There is the seduction of the spoiling gaze and the graduations of imperceptibility with which it occurs: "And all by such slow and insensible degrees to be sure as to pass unperceived even by those most concerned if this notion is maintained" (*Lost Ones* 39). And the notion here is—dilating over the unceasing repetitions of cylindrical thought, the obsessive speculation—"the difference *considered*" (emphasis mine), that is, the *différance.* It is "not one of speed," quicker and quicker, as with the words pouring from the Mouth of *Not I,* but of "space travelled," a harrowing space of undecidability in which the endurance of perception or "cylinder alone are certitudes to be found and without nothing but mystery" (42). But not the mystery of the Logos that keeps the pronouns in place.

For there is in the cylinder, like some protoplasmic irritability, an impatience with repose. It is that certitude of nothing but mystery which, with the speed of subjectivity, keeps identity at bay, as at the moment of my daughter's birth. Is it possible that we were, from that instant, even before, always already loving someone else? And is she, the one we're loving now— "what?. . . who? . . . no! . . . she! . . . SHE!" (*Not I* 23)—other than the one who remained, "begging the mouth to stop" (20) in the painfully loving delirium of the equivocal bearing down—"when suddenly she felt . . . gradually she felt . . . her lips moving . . . imagine! . . . as of course till then she had not . . . and not alone the lips . . . the cheeks . . . the jaws . . . the whole face . . . all those— . . . what . . . the tongue? . . . yes . . . the tongue in the mouth . . . all those contortions without which . . . no speech possible" (18–19)—the lifelong labor to bring it into the world?

But here, unavoidably, the pronouns slipping into the figure of speech,

I do seem to be speaking of something like a text, as if it were a dubious birthright, as in the opening of *Molloy*, or the ecstasy of "writing aloud" at the closing of Roland Barthes's *The Pleasure of the Text*: "the pulsional incidents, the language lined with flesh, a text where you can hear the grain of the throat, . . . a whole carnal stereophony: the articulation of the body, of the tongue, not that of meaning, of language, but rather "the breath, the gutturals, the fleshiness of the lips, a whole presence of the human muzzle," as monstrous in short as *jouissance* can be.[14] It's next to impossible to think of Beckett and not get caught up in the compulsive textualization of displaced bodily parts, the tongue in the uterus, the speechless infant in the mouth, the writing before the letter on the matriarchal wall, going through similar contortions to achieve self-presence in the living present, that pure auto-affection which, like the writing of the unconscious in the libidinal economy of the womb, does not inhabit or borrow from anything outside itself. "This difficulty," says Derrida in his commentary on Husserl, "*calls* for a response. This response is the voice [*la voix*]. The voice is richly and profoundly enigmatic in all that it here seems to answer,"[15] as in *The Unnamable*.

But what exactly is it answering—"Where now? Who now? When now? Unquestioning. I, say I. Unbelieving" (*Unnamable* 3). And: "How could you have responded if you were not there?" says another voice, enigmatic, in *Footfalls* (*Ends and Odds* 48), as you find yourself answering, I *was* there, I thought, or thought *I* was, supportively, as they say—but when the tiny little thing *wouldn't* come out, for all the labor, in a devouring helplessness at the edge of speech, somewhere between prayer and *pensum*. It was a kind of perceptual prurience, I thought, watching myself watching the bloody show. There I was, the eye of prey, the self-victimizing consciousness which is the monstrosity in the vicinity of birth, "the infinitesimal shudder instantaneously suppressed," in the silence of the rotunda after the mirror mists, "Only murmur ah, no more, in this silence," in *Imagination Dead Imagine* (66).

In Beckett we are always looking at what, perhaps, should not be looked at. We're not quite sure why not, since it isn't as if we haven't seen it before—only, like the deepest memory of dream, what we're looking at is something forgotten and only thus remembered. Thus, too, in the *Ghost Trio*, the faint and impersonal voice that "will not be raised, nor lowered, whatever happens," responds to the difficulty that calls for it by asking us to "Look. (*Long pause.*) The familiar chamber." And we see it ghosting out of remembrance in the faintly luminous light of no visible source, as a video image. There is the intimate estrangement of that voyeuristic medium around which the family gathers, not only the chamber but the miniaturized chamber drama. It is the old Freudian family romance, elliptically there, *close-up,* like the grain of the voice that is always more material as an image on the screen, however impassive, in the image of the voice, seen, in the dust, the floor, the wall, which, having seen, as the voice says, "you have seen it all" (*Ends and Odds* 55).

Despite Othello's lust for ocular proof, seeing is not necessarily believing. As we've heard in recent years from the human sciences and literary theory, *seeing is interpreting.* And the problem with interpreting is that the thing to be interpreted presumes an enigma even if seemingly self-evident, like "the kind of wall" in *Ghost Trio* (55). Without any system of synchronization between the perceiver and the perceived, it seems impossible to know whether it's a thing in itself with an identity of its own or an interpretative subject *preselected* by thought within the tautological enclosure of its self-reflection: eye of flesh, eye of prey, subject closing upon object, hunter and hunted, mirror upon mirror mirroring the bloody show? or *projected* as an object by the perceiving subject in accordance with the logic of its own desire?

All the preying ramifications of perception in Beckett are variations on the blindness that came to focus in the image of Hamm: the blindness of insight of the solipsistic subject, hooded, and supplied with a stancher for emblooded eyes. The consciousness of Hamm is like a camera obscura. The lens, however, is blocked off to our sight, so that what we experience as he looks darkly toward us is ourselves looking at what only meets the eyes but does not, if his eyes *are* sealed, look back. So there we are doubly looking, picking up the obscurity on which our eyes seem to rest, *un*-enlightened. "I see my light dying," says Clov (*Endgame* 12), and thus do we, the light of the perceptual system without synchronization illuminating not the voice that comes from who knows where, but *only a surface that speaks.* All vision is both projective and introjective, and what comes back, then, from the seductive blankness of Hamm like an empty signifier over the stream of the look is what, projected there, is deposited back, as in film. What settles on the imaginary plane of perception is marked, as Christian Metz observes of the identification of spectator with camera in the cinema, by "our relation to the world as a whole and . . . rooted in the primary figures of orality."[16] As we gaze upon Hamm he seems to be—through too much historical consciousness in a play that never forgets—an arrested version of orality, no more than a figure of speech.

"Who perceives, who enunciates the difficulty?" asks Derrida in his essay on Foucault, "Cogito and the History of Madness" (*Writing and Dif-*

ference 37), into which my daughter, tiny little thing, is with the infinitesimal shudder of the eye of prey instantaneously caught up. I should have said shutter, if you'll forgive the pun, because they now let you take pictures in the delivery room. Even now, loved as she is, she is being *stared at.* It is the hauntedness of being the *being-perceived* in the beginning which is in Artaud—whom Derrida has studied as a mirror of thought—the reason for madness. It is also the ontological basis of what for Artaud is Original Sin, the idea of an *audience,* that specular entity whose name suggests the Word, the thing *heard.* The audience—*the ones who look*—is the look of the Law. It is the audited reflection of originary division and primal separation. What occurs in the susceptible body of the speechless infant as fecal matter signifies for Artaud a kind of dismemberment, or *sparagmos.* It is a sign of the original bloody show in the ritual drama, the loss of precious parts of ourselves that are only *re*-membered in dreams. It is the preying eye of the specular ego that depreciates us and soils us in the name of a lethal power that steals both word and flesh. It is the insinuating difference in a structure of theft, or rather the double that inserts itself between ourselves and birth, the "subtle subterfuge which," as Derrida says, "makes signification slip" (*Writing and Difference* 177), the nothing that posits itself between us and origins, what comes to be the history whose name is death.

It is in this thievish space of privative being that, in the very deepest sense, the spectator is constituted and—for Beckett as well as Artaud—the theater gives birth to its Double, the self-reflexive subject of thought, the thinking subject stealing thought away, eye of flesh, eye of prey, bringing death to the bloody show.

VLADIMIR: We must have thought a little.
ESTRAGON: At the very beginning.
VLADIMIR: A charnel-house! A charnel-house!
ESTRAGON: You don't have to look.
VLADIMIR: You can't help looking.
ESTRAGON: True.

(*Godot* 41)

In Beckett's earliest attempts at drama—deconstructing the well-made play and playing within the play—this holocaustic association was already there. *Eléutheria* foreshadows an equivocal strategy with respect to the theater as an agency of the economy of death that, for the bourgeois audience, gazing on death, is written on the price of its ticket. When, in the last act, Victor has defined liberty as "seeing yourself dead," there is a final curtain in which, reconciled neither to the Krapp family romance nor to suicide, he lies down on his bed after looking long at the audience, "his thin back turned on humanity." As for seeing yourself dead, that's the problem of representation that plagues Artaud and deconstructionist thought. "You can't see yourself dead," as Victor says. "That's playacting."[17] Which is the vice of representation in the dominion of death, that death can only be *represented*. Which is to say it can only be theater, falsifying theater, that repeats it over and over, an interior duplication of the division, the *sparagmos,* the originary bloody show—in which we must have thought a little at the very beginning to make a charnel house that seems without end.

"Will you never have done? (*Pause.*) Will you never have done . . . revolving it all? (*Pause.*) It? (*Pause.*) It all. (*Pause.*) In your poor mind. (*Pause.*) It all. (*Pause.*) It all" (*Footfalls* 48). Whatever it is that is being revolved, it seems to steal "the simple presence of its present act from the theater, from life," as Derrida says, rehearsing Artaud, "in the irrepressible movement of repetition" (*Writing and Difference* 247), through which Beckett and deconstruction try to work. It is the structure by which they are inhabited, in order to attain the "repetition of that which does not repeat itself" (250), the prerogative of being in its unrepeatable plenitude, the pure *"present indicative of the verb 'to be'"*—not I, not Other, but *it,* perhaps *it all,* "the pure and teleological form of expression insofar as it is logical," as if an enigmatic *third person* were the real determinant (as Heidegger thought) of the infinitive of being (*Speech and Phenomena* 73). "It is here that *speech* is necessary," writes Derrida (74), and with speech, the inaugurating word, tautological, as in the speechless infant, "the one the first and last time curled up." One cannot deconstruct this movement of appearance that is the movement of consciousness itself entering history, "without descending," the little fabric vanishing, "across inherited concepts, toward the unnamable" (77), as Derrida says, and as Beckett does.

In Beckett as in the Logos, the beginning is a word, though when push comes to shove, as in the difficulty of my wife's delivery which also called for a response, it seemed a far cry from that. "Astride of a grave and a difficult birth." To bring my daughter into this world, godforsaken world, they had to use the forceps. They were inserted one at a time, "Down in the hole, lingeringly" (*Godot* 58), large shining cusps of surgical steel, as if the Hinge were rounded. They left a mark on my daughter's cheek. It has already disappeared, but as I keep revolving it all it will (I'm afraid), like the "shudder in the mind" in *Footfalls,* be indelibly remembered in its vanishing like the inscription of the seminal trace: "The semblance. Faint, though by no means invisible, in a certain light" (*Ends and Odds* 47). As if it were written, as it now is. And so, as the bloody show continued, that remarkable conception, it was as if an immaculate negation also came forth, but *only as a text.* It came from something unnamable which remained in the womb, like the voice in the *Fizzle* which gave up before birth, though "birth there had to be," for it's impossible otherwise, "I didn't wail, I didn't see the light it's impossible I should have a voice, impossible I should have thoughts, and I speak and think, I do the impossible, it is not possible otherwise, it was he who had a life, I didn't have a life, a life not worth having, because of me he'll do himself to death, because of me"—what?. . . who? . . . *not* she!—"I'll tell the tale, tale of his death, the end of his life and his death, his death, his death alone would not be enough, not enough for me. . . ."[18]

Nor me. And as the pronouns merge in this reflection, confusing gender and person, slipping from the loving scrutiny of a particular birth to the birth in which love is only scrutiny, the eye of prey, I find myself thinking neither of her nor of him but of *me,* myself my own object in the reflection, an interior space of being where whatever it was that was left behind, the *remainder,* the forgotten part of being, is summoned forth. And as I think of her now, picking her up in thought like the "tender mercies" remembered at the end of *Not I,* "nothing but the larks . . . pick it up" (23), the scrutiny returns again, and the brain, "the beam . . . flickering on and off," scrupling, "starting to move around . . . like moonbeam but not . . . all part of the same . . . keep an eye on that too . . . corner of the eye . . . all that together" (20–21) repeating, crossing gender and time, becomes me, and I *am* now speaking of the paternity of a text, "the words . . . the brain . . . flickering away like mad" (22–23) yet something also begging it to stop "unanswered . . . prayer unanswered," keeping an eye on that too, we pray, we prey, words flying up, thought remaining below . . . pick it up.

(1985)

6

Barthes and Beckett
The Punctum, the Pensum,
and the Dream of Love

Pathos has had a bad name in the history of the modern; sentimentality worse. Until the last books of Roland Barthes, they seemed like insipid residues of humanism in the era of the End of Man. An honorable exception was always Beckett—the congenital last holdout of humanism—who couldn't shake the pathos for all its running sores, the laughter of mutilations, and whose cruelty never prevented you from having a good cry, right up the *risus purus,* the laugh laughing at the laugh. If the writing of Barthes—dry, obtuse, *matte,* fatal, as he describes it—seems to come from "a gentle hemorrhage"[1] in the discourse of desire, the grotesque comedy of Beckett seems to leak from a defective bypass in the braininess of a bleeding heart. "Nature!" exclaims Hamm, rapturously for a moment (*pause*), forgetting his painkiller. "There's something dripping in my head. (*Pause.*) A heart, a heart in my head."[2]

Barthes, too, has a heart in his head, as he suggests in his quasi-autobiography, *Roland Barthes by Roland Barthes,* in the *pensée* entitled "L'amour d'une idée"—Love of an idea. *Love* and *Idea:* we might almost say, before loving the idea, a fatal coupling! For at a time when all our thought, and certainly theory, seems infatuated with the sexual, love seems obscene, as Barthes observes in *A Lover's Discourse,* because it prefers the sentimental (175). He prefers it himself with a certain exuberance. "I take for myself the scorn," he writes, "lavished on any kind of pathos: . . . like the Nietzschean ass, I say yes to everything in the field of my love" (166–67). If sentimentality is still to be thought of as an emotion disproportionate to its motive and somewhat immune to considered judgment, Barthes seems to indulge himself to the point of infatuation, and not only about the idea of love: "For a certain time," he writes in "Love of an idea," "he went into raptures over binarism; binarism became for him a kind of erotic object. This idea seemed to him inexhaustible, he could never exploit it enough.

That one might say everything with only one difference produced a kind of joy in him, a continuous astonishment. Since intellectual things resemble erotic ones, in binarism what delighted him was a figure"[3]—as it does in the figurations of love in *A Lover's Discourse,* the goings and comings of love, the ubiquitous plottings, the strivings and contrivings, the measures taken, what keeps the lover's mind racing through all the contingencies, cantillations, and vicissitudes of love. Speaking, however, of Exuberance, the Blakean figure by which the amorous subject negotiates the place of love in an economy of pure expenditure and utter loss, Barthes warns in a parenthesis that, "if we would glimpse the transgressive force of love-as-passion," we must remember "the assumption of sentimentality as an alien strength" (*Lover's Discourse* 84).

This strength is what we see in *Camera Lucida,* not only in his refusal to reduce himself-as-subject before the photographs he studies, but in the memorial to his mother in that somewhat Proustian book. He does not weep, he says, in another parenthesis, expecting that Time will simply dissipate the emotion of loss. Meanwhile, he does not refrain from summoning up in bereavement the language of sensibility and irreducible affect. He wants to mourn his mother in the untenable words of the ego's old dispensation: as *being, soul, essence,* a quality of life; in a world suspicious of love and substance, the *substance* of the beloved, rather than a reflection of structuralist activity or an illusory Figure of Speech; not the Mother, but *his* mother, the only mother he can mourn. Since the classical phenomenology in which he'd matured had never, so far as he remembers, spoken of desire or mourning, he has to look elsewhere for a way to cross the hysterical division of History—which *is* hysteria, marked and affirmed by Death—in order to recover an Image of his mother that would be immediately steeped in the particularity, the *singularity,* of his pain, what would preserve for him the "radiant, irreducible core."[4] Against his Protestant instincts, which refused the Image, and his demythologizing past, which exposed it, he would give himself up to the solitude of the Imaginary, the Image-repertoire, in order to keep with him, "like a treasure," his desire and grief.

So, too, with the anticipated *essence* of Photography, to which he was drawn as *Spectator* for "'sentimental' reasons," and which he wants to explore not as theme or question but as a *wound*—a wound that he willingly suffers with nostalgia and a pensiveness that is the recuperative medium of the insufficiency of remembered love. We may have quite different feelings or amorous sentiments about the details of the photographs he examines—the sheet carried by a weeping woman, the black sailor's crossed arms, Bob Wilson's sneakers—but what is undeniably moving in the book is his account of how, when it was impossible "to participate in a world of strength," appalled by social life, he lived in his mother's weakness before she died. Nursing her as he did, bringing the favored bowl of tea to her lips, he experienced her, "strong as she had been," his inner law, as his feminine child: "I who had not procreated, I had, in her illness, engendered my mother" (*Camera Lucida* 72). Barthes had written in *A Lover's Discourse,* not very long before, that he had learned very early, as a normal person, to endure the loss of a beloved object, since he was accustomed to being separated from his mother. But he knew that the separations remained a source of suffering, approaching hysteria. As a "well-weaned subject," he could feed himself, "*meanwhile,* on other things besides the maternal breast" (14), but as if in retribution for his having said so the *meanwhile* wasn't long. Once his mother died he resigned himself to awaiting the remainder of a life that would be "absolutely and entirely *unqualifiable* (without quality)" (75) before his "total, undialectical death" (72). Which came much too soon to confirm him in its imbecilic negation, as Sartre said of it in his epitaph on the death of Camus.

Like the narrator in Proust, Barthes insisted in *Camera Lucida* not only upon his suffering but the profundity, the *originality* of his suffering. He was unashamed of its excess, as of the tainted idea of *origin* in the claim of originality, which in the creed of poststructuralism is as suspect as pathos. Even if the emotion of loss, amortized, were to vanish in time, the gradual labor of mourning would not—he couldn't believe it—relieve the pain. It is the economics of grief, including a dialogue with Freud carried over from *A Lover's Discourse,* that is the perceptual field of *Camera Lucida,* as it is a kind of econometrics of grief that is the obsession-compulsion of all of Beckett's work, driven as it is by the desire for what is *not-there* and, chances are, never will be. It is the immanence of an indecipherable and irrecoverable loss that is both stochastically and, as in *The Lost Ones,* almost statistically explored.

Of what Barthes had lost we have only the reflections on the Winter Garden Photograph, the sepia print of his mother as a child of five, which he did not reproduce among the other photographs in *Camera Lucida.* While it achieved "utopically, *the impossible science of unique being*" (71), even the shared values of science couldn't keep the photograph from existing only for him. Were we to see it, he says, it would interest only our *studium,* the term he uses for acculturated concern, for the *studium* is in the category of liking rather than loving. As amenable cultural subjects we might be attentive to the photograph's local color, the little girl's clothes, the period, photogeny, "but in it, for [us], no wound" (73)—which is what he calls the *punctum,* a fissure, sting, cut, hole, tear in the *studium* of a photograph, the eruptive detail, the accident that bruises, the unnamable thing that *pricks* and which, if he can name it, won't prick him at all (27, 51). In the old semiological jargon the *studium* is coded, the *punctum* is not. As if the image were launching desire past what we have permission to see, the *punctum* seems to be leading us, in the absence of a transcendental signifier, to "a kind of subtle *beyond*" (59). This, too, is a little shameless in the phenomenological bias of postmodern thought.

Barthes concludes the study of Photography with a summary of the *punctum* as "a sort of link (or knot) between Photography, madness, and something [he] did not know," which— summoning up another sentimental phrase—he ventured to call "the pangs of love." In certain photographs that pricked him, through the action of the *punctum,* which also attests to bodily loss, spoilage, devastation of the autonomy of a pleasurable self, he heard the almost unfamiliar music of an old-fashioned emotion whose name he remembers as Pity (116).

He might have been forewarned by Beckett. "Yes, one day you'll know what it is," says Hamm, in his oracular vision of an infinite emptiness, "you'll be like me, except that you won't have anyone with you, because you won't have had pity on anyone and because there won't be anyone left to have pity on" (*Endgame* 36). It's a prospect of life as utterly unqualifiable because—in the economy of death: even at the start "finished, it must be nearly finished" (1)—the grains of accumulation seem to be nothing but loss, ineluctable and pitiless loss. "It's not certain," says Clov (36), undercutting the apocalyptics, as if he'd pricked the *punctum.* But then, seeing his light dying, he seems to be dying himself as if immobilized with compassion. Something is taking its course, engorged with time, making his body a total wound. Barthes never accumulates anything like the empowering magnitude of this incapacity in the concept of the *punctum,* but as he moves through the earlier affective intention of his book to distinguish a cultural field (the *studium*) from the unexpected flash or hallucinatory rip across it (the *punctum*), he discovers a higher order of *punctum,* the source of Pity, not merely the infectious detail, the charm, but a deadly stigmatum in the brain scan, a definitive click, then *flat Death* in the photograph, "the lacerating emphasis" of Time, the *thing-which-has-been,* not as form but unfiltered intensity, its "pure representation" (92, 96).

It is here that the *punctum* is intersected and deepened by what we may feel in *Waiting for Godot* when Didi is gazing at the sleeping Gogo, *being-seen* in his speculation, as if he were sleeping himself, looked at, positioned where his thoughts are, "Astride of a grave and a difficult birth. Down in the hole, lingeringly," as if perception were the grave digger putting on the forceps.[5] So Barthes, when he gazes at the handsome portrait of the handsome young man waiting to be hanged. What he sees is an anterior future, the *sentencing* of a past, contemplating with horror a subtle *behind* that is appallingly beyond, proleptic, the absolute past of the pose that foretells a future death. "What *pricks* me," he says, "is the discovery of this equivalence. In front of the photograph of my mother as a child, I told myself: She is going to die: *I shudder like Winnicott's psychotic patient, over the catastrophe which has already occurred*" (*Camera Lucida* 95–96). It's as if through the accretion of remembered loss in the photographs that pricked, Barthes went through the *punctum* and out a black hole to the seminal side of representation and thus directly into the unconscious, whose processes are indestructible and where, as Freud said in *The Interpretation of Dreams*, "nothing can be brought to an end, nothing is past or forgotten."[6] Barthes, who hated dreams and distrusted fantasy and had looked askance through much of his life at the deceits of representation, was now at the imaginary source, possessed by the Image-repertoire. "I entered crazily into the spectacle, into the image," he confesses, "taking into my arms what is dead, what is going to die, as Nietzsche did when . . . he threw himself on the neck of a beaten horse: gone mad for Pity's sake" (*Camera Lucida* 117).

It is this ecstatic burden of the tragic pathos, its madness, abject, stupid, the nearly forgotten, discredited, old-fashioned emotion that brings the Barthes of *Camera Lucida* into the camera obscura of Beckett, the eminent domain where Hamm sits, in his deconstructive blindness, veiled by a kind of Veronica—blood and tears inscribed over the blacked-out lenses of the scopic eyes—as a figure of almost boundless, commiserable, but incommensurable love:

> You weep, and weep, for nothing, so as not to laugh, and little
>   by little . . .
> you begin to grieve. . . .
> All those I might have helped.
> (*Pause.*)
> Helped!
> (*Pause.*)
> Saved.
> (*Pause.*)
> Saved!
> (*Pause.*)
> The place was crawling with them!

(*Pause. Violently.*)

Use your head, can't you, use your head, you're on earth, there's no
  cure for that.

(*Pause.*)

Get out of here and love one another. Lick your neighbor as yourself.

(*Endgame* 68)

It turns mordant, of course, in Beckett, as all humanity (the audience bearing the brunt) takes on the aspect of the beaten horse. But the impossible
Pity is impossibly there. As Hamm covers his face with the stancher, ending
the play that from the beginning is haunted by the sense of an end, he
"remains motionless" (84) as Barthes "remained motionless" (*Camera
Lucida* 73) in the inexhaustible commemoration of his mother through the
unweeping diminuendo of the emotion of loss, which does not erase the
image of what is lost forever, the pain still unappeased.

"Day after unremembered day until my mother's death, then in a new
place soon old until my own," says the narrator in Beckett's *From an Abandoned Work*. "I gather up my things and go back into my hole, so bygone
they can be told. Over, over, there is a soft place in my heart for all that is
over, no, for the being over, I love the word, words have been my only
loves, not many."[7] Over and over, trying to mitigate the suffering that proceeds "*from who she was,*" Barthes tries to replenish the sense of banality
in his grief, the recurring pathos, "what everyone sees and knows," with
the originality of an emotion that belongs only to himself (*Camera Lucida*
75–76). Overwhelmed by the truth of the image in the Winter Garden Photograph, he would henceforth consent to combine two voices, like Beckett,
"the voice of banality" and "the voice of singularity," converting the problem of grief into a problem of language. "Language is my skin:" he had
written in *A Lover's Discourse*, "I rub my language against the other" (23).
And in *Camera Lucida*, immediately after the assertion that life without his
mother would be unqualifiable, he writes, "It was as if I were seeking the
nature of a verb which had no infinitive, only tense and mode" (76).

But painful as it is, it is an arduous task, a work in danger of being
abandoned. For he cannot transform his grief, it can only be *indulged,*
because the photograph, *his* photograph, is without culture, and looked at
over and over, it allows him to experience the grief only at the level of the
image's finitude, which in photography does not, as in film, move on pro-
tensively to other images. Like the death he had predicted for himself, the
photograph is undialectical, without the power to redeem the corruptible,
converting the "negation of death into the power to work." What he sees in

the photograph is "a denatured theater" where death escapes the gaze and cannot be interiorized. There is in the photograph an "unendurable pleni-tude" that, instead of being "in essence, a memory (whose grammatical expression would be the perfect tense)," is rather blocked memory, which keeps it from being spoken. What he sees there is "the dead theater of Death, the foreclosure of the Tragic," the pathos, which denies him the catharsis he is looking for, the conversion of grief into mourning (90–91).

In *A Lover's Discourse,* however, love is another matter in another theater. "Enamoration is a *drama,*" Barthes had written, restoring to the word *drama*—through Nietzsche on *The Case of Wagner*—the archaic meaning of an enraptured stasis in great declamatory scenes, which exclude action or keep it behind the scenes. For Barthes the amorous seduction of the lover's discourse *is* such drama, a "pure hypnotic moment," hieratic, "this declamation of a *fait accompli,*" like, you're on earth, the loved one's left you and there's no cure for that except the little sacred history— "(frozen, embalmed, removed from any *praxis*)" (*Lover's Discourse* 94)— which you rehearse over and over until through some miracle of mortification it seems to break through the glazed encasement of the mnemonic embalming fluid. It is not merely the alphabetical arrangement of "the great imaginary current, the orderless, endless stream" (7) of *A Lover's Discourse* that causes the enamored figure of Drama to be followed by that of the Flayed Man, "a mass of irritable substance" (Barthes quoting Freud) whose brain and skin are shredded by the rigors of love. Like Hamm. Or Artaud. The origin of the memory of a drama of mysterious ori-gins—the "essential drama" that Artaud remembers and his ravaged body represents—is this irritable substance, whipping its innateness, a jet stream of bleeding image in the cruel service of the violence of thought, not the log-ical stoppage of thought but *the cause by which the mind can think.* The thinking occurs, however, as in the mise-en-scène of the unconscious, an alchemical space of unremitting desire, through the filiating detour of immemorial dreams. We are reminded by Artaud and Freud that the uncon-scious—with its ruptures and disjunctures and bloody eyeballs of the oedi-pal drama, that *punctum*—is our oldest *mental* faculty. There is, thus, a genetic violence in the lover's discourse, a blindness, a madness, which thinks carnally at every nerve end of thought "through all the filters and foundations of existing matter" toward the rare and irreducible beauty of a prodigious love, the orderless, endless stream becoming—as Artaud reimagines the Mystery for his alchemical theater—the "complete, sonorous, streaming, naked realization. . . ."[8]

Here, too, the prodigiousness of what's remembered seems a function of what is forever lost. The scale may change, but the violence of thought remains. As Lacan suggests, the aggressivity arises along with the image of the other in the *déchirement,* the tearing, the rending, the laceration, the initiatory splitting off of the self-enamored subject in the drama of the Mirror Stage. We have already seen that Barthes, pensive over the photograph, thinks of it as a kind of theater. If it draws less blood than Artaud had in mind, there is still a violence in the *punctum,* the cut, the tear, as there is in the disorder of repetition that makes Photography, according to Barthes, essentially indescribable. Not the content of the photograph but its sovereign contingency, the rudimentary Encounter with the Real (Lacan), its irruptive occasion. As Barthes sees it, the photograph is violent because "it *fills the sight by force.*" Realizing that the word *violent* may be extravagant, he adds: "many say that sugar is mild, but to me sugar is violent, and I call it so" (*Camera Lucida* 91). It's a nuance of his preciosity, this violence, something febrile, oversensitive, what we used to associate with the nervous system in a case of tuberculosis. Yet one feels he *does* feel as he says, grains on the teeth, just *that,* as the *punctum* of the photograph is just *this,* well weaned as the subject is.

So—again the scale reduced from the prodigious conception of Artaud's theater, the acuteness of which depends upon an originary and essential separation—Barthes is sitting, alone, at a café on the Piazza del Popolo in Rome. He is on a holiday, part of the spectacle that he is also watching, *feeling watched,* with a sense of pronouncing himself through a fantasy. Everything around him—the bustling world of theatrical Rome, whose plenitude is its system—changes value in respect to a function, the Image-repertoire, which he has entered like a sanctuary, those dismembered fractions of perfected love. There is the streaming realization that he has cut himself off from the world, which seems *unreal,* so that he may surrender himself to the Image. Bereft, withdrawn, he may, as the lover does, hallucinate in a solitary drama "the peripeteias or the utopias of his love." But there is a second phase that is not quite a fantasy. He is "not 'dreaming' (even of the other)," nor is he deceived. He realizes that "no imaginary substitution will compensate" for the loss of love (*Lover's Discourse* 90). Speaking of another *punctum,* or syncope, "the noise of a rip in the smooth envelope" of the loved one's Image, Barthes knows that in that rip he may hear the menacing rumble of "*a whole other world,* which is the world of the other"—and no longer the pure amorous field (25–26). With the horrible ebb of the Image, there is the realization that "the horror of spoiling is even stronger than the anxiety of losing" (28).

We are all familiar with the litany of that spoilage in Beckett, which seems to arise out of nature like the stink of History. "What dreams! Those forests!" says Hamm, after the cracked "a—bsolute" of his opening yawn (*Endgame* 2–3), awakening into the nightmare of History from the dream of love, the loss of which can become so intense that even the dream of it disappears. There is a part of the lover's discourse that seems to occur in the zone of zero of Beckett's play or at the freezing point of the rotunda, "a ring as in the imagination the ring of bone," in *Imagination Dead Imagine* (*First Love* 63): "Everything is frozen, petrified, immutable," writes Barthes, not Beckett, "i.e., *unsubstitutable:* the Image-repertoire is (temporarily) fore-closed" (*Lover's Discourse* 90–91).

But only temporarily. The Flayed Man is too irritable for that. His "exquisite points" are excited by the faintest thought of love, as in *Imagination Dead Imagine* the most minimal sign of life awakens into being against the desire for a stilling of the "countless rhythms" of being, a respite, petrification—"not dead yet, yes, dead, good, imagination dead imagine" (63)—or against the desire for a homeostatic silence, as in *Ping,* where the "Traces blurs light grey eyes holes" are like a polygraph of the *puncta,* "light blue almost white fixed front a meaning only just almost never ping silence," and then before the end of *Ping,* "one second perhaps not alone unlustrous black and white half closed long lashes imploring ping silence over" (*First Love* 72). The pings over the "all known all white bare body" of distilled and humiliated desire, love's body, "Hands hanging palms front white feet heels together right angle" (69), are like the "map of moral acupuncture" over the defenseless body of the Flayed Man in *A Lover's Discourse,* that mythic figure of the most vulnerable love which, even when crushed, still twitches with desire (95). It's as if the exquisite points of these two exquisite writers, Barthes and Beckett, were nodes of protoplasmic irritability, the malaise at the selvedge of nonexistence that refuses not to be. It is this refusal of the death instinct *in* the death instinct that Freud tried to understand in *Beyond the Pleasure Principle,* where he also makes the astonishing suggestion that we are more than half in love with death, since death is the *aim* of life. In the circuitous detour of thought that seems to reflect as it reflects upon the circuitous paths to death, Freud surmises that the desire to return to an earlier state of things is so that, with something more or other than pleasure, the organism may die only in its own fashion.[9]

What more can the lover desire? Out of the closet, all known silence over, moving toward the subtle *beyond* of the *punctum,* where he engenders in death a feminine child, without procreation ("Accursed progenitor!" says Hamm [*Endgame* 9] to the amputated remains of the phallic father), Barthes in *A Lovers' Discourse* is also beyond the simpler-minded *jouissance,* the less costly erotic play of *The Pleasure of the Text.* He is at least more equivocal about it, anachronistic, since the lover is not a man of good conscience, who rejects the bait of analogy and the alibi of representation. He is rather entranced by the Imaginary, a *lunar* child, not playful in the old way, but tender, easily bruised in his exquisite points, experienced in anxiety, waiting, and impatient with the arbitrary play of signifiers that seem, in his hypersensitive irritability, worse than an alibi, not only a fissure in the subject like the *punctum* but a tissue of appalling lies. "One is no longer oneself, on such occasions," writes Beckett, already versed in the failures of love, in *First Love,* "and it is painful to be no longer oneself, even more painful if possible than when one is. For when one is one knows what to do to be less so, whereas when one is not one is any old one irredeemably. What goes by the name of love is banishment, with now and then a postcard from the homeland, such is my considered opinion, this evening" (18).

In a sequence of *A Lover's Discourse* entitled "The World Thunderstruck," Barthes may not share the tone, but he shares the considered opinion, the loss of the home of love, the horror of being split off not only from the loved one but from any conception of himself, self-banished, betrayed, abandoned. He articulates the suffering of a complete withdrawal, the vertigo of a terrible absence. "In the first moment I am neurotic, I unrealize; in the second, I am psychotic, crazy, I disrealize" (91). It seems like a kind of death, but if he can manage, "by some mastery of writing, to *utter* this death," *think* about it, as in the pensiveness of *Camera Lucida,* in which he engenders his mother in her dying, he can die first in his own fashion and then begin to live again—although we have seen that there is no guarantee of any real quality to the life before the total undialectical death. "Strange notion in any case, and eminently open to suspicion," writes Beckett in *The Unnamable* of the obligation of the *pensum,* "that of a task to be performed, before one can be at rest. Strange task, which consists of speaking of oneself. Strange hope, turned towards silence and peace."[10]

There is, then, in the craziness of the spectacle, where Barthes took into his arms the thing that is dying, something *pensive* in the *punctum* which reminds one of the *pensum,* that curled-up worm of encyclical thought, the mortal coil, the intractability of *The Unnamable,* which keeps the discourse from coming to an end because the lesson has been forgotten and which—like the stigmatum of the *punctum*—may have been a punishment for the misfortune of being born. No telling what it is, says Barthes, whose last words in *Camera Lucida* speak of "the wakening of intractable reality" (119). "But was I ever told?" asks Beckett (*Unnamable* 30), how intractable it is, the irruption of love in the memory of the dead.

In Beckett there is an inversion of the sentiment that the dead live on in our memory of them. Reflecting in his essay on *Proust* on Marcel's memory of his grandmother—the involuntary memory that restores what, he then realizes, is *no longer there*—Beckett writes: "The dead are only dead in so far as they continue to exist in the heart of the survivor. And pity for what has been suffered is a more cruel and precise expression for that suffering than the conscious estimate of the sufferer, who is spared at least one despair—the despair of the spectator."[11] It is the despair of the spectator that is, however, introjected in the work of Beckett, which is, not only the plays, obsessively and painfully conscious of being observed. There is at the same time disdain for the trust in observation which thinks, like the lover gazing at the loved one, that if you look long enough and hard enough you will really *see*. What you will see, if you use your head, is that there's no cure for that. As for the despair of Beckett, it is thickened by the irony of the memento mori: that we seem to be living not only in the memory but the mastery of the dead, who utter without pity for the living the death we think about. "Speak, yes, but to me, I have never spoken enough to me," says the voice of *The Unnamable*, "never had pity enough on me, I have spoken for my master, listened for the words of my master, listened for the words of my master never spoken, well done, my son, you may stop, you may go, you are free, you are acquitted, you are pardoned, never spoken. My master." Whatever's dripping in the head, the heart in the head, "There's a vein I must not lose sight of" (30–31).

It's a vein that Barthes did lose sight of now and then, understandably, as we see in *Barthes by Barthes,* as he speaks of his childhood, the dead father's name on the blackboard, "the figure of a home socially adrift: no father to kill, no family to hate, no milieu to reject: great Oedipal frustration!" (45). Which is why the Imaginary of Barthes is ever so different from that of Sartre, to which he pays homage in *Camera Lucida.* Sartre's father also died early, but he thinks of that death in *The Words* as a fortunate disburdening, so much so that he claims to have been told by a psychiatrist that he has no superego. Barthes does, which accounts for the frustration, as well as the earlier allure of *jouissance,* anti-Oedipus, schizoanalysis, the feminine, and the infinite galaxy of signifiers in a field of lubricious play, that absolute flow of becoming in the libidinal economy of an imperium of Desire. But if there's madness in *Camera Lucida* it is the madness of a final realism. This realism is "absolute and, so to speak, original," and nevertheless *bespoken,* that is, spoken *before.* It accedes, then, "to the very letter of

Time: a strictly revulsive movement which reverses the course of the thing" (119), as it also keeps its distance, which has wavered in Barthes before, from the clamor of anarchisms, marginalisms, polysexualisms, radical feminisms, which want to abolish the images in order to rescue desire from the phallocratic grasp of logocentric mediation–"you are free, you are acquitted, you are pardoned, never spoken"—without which, the *being-spoken,* painful as it is to say, there wouldn't be any desire.

As Beckett has always known, even when kicking against the pricks. "It follows," says Barthes, "that in any man who utters the other's absence *something feminine* is declared: the man who waits and suffers from his waiting is miraculously feminized" (*Lover's Discourse* 14). It may not, as in Beckett, be the best of all possible miracles, but the feminine shift, drift, or habitation is always there, as when Molloy finds himself in an originary longing somehow in his mother's room. Yet, as we see in the feminized figure of *Enough,* the feminization is not enough, for there's still the fatal couple, his old hand on her old breasts: "I did all he desired. I desired it too. Whenever he desired something so did I. He only had to say what thing. When he didn't desire anything neither did I. In this way I didn't live without desires. . . . When he was silent he must have been like me" (*First Love* 53).

The Unnamable and the amorous subject have this in common: they cannot be reduced to the subject as describable symptom. And if one is forced to make fine distinctions about them, as in the present discourse, that's because they are forever making fine distinctions about themselves, tautological, oversubtle, reversing the amorous field—even when, as in Beckett, they seem desperate to hold within the alienation of language their ontological ground. "I was so unused to speech," says the garrulous narrator of *First Love,* "that my mouth would sometimes open of its own accord, and void some phrase or phrases, grammatically unexceptionable but entirely devoid if not of meaning, for on close inspection they would reveal one, and even several, at least of foundation. But I heard each word no sooner spoken." Which is the problem, hearing it, undoing the undying love. For, as they say in the discourse about discourse, as the signifier approaches the signified, becoming the *thing-heard,* it seems to shake the foundation, and becomes in the very logorrhea the bereft and helpless comedy of the originary constipated Word. In this sequence of *First Love* the narrator awakes from the observation about the word no sooner spoken with the woman renamed Anna beside him, naked, a stewpan she gave him as a bedpan in his grasp. "It had not served," he says. "I looked at my member. If only it could have spoken! Enough about that. It was my night of love" (31).

If it's not a satisfactory night, that's because—however we come, like Barthes, to the love of an idea—we love in the idea of love, loving ourselves loving. Moreover, as we see in Barthes and Beckett, there is something wanting in love, which we think of as a thing of silence, if it is not entirely spoken. If not for the words of love, failing as they do, there might not be not only a lover's discourse but—even in silence—anything like love at all.

Yet: no metalanguage, Barthes insists, in explaining how *A Lover's Discourse* is constructed. He wants to speak, as close as rhetoric permits, to a primary language. But that's an aspiration of the discourse which always frustrates its end, as in *The Unnamable,* where "the search for the means to put an end to things, an end to speech, is what enables the discourse to continue." In Barthes, the continuation eventually annuls the object of desire, so desire may desire itself. In Beckett, the discourse wants to serve another purpose than desire, "In the frenzy of utterance the concern for truth"— and a certain nostalgia for its profundity. "But not so fast," he says, like Lucky about his own autistic frenzy. "First dirty, then make clean" (*Unnamable* 15). But even when the language is clean, transparent, as it can be in Beckett, it still shifts and confounds, like the thought of love itself, intractable, unreal, the speech of one addressing another who, in order to be there *as* other, *never speaks.* This makes of the amorous subject and the unnamable not a psychological but a structural portrait, which is not quite what Barthes wanted for his mother.

The discourse in each case has no case history. Nor is there anything like the specificity of History in the Winter Garden Photograph. It is a discourse that "exists only in outbursts of language, which occur at the whim of the trivial, of aleatory circumstances" (*Lover's Discourse* 3). It's as if, for the unmooring moment, all other categories were abolished and there were, in the play of amorous feeling or its other, *desperation,* nothing but the Imaginary from which to speak, out of the momentum of "*an extreme solitude*" (1). It is this solitude from which the unnamable thing is generated, the other becoming the site of love where love embraces desperation. For Barthes the other is, for all the power of his love, what occurs *without* him. That is why for all his love he feels annulled by the *other's* suffering. It is this realization that, in the movement of desire, calls for its finest tuning, a certain distancing by means of which the *disappearance* of the other is made endurable.

As for Beckett, the excruciating pathos that remains virtually unrelieved, despite all the measures taken, is the insufficiency of any distance, which can never be enough, *not distance,* for he is not convinced that the other occurs without him: "he did not like to feel against his skin the skin of another," says the figure of *Enough*. "Mucous membrane is a different matter. . . . If the question were put to me I would say that odd hands are ill-fitted for intimacy. Mine never felt at home in his. Sometimes they let each other go. The clasp loosened and they fell apart. Whole minutes passed before they clasped again. Before his clasped mine again" (54). At night, before they disappear in the dawn, they walked in a half-sleep and the other touched "where he wished. Up to a certain point. The other was twined in my hair" (60). The amorous distance, says Barthes, can be given a certain name: *delicacy* (*Lover's Discourse* 58). Even such delicacy exists for Beckett only in the propriety of an impeccable distance in the intimacy that always fails. From things about to disappear, he says delicately elsewhere, he turns away in time, but to watch them out of sight, no, no, he can't do it—even if the pathos returns.

Whether desperate or enough, the amorous subject shares with the Unnamable the desire "to slip," as Barthes says, "between the two members of the alternative: . . . *I have no hope, but all the same* . . . " (62). They drift, slip, slide, perish, with anything but imprecision, choose not to choose; between to be and not to be (in love, in life): *to be continued*. . . . If, however, the lover—the lunar child, off in the moon—" 'offers' nothing in the play of the signifier," as Barthes once proposed it with more or less gratuitousness for the postmodern text, that's because the lover is "under the ascendancy of the Image-repertoire," where, as "forms of coalescence" (imitation, representation, or the dodge of anamorphosis), the analogical demon presides (96). The *bête noire* of the autobiography of Barthes— which starts with photographs that *"will never be anything but imaginary"* (*Barthes by Barthes* 3)—is analogy, which adds to its curse its irrepressible attachment to the Nature that seems to have forgotten Hamm, though Hamm, that fractured and irrepressible actor, has never forgotten Nature. Barthes says about the demon of analogy, shifting from third to first person, "it is actually the imaginary I am resisting: which is to say: the coalescence of the sign, the similitude of signifier and signified, the homeomorphism of images, the Mirror, the captivating bait" (44). But for the lover there is no resisting analogy, since the lover suffused with amorous feeling embraces the play of figuration in the Image-repertoire. "The art of combining is not my fault," says the aging and ever-desiring subject of Beckett's *Enough*, breasted, with Aquarius hands. "It's a curse from above. For the rest I would suggest not guilty" (54).

Barthes is not quite not guilty, however, in *Barthes by Barthes*, as he confesses to being "troubled by an *image* of himself," suffering when he is named. But as the lover in *A Lover's Discourse*, he wants to be named, spoken, at least upon the loved one's lips, repeated to satiety. He looks in the Mirror, takes the bait, has a craving to be engulfed—a far cry, poetic as it was, from the semioclastic mission and style of the earlier Brechtian Barthes. The one who speaks in *Barthes by Barthes,* as if a character in a novel, conceives of the perfect human relationship in a vacancy of the image, which is always on the side of domination and death (43). The one who speaks as lover to the other who does not speak is always already dispersed, ungathered, suffering a loss of structure, the gentle hemorrhage from the body. The one who melts, thaws, resolves into a dew, is drawn to the "dream creature *who does not speak*" and who, in dreams, is the silence of death—which causes the lover to feel, with death silent, there, already beside him, that there is no place for him anywhere, even in death.

By contrast, the subject of *Barthes by Barthes* is attracted, as in Morocco, to a dryer climate and another plenitude, undreamed, unglossed, free of assigned image, interpretation. It is exhausting, true, this matte quality of relationships, but "a triumph of civilization or the truly dialectical form of human discourse" (43). The lover's discourse is, as we've seen, not dialectical. There is no order to the figures except the arbitrariness of nomination and the alphabet. They erupt, twist, writhe, flail, sweat into each other, collide, subside, explode again, no first or last figure, *no love story,* and with no more system than a "flight of mosquitoes." Yet they have a vibratory cohesion, the mythic stamina of the Erinyes (*Lover's Discourse* 7), who exhausted themselves as Furies before they turned into goddesses of love, still vigilant on behalf of the Mother.

The strange "exercises" of the mother in the window of *From an Abandoned Work* are like the figures of the amorous discourse, which are not figures in the rhetorical sense but, as Barthes describes them, gymnastic or choreographic. The fragments of discourse are in their figuration like the statuary of ancient athletes, "what in the straining body can be immobilized" or arrested (*Lover's Discourse* 4). But it is, as Beckett knows, a kind of "lunatic sport," these exercises, for "underneath each figure lies a sentence, frequently an unknown (unconscious?) one, which has its use in the signifying economy of the amorous subject" (5–6). Dubious use, dubious subject. This, for Beckett, is the *pensum,* the onerous task which may, for all he knows, proceed from what-she-was, the mother "waving, waving, waving me back or on I don't know, or just waving, my sad helpless love, and I heard faintly her cries." The cries mingle with the cries with which the universe of discourse is suffused, so that perception also seems to be made helpless by the mother who, though so "white and so thin I could see past her" (*First Love* 40), was never sufficiently *still* to allow perception at all. So it is that in Beckett the figure which is, in Barthes, the lover at work is the figure of an abandoned work.

Waved back or on, he doesn't know, only to be known, his sad help-less love. The lover's discourse in Beckett is a broken monologue of one who, if he couldn't love well, loved only too much, and still loves, first love, always, always in vain, thus the straining outbursts of the frustrated body of love, the trivial, the aleatory, which in Beckett is also anal. For him, as for the aging Yeats, love has pitched his mansion in the place of excrement, as in that straining figure that Lucky makes when they order him to dance—the Scapegoat's Agony? the Hard Stool? Pozzo says, "The Net. He thinks he's entangled in a net" (*Godot* 27). And indeed, when he begins to speak it's in the onrushing momentum of love, quaquaquaqua, the lunatic sport, as if the entire lover's discourse were uttered at once; in the apparent gibberish, the entire network: an intellectual history of the phallogocentric tradition, its breakdown, Fartov and Belcher, etc., like the death of the God of Love. All of what rushes through the mind in Lucky's speech is, as Barthes says, "marked, like the printout of a code" (*Lover's Discourse* 4) or—in that other, scatological tradition—the contents of a cloaca. The words have specific uses, but underneath each figure lies a sentence, one long almost unendurable sentence.

This sentence, or rather "syntactical aria," is the *pensum,* the sub-stance of a judgment, the *burden* of the aria, or song, for there is always in the lover's discourse the plaint, the unfulfillable words of love, as if in the absence of the Word there are only words, words, words. It is no mere coin-cidence that when Barthes writes of the sentence-aria running through the head, it constitutes the figure of *Waiting,* since the sentences are matrices of suspended figures which utter an affect that is forever breaking off. As with the waiting in Beckett's play, if the other doesn't come, the other is halluci-nated, for waiting is a delirium. "The words are never crazed," says Barthes, "(at most perverse) but [as in Lucky's speech] the syntax is: is it not on the level of the sentence," he asks, "that the subject seeks his place—and fails to find it or finds a place imposed upon him by language?" (6). The thing which runs beneath the figures of love is a verbal hallucination, "a mutilated sentence"—the *pensum.*

It spawns itself in Beckett as the obsessional love lyric of self-corrosive thought in love with the thought of loving. To love love, to be in love with loving, is—as we also see in Barthes—to abrade with apprehension the object of love, *to annul it,* as if the death of love were pronounced in the marriage of true minds. The lover's anxiety, says Barthes, is "the fear of mourning which has already occurred at the very origin of love." When

FIG. 10. The lover's discourse in Beckett is a broken monologue of one who if he couldn't love well loved only too much, and still loves, first love, always, always in vain. . . . (Robert Symonds in *Krapp's Last Tape*, directed by Jules Irving at The Actor's Workshop of San Francisco, 1960)

Barthes then describes the mourning at the loss of love, he realizes that what he is lamenting is the demise of "a beloved structure, and I weep for the loss of love," he says, "not of him or her" (30). So, the lamentations of Beckett are the mourning *of* the Image-repertoire itself, the beloved structure. There is a sort of perverse pleasure in the broken images of love, as well as the unbearable ambiguity in the remembrance of the thing annulled.

"As to whether it was beautiful, the face, or had once been beautiful, I confess I could form no opinion." The narrator of *First Love* had also looked at photographs, with faces that he "might have found beautiful had [he] known even vaguely in what beauty was supposed to consist." His father's face on a death-bolster had suggested a possible aesthetic, but "the faces of the living, all grimace and flush, can they be described as objects?" (27). Anything like objects of love? There is a certain advantage, Barthes suggests, in the annulment of the other by love, since it may be absorbed with a certain eloquence into the abstraction of amorous sentiment. One may be soothed by desiring what, being absent, can no longer threaten or harm. But then there is a turnabout, and the absence is desired. It is disannulled in the amorous sentiment that is the sufferance of desire, as if the delicate awakening of love occurred in a kind of libidinal reversal, at the dew point, the pathos of a seminal flow: "I admired in spite of the dark," says the figure of *First Love*, "in spite of my fluster, the way still or scarcely flowing water reaches up, as though athirst, to that falling from the sky" (27).

But what begins (again) with such delicacy becomes monstrous in love, the waters never quite meeting in the consummation of desire. Nor is it really, in Beckett, as in *A Lover's Discourse*, that the waters merely recede and the other departs, turns away, fails to show, withdraws. Rather, and more oppressive yet, the other approaches. Even in recession the other approaches, "the other advances full upon me. He emerges as from heavy hangings, advances a few steps, looks at me, then backs away. He is stopping and seems to be dragging invisible burdens. . . . He raises his eyes and I feel the long imploring gaze, as if I could do something for him" (*Unnamable* 14). If Barthes rehearses what it is to be in love, Beckett conveys the terror of *being-loved*, the one who is loved gratuitously and asked to love *in return* without ever knowing what it is that we call love, for which one invents the obscurities that supply its rhetoric which always fails, like the very idea of love. It's as if the approach of love incapacitates the very thing that loves. As for the mother who loves, can one learn to love like that? From innate knowledge? asks the voice of *The Unnamable*, "is that conceivable? Not for me" (12). The dysfunction seems to be in the knowledge of love itself, what cannot be known without love so that love itself might be known.

"But I seem to have retained certain descriptions, in spite of myself," the Unnamable goes on: "They gave me courses on love, on intelligence," the curriculum of the *pensum*, "most precious, most precious." But what has that to do with love? "I use it still, to scratch my arse with" (13). And yet there's a point in Beckett when the arse is sufficiently scratched to become the *punctum* in the *pensum* "once known, long neglected, finally forgotten, to perform," before there's an end, "gaining ground, losing ground" in the labyrinthine torment that can't be grasped or limited or felt or suffered, "no, not ever suffered" (36)—and yet, when the very possibility of love is foreclosed, there is the "luminous none the less" (16), the pathos in the *punctum* which comes from the heart in the head.

Among the stars and constellations, the protagonist of *First Love* can only make out the Wains, first shown him by his father. He has also discovered the tenderness of the earth for those with no other prospect but her "and how many graves in her giving, for the living"—including the newborn child whose cries he plays with as he once played with song, "on, back, on, back, if that may be called playing" (35). Freud called it so in the child's *fort/da,* the reclamation of the mother by the throwing out and drawing back of the grandson's spool, like Krapp's spool, *spoool,* a way of averting the cries—weeping is not crying—"cry is cry, all that matters is that it should cease. For years I thought they would cease. Now I don't think so anymore. I could have done with other loves perhaps. But there it is, either you love or you don't" (36). In this sense, but I won't presume, I'm not sure that Barthes did. It seems like good plain sense, this remembrance of first love, at the tortuous end of a lover's discourse, but it is torn with an alien strength, on, back, on, back, from the curse of a bleeding heart.

(1986)

7

The Oversight of Ceaseless Eyes

You're sure you saw me, you won't come tomorrow and
tell me that you never saw me![1]

That desperate line from *Godot* seems, in the recessive distance, if anything
more forlorn and, in the context of recent thought, just about doubly
absurd. For even if Didi were seen, as he (dubiously) appears to be, he is
after all only an appearance, and what does the seeing amount to—what
does it *mean?*—if we can't quite count on an identity, an *I* that goes with
the *me*, an autonomous self or ego, as the stable subject of sight. The issue
is recurrent in Beckett, explicit in other plays, where in all the rushing
words the void keeps pouring in, as with the retrospective subject of *That
Time,* which, "never having been" in the first place, is "never the same but
the same as what for God's sake did you ever say I to yourself come on now
(*Eyes close.*) could you ever say I to yourself in your life. . . ."[2] Well, then
(*eyes open*), should one speak of the object? And even if that were stable,
says a more theoretical voice, "exemption from intrinsic flux in a given
object does not change the fact that it is the correlative of a subject that
does not enjoy such immunity. The observer infects the observed with his
own mobility."[3]

This may sound like an echo of Heisenberg in the language of Lacan,
but it is once again from Beckett, in the precocious essay on Proust. If the
garrulous nothing of *Waiting for Godot* was an aporetic enactment amid
the slippage of the signifiers, the slim volume of Proust—with its "contempt
for the vulgarity of a plausible concatenation"—was an already exhaustive
preface to poststructuralist themes and the specular obsessions of the discourse of desire. The loss, the lack, the rupture, all of it is there, the break
in origins and the originary trace, and—in the "gaze [that] is no longer the
necromancy that sees in each precious object a mirror of the past" (15)—the
terror of separation and uncertain signs. "Moreover, when it is a case of
human intercourse, we are faced by the problem of an object whose mobility is not merely a function of the subject's," but even more irreparably than
the allure of "otherness" implies, "two separate and immanent dynamisms

related by no system of synchronisation. So that, whatever the object, our thirst for possession is, by definition, insatiable" (6–7). If the desire for possession is bound up with the gaze ("the eyes with gazing fed": from Shakespeare's sonnets to feminist/film criticism), there remains the troubling question—suggested not only by Marcel gazing at the sleeping Albertine, but also by Didi (with the look of being looked at) gazing at the sleeping Gogo—as to *who* is really doing the seeing in the specular play of an absence that is the principle of sight.

"You don't have to look." "You can't help looking." "True." Never mind *who* for the moment; looking at *what*? As the tramps gaze over the forestage in the exchange of ceaseless eyes—veering wildly in their imaginings from "the very beginning" (the primal scene?) to "the last moment" (the one before or yet to come?)—they see "A charnel-house! A charnel-house!" which seems to arise through the maw of the audience from the recursive deadliness of thought itself. "What is terrible is to *have* thought" (*Godot* 41). And if you think of it it's appalling, the more you *think*, feeling it coming all the same, the end or the beginning ("The very beginning of WHAT?" [42]), as Didi said at the outset, "(With emphasis): AP-PALLED." You can't help looking, true, but any way you look at it, it can't be seen because, as Gogo says after peering into his boot, staring "*sightlessly*" before him, "there's nothing to show" (8). And there's the rub, which leaves us—like the claim of Hamlet to what "passeth show"—with the equally ceaseless problem of interpretation, that estranged enterprise of the mind, somewhere between "the luminous projection of subject desire" (*Proust* 1) and the desire to make (objective) sense of whatever it is we see or, even more so, what we don't; or what with more or less hysteria, like Gogo waking from his dream, we're not quite sure we saw. In that respect, it is meaning we want to possess (to have thought, then, is *not* to have it) and more than that, insatiably, the *meaning* of meaning, an ancient philosophical problem focused radically again in the theater with an incursion of the absurd (returning to the question of *who:* "Do you think God sees me?" [49]), in the now-canonized elusiveness of *Godot*.

Meanwhile, one of the ironies of the postmodern—the theatricalized period that followed upon the absurd—is that what seemed in Beckett infolded, secretive, encrypted, narrowed down to a needle's eye, became in a warp of specularity among the staples of MTV, as if the repressed contents of the unconscious, exploded, were released to the world at large. If that, in theory, mitigated somewhat the existential anxiety (and Beckettian pathos) that came with the absurd, it burdens the question of meaning with almost more than we can possibly see, a virtual pornography of sight that has begun to seem obscene. I want to come to that shortly, along with the repercussions in newer kinds of performance, beyond the perimeters of the scene established as theater. But let's for a narrower moment reflect on that, as it were through the theater (the site of seeing) reflecting on itself. With the minimalism of Beckett in mind, what I am most particularly concerned with is the subtle thing the theater came from before it widened into theatricality, an *excess of theater* that from the very beginning—escaping the desire for "ocular proof" (*Othello* 3.3.363)—always threatened to undo the form. It is precisely this excess, inappropriable as meaning, that has been compulsively remembered through the entire history of the drama, as if the paranoia of its major figures, from Sophocles' Oedipus to Genet's Irma, has proved contagious and possessed the dramatic text. It's as if the text itself, distrusting theater, were suffused with a certain anxiety about the prospect of its performance. There are any number of symptoms carrying over to theater practice and the dynamics of the relation between actors, directors, playwrights, critics, and scholars. Each (like Beckett himself)[4] has been invested in or protecting a certain meaning. As the god of the theater, Dionysus, should have suggested in "his" own nature, whatever the most certain meaning is, it can be right there before your eyes, but—because it's essentially *imageless* (as Nietzsche said of Dionysus)—in any event it always escapes.

"The meaning of meaning is Apollonian," says Derrida in his essay "Freud and the Scene of Writing," "by virtue of everything within it that can be seen."[5] As we reflect upon (and within) this Apollonian heritage—switching back and forth between the seer and the scene—we are inevitably drawn into the dialectical wordplay between the visible and the invisible, where in the very sinews of perception the spectacle appears as a trace or decoy, the ghostly, reverberant *surface* of the seen. Theater is made from this play of meaning in a structure of becoming, the passing form of an invisible force, where we lose meaning by finding it, and there is always something *repressed*. So it is, with all its duplicity, in the camera obscura of *Endgame,* which—to the degree that Beckett's theater is a reinterpretation of the form—seems in its spectral beginning like the ontological moment, the *precipitation* of appearance, or the materialization of theater from whatever it is it is *not*.

What meets our gaze is what we do not see. That's what appears to be self-reflexively dramatized in the teasing revelation of the blinded Hamm, who, even when unveiled, remains behind his glasses, (un)canny, logorrheic, intertextual, the object (or objective case: the "*Me*" who is going to play)[6] of subjectivity, a signifying presence with no reality except as a *figure of speech.* What we might have seen there, however, is what we have since encountered in the semiotic terms of the newer psychoanalysis: that there is a double articulation to theatrical fantasy, arising from the linguistic structure of the unconscious, that is *founded* in repression. (Here we touch upon what, not only in Beckett, is a truth of theater that is archaic in theater, and that is *the theater's fear of its own presence,* what is both repressed and articulated at certain astonishing moments in its canonical history.) What appears to be theater occurs in the difference between manifest and latent, surface and depth, the "spacious breadth" of the division in "a thing inseparate," as Troilus says in that mad discourse on the scene of betrayal (*Troilus* 5.2.144), the succession of signifiers that constitute performance. The unconscious signified arises from some pitfall of this inseparate thing, the gap or absence in which it resides (with dimensions too fine for the insertion of "Ariachne's broken woof" [5.2.148]), the orifice between the signifiers, not in order to express what has to be said but in order to indicate, *by veiling it,* what needs to be hidden.

Caught up in the strange logic of this succession, what we think of as "living theater" is, in the repetition of its seminal moment, a representational problem. This problem was compounded, after the advent of Beckett (but in a sort of misprision), in the dissidence of the sixties, which, scorning the hidden and wanting nothing repressed, aspired to unveil it, as in the desublimating redundancy of the Living Theatre, which literalized the succession in its signifying bodies—the naked inscription of Paradise Now—and the solipsistic images of the spectacle's excess. The utopian mission of the sixties (sublimated in theory and persisting today in the discourse of desire) was to liberate the unconscious onto the public scene, acting out the imaginary in a perverse romance with the media and the strategy of appropriation of the fantasy machine.

For the audience in those exhilarating days—the old dramaturgy rejected, everybody making the scene—the profusion of images offered a double prospect: that it might become the spectacle and, as Rousseau projected it in his letter to D'Alembert, that the spectacle would be a community. What it got instead was *commodification.* And never more abundantly so. For there is nothing that carries with it so readily as image that consumable equivalence that is—as Danton perceived on the "thin crust" of the promenade in Buechner's play[7]—the circulatory principle of bourgeois exchange. Today, on the lucrative fringes of what used to be the counterculture, this is by no means an embarrassment, as we can see in the Day-Glo salability of the (new) psychedelic glamour on the periphery of Tomkins

Park, passing from the desolation of the East Village to the dazzle of the Palladium. (Given the quick inflation of the art, not to mention the real estate, in the East Village, it has passed, besides, into the mainstream galleries of bourgeois exchange even faster than I have been able to take note of it in the slower movement of this scene of writing.) Whether or not the society of the spectacle is a culture of narcissism, there is nothing more indicative of a commodity-conscious culture, designer fashioned and hyped on style, than the high performance of high visibility that we see now in the arts, whether the spotlighted neo-abstraction in the disco Kamikaze or the '61 Cadillac, overpainted and supercharged, the Suprema Ultima Deluxa of Kenny Scharf. The circulation of appearance is made all the more spontaneous when replicated by the media, with images of other images and, in the new bohemia or avant-garde, images of the artist-as-image who is, along with the audience-as-spectacle, remaking the scene for somewhat glossier consumption, as if mediation were natural law and—born again in quotation—the sixties were never repressed.

It is a scene in which "the eyes with gazing fed" are glutted by the gaze that, seeping from the unconscious, saturates the world. What is happening in the theater can hardly compete with these newer modes of performance on the spectacular scene of bourgeois exchange. (Certain of those modes of performance were, in the late fifties and early sixties, developing in and around The Actor's Workshop of San Francisco at the same time we were producing Beckett, who attracted to the theater, as other playwrights didn't, artists from other forms. To this day certain tendencies in performance art would seem to be extractions or extrusions of verbal or gestural properties from Beckett's theater as well as scenic images, such as Winnie in the mound or the Mouth of *Not I* or the heads in the urns of *Play*.) While the solipsism and excess persist, now more than ever as a matter of style, they do so at their best with a no less beguiling and often chastening irony, like the expensive labor in the enchantment of Christo's Parisian epic, a marvel of high fashion, the repackaging of the Pont-Neuf. The implication of the conception is that it was already packaged, by the culture of guidebooks and the eroding traffic of ceaseless eyes. Also viewed by multitudes (some of those in Paris for the spring collections), Christo's polyamide spectacle was a semiotic veil over the history into which—stretching and fretting its magic hours upon the bridge or laving its sides in a watery splendor with light reflected from the Seine—it was committed to disappear. Here, after the sublimity of its little moment, the ordinary monument was restored, with whatever ambiguous residue from the spectacular transformation.

But some of those captivated by the expanse of spectacle in our lives

FIG. 11. To this day, certain tendencies in performance art would seem to be extractions or extrusions of verbal or gestural properties from Beckett's theater, as well as scenic images, such as Winnie in the mound. . . . (Beatrice Manley as Winnie in *Happy Days,* directed by Lee Breuer at The Actor's Workshop of San Francisco, 1961)

also think of it as an unabating infatuation that threatens to engulf the real, if it has not already done so. This is something else again—not the old fear of deceit in the image, an aversion to appearance, but rather as if the Platonic cave were a breeder reactor whose core was toxic waste: what we're looking at, it appears, is the end of representation that, by runaway reproduction, has at last undone itself. For Jean Baudrillard there *is* an obscenity in all this, "no longer the hidden, filthy mien of that which can be seen," but rather "the abjection of the visible," its nullity. This arises from a universe of systems and stretches over it, mirroring our technologies, "their sleek and accommodating distances, miniaturized."[8] In the accommodating spectacle of this reduction, the giant wrappings of Christo, which suggest the engulfment, would be another hapless gesture, the mimicry of redundancy in a network of redundancies. Nor is this anymore the return of the Same. Too attenuated to be the return and insufficient to be the revenge, it is no more than a minor mockery of representation, now bleached, nullified, and liquidated by the information system. Which system is mocked over and over, it would seem, at some subliminal level of its network of redundancies, "their object, duration, frequency and harrowing nature," in the recursive non sequiturs or glutted (in)consequence of Beckett's self-nullifying prose, with only the unnamable surviving the liquidation.[9]

(There is likely to be—as there has been, among some with a theoretical investment in the prospects of mass culture—more or less resistance to this bleak and imploded view. But should it require confirmation, think for a moment of any of those recurrent catastrophic events, out of the realm of pure contingency, or the unnamable itself, that seem to constitute the threshold or outer limit of the system of representation. Recall, for instance, the seeming innocence with which the space shuttle *Challenger*—carrying the teacher whose pupils were at school watching over television—exploded into the white radiance of eternity or the ultimate communication, the apotheosis of visibility. We all remember the image, with instant replay, parsed and graphed, replicated by the hour, but perhaps have forgotten how it was absorbed by the media and a media-conscious administration into the construct of a national emotion, or some appropriate facsimile, for which only televised disaster seems to be the sufficient cause. Meanwhile, in what has become a national habit, the almost universal urge for image, augmented by the right to information, seemed to be honored over privacy in the supremacy of the networks, which will sometimes exact the image even from a victim like an ethical obligation. More often than not, that we are all there to be imaged is assumed as a reflex that won't refuse.[10] Thus, the watching students and the family, seen viewing the explosion in its horrific instance or pursued by the cameras after—or even, no doubt, watching their own images later on—were quickly deprived of the continuity of devastation or a pure moment of unmediated grief.[11] Without minimizing the widespread decency that follows disaster or the sensitivity in the commentary that is aware of these ironies, there was one that was sure to go unmentioned as the images of the fireball, relayed by satellite, encircled the globe. While it's obviously in order for all systems to be shut down [as that wasn't] when there's the slightest trace of a malfunction before the launching, when the perfectly imaginable horror does happen in flight, it seems just about inconceivable for all network coverage, that other system—from which, after all, the space program is inseparable—also to be shut down, letting all emotion settle into a nonspectacular interval of national silence. But that quite naturally has to wait—the silence—for the moment of prayer and meditation in the unison of the memorial, when we mourn together over television, with cameras on the grieving families.)

What makes them obscene, in Baudrillard's view, is that the images never cease. Nor do they cease to be commodities (like the pictures in a well-known children's book—called *I Spy*—which my daughter used to insist we look at, over and over). Brought to a pleurisy by reproduction, the tumescence of image virtually exceeds the real, the very boredom of the endless replications inducing a fascination that, so far as we can see, might exist without an image, in the disembodied passion of the look. The trouble is that, thus fascinated by the fetish/image, we can hardly be expected to see anything very far.

It is the paradoxical stupefaction of these mediated spectacles, "the glazed extreme of the body," that crosses into the obscene, an advanced state of the disease of catatonia among the spectators of what Brecht called the *culinary theater*. "True, their eyes are open," he wrote in his notorious description, "but they stare rather than see, just as they listen rather than hear. . . . Seeing and hearing are activities, and can be pleasant ones, but these people seem relieved of activity and like men to whom something is being done."[12] What happens offstage in this audience Beckett put onstage in *Waiting for Godot,* where in the stunned proceedings nothing happens twice. But in the empty scene that Baudrillard is describing nothing happens again and again and again, filling "the viewfinder," until "we are saturated with it." This evocation of a glutted emptiness is preceded in Baudrillard's essay "What Are You Doing after the Orgy?" by an outré form of culinary theater, at the S/M end of the spectrum of performance art, though it also happens to be "real." As the event was reported, a young Japanese dismembers a white and nubile woman with a kitchen knife and, as he eats the "delectable parts," tries to reassemble her *image*. He also takes Polaroids at every stage to be sure that he won't forget (43).

This, to be sure, is the worst possible case of the society of the spectacle, which is also, as the case is made, the termination of the social in the indeterminate Mass. Whether or not the social is ended, this indeterminacy is now something more extensive than an aesthetic of the aleatory on the margins of the avant-garde, worked out by a throw of dice through the Book of Changes, as it once was by John Cage. Since the sixties art has not only had to navigate the sometimes collapsing, then reappearing, rather indiscernible lines between manifest and latent, surface and depth, nature and culture, but to situate itself between high culture and mass culture, popular culture and subcultures, and the overall diffusion of culture in which we have seen the accumulation of a vast array of spectacles as the most favored commodity of consumer capitalism.

What we encounter in this diffusion are performance events that, like *The Marble Fog* of Robert Longo at the Brooklyn Museum, are seduced by the fascination-effect of the world of simulation even as they expose it.[13] The effect is spectacular but not at all specific, as the fog (like history) dissipates, along with whatever remains of the solidity of tradition, the ideological status of recycled forms. The audience may be deliberately confused in such events by the pastiched blurring of the living and nonliving, presented and represented, but it is an audience for the most part born to the specular mania of the postmodern. It grew up in a confusion of genres, consuming the bricolage. The tableaux of Longo—like some doubly glazed and panoramic distension of the art that fascinated Diderot—are very much aware of this. In the performative bravura and monumental borrowings of their oversized theatricality, they are a sight to be beheld. Longo is himself ambiguously entranced with the quotable resources from myth, history, and the media available to the spectacle, but the viewer is also being asked—with more or less factitious terror in the swarm of uncertain signs— to examine the manipulative powers of the signifying apparatus. The combinatory devices of his performances can be mesmeric as they hint at meaning, but they are also concerned with the disarming ways in which alienation and mystification, the seductive staples of commodification, are bound up with spectacle.

There is in such performance a somewhat elusive attitude toward the further release of simulations and the over-rehearsed images from a kitsch and archaic repertoire. The argument is that cultural forms and myths are being recycled in order to deconstruct them. There is something discomfiting in the claim that amounts to a double bind since—as in the work of Riefenstahl or Syberberg or theory's obsession with classical Hollywood films—the persistent glamor of the showing, the embossed past and emblazoned kitsch, the renown of the empty signifiers, keeps the myth attractive. Recent performance art is, however, much less ambiguous about the revealed mechanisms of representation that account for the mystifications. It is also a good deal less embarrassed (aesthetically and sexually) about what we used to call having it both ways, which is not exactly what formalism meant by resolving paradox in ambiguity. In Longo's work the various arts are not merely overlapped or blended, as in the earlier multimedia (though it could be said that the photographic and filmic images are in the most favored, absorptive position).

The resurrected images and iconic forms of Longo are not "fused" into the appearance of an autonomous work in the modernist sense, or in a

Beckettian sense poignantly wobbling between the modern and postmodern. They are, rather, given the off-the-wall look of an assemblage of appendages hoist by their own petard. Incongruous elements are, simultaneously, kept free-floating and endowed with gratuitous aura, artfully aggregated and hyperbolically juxtaposed, in a sort of elephantiasis of surfaces whose effects are neither an account of history nor, if history's causes are known in its effects, a reliable record of why and by whom. As with the collaborative activity of a movie, Longo often includes his coworkers in a list of credits, but in Aristotelian terms the formal cause is absent. In the aesthetics of the postmodern that absence is not without virtue. The ideological dilemma, however, of the Longo spectacle is expropriation of the expropriators, as with Laurie Anderson at the Grammy Awards after recording for Warner Brothers. Like Longo, Anderson is able to include the dilemma with more or less irony, or disarming humor, in her work, as she did in *United States;* but it's as if their technical operations were programmed by and for a supply-side economy. As for the audience, in the rather glamorous means by which we are made aware of the fetishizing attraction of the exchangeable image, we find ourselves consuming, not altogether distastefully, another unliving if upgraded commodity.

It seems to be the inevitable outcome of the postindustrial reification of image that is the reign of representation. In recent theory the critique of representation is rabid and powerful. As if they'd discovered what always eluded Artaud, a body without organs, certain variants of poststructuralist discourse—polysexual, schizoanalytic, radically feminist—are still engaged in the probably vain anti-oedipal and tautological enterprise that proposes to bring representation to an end. (In somebody like Karen Finley, the gender-busting audacity of her assault on logocentrism amounts, in a sort of apocalyptic delirium that knows it won't end, to shitting on representation or sticking it up her ass.) But so long as there is a spectacle, it may be well to recall the Situationist thesis, formulated by Guy Debord at a time when radical transformation seemed not only urgent but a more likely possibility: "The spectacle in general, as the concrete inversion of life, is the autonomous movement of the non-living."[14] Artaud was enraged by the repetition of this autonomous movement that inhabits the recurrent discourse on repetition in the libidinal economy of deconstruction. As for the articulation of "the living upon the nonliving in general, origin of all repetition,"[15] whose trace is material and immaterial at once, it sounds like a definition of performance that brings us back to the unconscious. As in the stagings of the unconscious—where we are actor/audience to a spectacle whose repetitions may escape us—we are always dealing in performance, the insubstantial pageant, with an (im)palpable signification whose truth is invisible and whose energy is opaque. "What's happening, what's happening?" cries Hamm in anguish. What else can Clov say but—though it may be with gratuitous cruelty—"Something is taking its course" (*Endgame* 13).

The (apparent) truth is that there is always a displacement at work in the form of its vanishing. The drama itself is an extended meditation on the idea that whatever it is we're perceiving has already passed us by. Its subject is *aphanisis,* the movement of disappearance that is, most radically, the manifestation of the subject. (The term was used by Ernest Jones for the disappearance of sexual desire, a fate not identical with castration; thus, aphanisis is the object of a fear even more profound than that of castration.) Shakespeare's sonnets are a virtual textbook on that proposition, and the perceptual impasse dramatized in the plays has been taken up anew in the performative nexus between psychoanalysis and deconstruction, as in this passage from Derrida: "The graphic image is not seen; and the acoustic image is not heard. The difference between the full unities of the voice remains unheard. And"—as we may see in the redoubled watching of the duplicitous scene with Troilus, the imperceptible fissure in the identity of Cressida—"the difference in the body of the inscription remains invisible" (*Of Grammatology* 65). The performance, in its signifying succession (not-signified), conceals and erases itself in the motion of its production.

This is the motion that teases us out of thought. No one sees the motion but the motion, as Ben Jonson wrote in one of his masques, and as Beckett assumes in the Zeno-phobic accumulation—"Grain upon grain," the millet seeds?—of "the impossible heap" (*Endgame* 1). And that motion—like the exertion of force between breaches that, to avert pain, arouses resistance—initiates and contains the problematic of the audience, which gathers around this paradox: that the pleasure of seeing—what Freud called *Schaulust* (seeing, being seen), with its implications of sado-masochism[16]—is constrained by the desire to see what cannot be seen (what passeth show in *Hamlet,* or the thing that's taking its course). That is not, as we tend to think, merely the primal scene, the bed of incest, but the seeing of the scene, the scopic drive itself (*the desire to see*)—the object of specularity that is really out of sight, like the ghost in the mother's chamber that only the son can see. Resisting ocular proof, it is the motion producing meaning that, to Apollo's eternal frustration, never lets itself finally mean.

(1989)

8

Quaquaquaqua
The Babel of Beckett

This may get more theoretical later; somewhat roundabout, but I want to begin with a sort of historicizing preface to what I had intended to say, for I came here directly from Paris, where I saw Beckett last week. He is in his eighties now and, as some of you know, has not been well. But while "the circulation," as he said, "leaves something to be desired," there were two neatly ready glasses on a small writing table, and we toasted each other with a shot of Irish whiskey (Bushmill's, to be precise), the particular occasion being, rehearsed as afterthought, that we had met almost exactly thirty years ago, winter it was, that time, was there ever any other time? as he might say, even if the circulation should happen to return. That time was the time I first went to Paris, the day after we opened in San Francisco, at the old Actor's Workshop there, one of the earliest stagings of *Endgame,* which I had directed.

I had known of Beckett's work, though it was hard to come by then, shortly after the war—I mean the last of those Great Wars, of course, World War II, after which for a while, that time, we didn't have any wars but, rather, "bandit raids" and "police actions," like that in Korea, whose landscape apparently resembled for those who had been there (San Francisco was a port of debarkation, and some of them showed up at our plays) the bleak denuded landscape of *Waiting for Godot,* with the same purposeless sense of a missing action or the repetitive expectation of an encounter yet to come. As for that other "preventive measure," not at first a war but an undeclared facsimile of a war, that eventually vain and demoralizing enterprise against insurgency in a jungle, *that* might have been a real war or a winnable war if, as General Curtis Le May wanted us to (or was that in Korea? that other time, I forget), we could have leveled them.

But in this case the preventive measure was a lingering mechanism of the Cold War, the Balance of Terror. If that was to become for Henry Kissinger the basis of détente and, within a huge global theater, the Doctrine of Credibility, it was also for Beckett the basis of his dramaturgy, where the issue of credibility, so germane to conventional theater, seemed to be utterly and hopelessly displaced in the dissolution of character and the dispersion of plot that became the disjunct paratactical strategies that we call postmodern today. What seemed to me evident then was that, at the psychic level at least, the nerve ends of perception itself, it was the Balance of Terror that Beckett was writing about (of course it was funny, always funny, the *risus purus,* laughing up the sleeve, the laugh, as he said, laughing at the laugh), along with the Energy Crisis, paralysis, debility, the exhaustion of Western culture, before the idea of an energy crisis was materialized as economic fact in the geopolitics of a postindustrial world, with what seemed inevitable in due time, the debility of a debit, in the distressing modulations of the microphysics of power and the ominous emergence of OPEC.

It was not quite price-fixing, however, that Beckett had in mind, though we shall come back in a moment to the matter of price. When he thought of a balanced terror it was in one respect Augustinian, as in his fondness for that nicely proportioned sentence of which Didi vaguely recalls a fragment, before he moves into his little hermeneutic study of the Gospels, the story of the two thieves, whereupon Gogo concludes on the basis of conflicting accounts by the apostles, all of which are variously believed, that people are really bloody ignorant apes. Here's the sentence, though in the faultiness of memory (from which I'm quoting) the balance may be faulty too: "Despair not, one of the thieves was saved; presume not, one of the thieves was damned." As you try to think of what would happen to the fineness of its balance if you tried to say it the other way around, let me move on a critical nuance to what else, relative to the generic terror, Beckett had in mind.

That might be described as an unmooring aspect of language itself, what Roland Barthes would later call the accumulative "terror of uncertain signs," though among those signs for Beckett is a certain certainty, the *pensum* of *The Unnamable,* the long sinuous if not insidious proposition of a double sentence: the sentence in *grammar* and the sentence in *punishment* pronounced by a judge in a court of law. It is a strange court, however, and an even stranger law, for if it seems eternally written it still needs *writing,* as it appears to do in Kafka, where it escapes interpretation. It's as if the writing itself were its mode of operation. And if the judges themselves are doubtful, confused, reluctant, or absent, what does that matter to the law? which is indelibly if invisibly, and entirely arbitrary, always already and watchfully there. *Every look is the law,* according to Kafka, and the subtlety of Beckett's idea of theater arises from the conjunction of language and the look, as in the stabbing and judgmental light of *Play*. Or when, with a sense of the air full of our cries, Didi is gazing at the sleeping Gogo—who is always disturbed by his dreams, the *specularity* of his dreams—while we are gazing at the gazing Didi.

I shall say more in a while about the look and the gaze—and if time permits, this time, may even examine the function of the gaze, its cross-eyed uncertainties at the beginning of *Endgame* and their relation to language, the elemental structure of the sentence, its subject and object, and the quiet but quite frightening balance of terror, if you think about it, in their disjuncture, subject and object: "Me—to play," says Hamm, with a great big yawn, as big as the Cartesian abyss, between the objective case in which he identifies himself, not *I,* and the infinitive that marks the drama. It is a sentence for which in another time one (not I) might have been punished—the ungrammaticality of it, or is it ungrammatical? In any case, Hamm *is* punished, or *acts out* a punishment, for Hamm may be a pretender, an Imaginary Invalid; indeed, we know he is, since he is only and always an actor in what, however, by Beckett's own testimony is his most "clawing" or punishing play, all the more severe from thinking too much.

As you can see already, I trust, the terms of the double sentence, the grammar and the punishment, are by no means unconnected, even at this moment, in the vicissitudes of thought. And, as I've tried to suggest briefly so far, they are also connected to the look and the gaze, as Nietzsche also knew who said that God is in the grammar, an all-seeing God that . . . *which* (should it be *that* or *which?* and should it, whichever, be capitalized for God?) *Who* (?) watches over our mistakes, as they still do with the *pensum,* which (that? without the comma, of course) is also the name for those little Cartesian books with cross-hatched lines in which children learn to write and do mathematics in French schools—as my little six-year-old daughter, back in Paris, is doing now. What Nietzsche, Beckett, and that stern taskmaster Hamm (a pedagogue if there ever was one) also understand is that God is in the grammar—and the look of the law—even when words slip slide decay, the syntax sprawls, the modifiers squint, and the structure of the grammar appears to disintegrate, everything falling apart, all the rules! nothing logical but aleatory, as it is in Lucky's speech, where we are nevertheless given a quite ordered history of the devolution of Western metaphysics since the Middle Ages, quaquaquaqua, beginning with the uttering forth of the existence of "a personal God," *this* time "outside time without extension who from the heights of divine apathia divine athambia divine aphasia," with the sublime indifference of an active forgetfulness, "loves us dearly but time will tell. . . ."

(I am particularly conscious of my grammar today because, on the plane from Paris to Washington, I was—when not rewriting this—reading the copyedited text of a new book of mine, in which the copyeditor had fastidiously checked all restrictive and nonrestrictive modifiers, changing *which* to *that* even where, knowing the rule, I'd rather not have that, which I tried to make respectfully clear in no uncertain terms by changing everything back.)

Be that as it may (in this Beckettian/grammatical context, is that a subjunctive or merely cliché?), be that as it *was* (?), it continues (reference? time? God?) *what* continues?—"let us resume," as Lucky says—*it* continues to exact the *pensum,* which also means, as Beckett dolefully writes, "a task to be performed," the egregious task of talking about oneself, "before one can be at rest." Strange compulsive paranoid self-reflexive task, and speaking of the look and the gaze, overseen by *whom?* and should *that* be capitalized? *can* it be capitalized, realizing as Marx did that capitalization, *capital,* has to do with money, as Beckett did when he didn't have any—and as we did in San Francisco when we first started to do his plays and very few showed up and some of those walked out because God was also in the dramaturgy saying it was incoherent and whoever gave you the idea that *this* was a play? sometimes punctuating the question by asking for their money back.

Those were the days—ah, the "old style" Winnie says—when people asked without embarrassment: *Who is Godot?* expecting to get a better answer than Beckett's own if I knew who Godot was I'd say so, which we, among others, repeated over and over, like T. S. Eliot's line about it being impossible, in words slipping sliding decaying with imprecision, to say what I mean, I mean him, saying what *he* means, until now both of them are somewhat clichés, habitually repeated ("Habit is the great deadener") to justify not the dark obscure of modernist language that/which deranges words into meaning, the meaning which like thought itself always escapes, but to certify instead, in those of little mind, the brain-damaged substance of words that—even if God *is* in the grammar, a merciful God—don't mean very much at all. And not because of the terror of uncertain signs or—to use the language of the law—any consciousness thereof quaquaquaqua, which is the repetitive burden of the *pensum* in Beckett, a virtual disease of consciousness, curled-up worm of encyclical thought suddenly unwinding in the labyrinth of the ear like the "mortal coil" of *Hamlet* running down the hill of heaven as low as to the fiends, words words words, the *intractability* of the Unnamable, repeating itself in its traces while searching the origin of the word, which is the *trace,* the origin of the memory from which it appears, as Derrida tells us today as he defines the fatal *différance,* which I won't try to define, words words words, which if they have any virtue at all, like what I'm saying now, only serve to keep the discourse from coming to an end because its subject is somewhat lost or the lesson has been forgotten, the brain pursuing them like mad, as out of the Mouth of *Not I,* the words that never cease, which may have been a punishment for the misfortune of being born.

In this respect, of course, Beckett is quite classical. Erudite as he is, and given to certain unexpected and surprising, even exotic locutions, like the *fontanelles* (in *Endgame*), his vocabulary is, not unsurprisingly, austere, hermetic, and constrained, like a vow of poverty. It resembles the language of no other dramatist so much as Racine, whose drama also proceeds, so to speak, from an exhausted *donnée,* as if it were all used up before it began. As for the punishment of being born, the burden is invariably that birth is the death of him—"ghastly grinning ever since. Up at the lid to come. In cradle and crib. At such first fiasco"—as we remember the ancients saying, in play after play, in similar punishments, so repetitively painful they're finally funny, siphoning the comedy out for another festival. (Beckett is also performed now in international festivals, but for his grievous hilarity there is only the recourse, as with Pozzo's watch, of a "deadbeat escapement.") "Better never to have been born," the ancient choruses would say after the madness of interrogation had subsided and there was nothing more to say.

"Nothing will come of nothing," said the father who was mad to the daughter who was dumb, until in the fugitive dead end of desperation there is the harrowing image of the gouged-out eyes, and "the worst returns to laughter." I am now speaking of *King Lear* (though the blindness of Oedipus still resonates in Hamm) and Beckett seems also to have taken the (dis)articulated wisdom of its ravings to heart. Over the last generation, however, the *pensum* seems to have been reversed in the productions of *Lear*—Peter Brook's, my own, those more recently in Eastern Europe and the Far East—that seem derived from Beckett: "Nothing will come of nothing," but there's still "Nothing to be *done*" (emphasis mine). Which is the evacuated datum from which the play, the waiting in *Godot,* the play within the play, proceeds: "I'm beginning to come round to that opinion." And that's where they came, *round,* as if the repetitions dismantled habit and wore away the clichés. Or came through exhaustion to the tautological outbreak of a virulent energy, like the dog that came into the kitchen to steal a crust of bread, in Didi's loud song that opens the second act:

Then cook up with a ladle
And beat him till he was dead
Then all the dogs came running
And dug the dog a tomb . . .
And wrote upon the tombstone . . .

Is that not in a sense what Beckett was doing?—"For the eyes of dogs to come:" etc., etc., in the resuming round:

I resume: what we have, then, in the *pensum* is a verbal hallucination, a mutilated sentence, "as a result of the labors left unfinished," by *whom?* who can say? Fartov and Belcher? Puncher and Wattman? one long almost unendurable sentence, like that which ends/rounds *The Unnamable* or, for that matter, Lucky's speech, quaquaquaqua, a sort of penitential insistence of runaway thought turning upon itself, for which they beat him up, and then—in the words of the Gospel—"Raise him up!" He thinks and they think, thinking of course to no apparent conclusion, as a result of the labors left unfinished, for who is ever finished with the apparency of thought? "Think! Think! Think!" the hapless figures say, squeezing their brains to a standstill even with the bowlers off. "You can think, you two?" says Pozzo, aghast at the possibility of thought, though "the trouble is," as Didi warned, "to have thought," leaving us with the ambiguity of tense and possession: to *have* thought, incredible! when thought is always escaping, to think and have it too.

As for Beckett himself, the more he thinks the more he apparently feels—as if the *pensum* were intersected by the price of OPEC oil—that for the *fact* of living itself (he would hardly say the *privilege*) we are always paying a price. William Carlos Williams wrote once of "the poetry of the movement of costs," and however mutilated the sentence the one inarguable apparency is that Beckett is a poet, whether he works in theater, prose, video, or film. He seems to understand, almost ontologically, the *economy* of each of these forms, its nuclear power. Speaking of which, and the poetry of the movement of costs, remember J. Robert Oppenheimer's poetic and Buddhist response to the dazzling white light of the Bomb bursting in air—from which, I suppose, as a result of the labors left unfinished, came in a splintered reverberation George Bush's "thousand points of light," which seems a far (disingenuously callow) cry from the dread of nuclear power and the historical point from which I started, assaying the cost, for Beckett, of World War II. It was not, I think, merely the era of existentialism nor its principle of the Absurd that caused him to echo the question that Winston Churchill, one of the great affirmative spirits of the age, had also asked, a question I remember quoting at the first rehearsal of our production of *Waiting for Godot,* when *Beckett,* as I've suggested, was hardly a household word in this country and barely known in the academy, which went through the customary stages of disdain and resistance before he entered the canon.

Anyhow, the question: "On this soil of Europe, yes or no, is man dead?" I must admit to thinking at the time—the rehearsal was in my house in San Francisco, just above the Haight-Ashbury district, where the counterculture was presently to assemble—that it was a somewhat un-American question. What would the House Un-American Activities Committee, which soon turned up in San Francisco (it was high tide of the McCarthy era), think of this bleak, encrypted, and morbid play? Never mind them, what would Walt Whitman think? or William Carlos Williams, who detested T. S. Eliot all his life for being too European? Not to mention, *this* time, the actors who were there, not one of whom, before we announced we would do the play (they thought I was mad) had *ever* heard of Beckett.

As for Europe, I can report from recent observation that, despite fallout from Chernobyl, which contaminated its soil, it appears to be quite alive and stirring. On the threshold, in the 1990s, of the European Economic Community, that great corporate merger of the national states that gave us Western culture, capital is moving in a hyperexcited economy of exchange, crossing barriers, channels, customs, languages, in a kind of recombinant DNA or redemptive mortgaging of Babel. But the question was, on this soil of Europe, is *man* dead? And they are still talking, at least in *theory* (what came to us as *deconstruction*), of the long-awaited end of man (corresponding to the repeatedly proclaimed end of ideology), that is, the tradition of bourgeois humanism (which even tainted Marx), with its logocentrism, phallic domination, Oedipus and his Viennese complex, and the old Freudian family romance, with its hermetic and suffocating nuclear family, at the center of which is the "fatal couple" and the structure of reproduction and representation—all of which is condensed by Beckett, in desiccated memory, into the video image of "the familiar chamber" of *Ghost Trio,* the door, the floor, the wall, its solipsistic emptiness, that *kind* of door, that *kind* of floor, that *kind* of wall, which, having seen, "you have seen it all," repeated over and over, in theater, in narrative, in film, and TV, where the soaps, *Dynasty, Dallas, Days of Our Lives,* bring the eternal chamber drama, magnified and extruded, extended, deferred, delayed, paratactically restructured, into the concurrence of popular culture and postmodern forms, like a demonstration of *différance.*

"Will you never have done? (*Pause.*) Will you never have done . . . revolving it all?"—the one tired, attenuated, interminable tale, however splintered or disjunct, as Beckett revolves it in *Footfalls:* "(*Pause.*) It?"—there we go with the grammar again, faulty reference, wouldn't they say? who? *they?* the indefinite plural, we all know *them*—"(*Pause*) It? (*Pause.*) It all. (*Pause.*) In your poor mind. (*Pause.*) It all. (*Pause.*) It all"—including the fiction that there is any reference at all, anything like a reliable subject and object, or even predicate for that matter, the worst of all possible words, perhaps, being not that feeble effort at the objectification of subjectivity in *It,* but the personal pronoun *I,* with which I started this talk today, a word that Lévi-Strauss, referring to the special complications of the French first person, called the most contemptible in the language, whereas in English we have what is maybe a more disturbing if telltale complication, the perfect assonance of *I* and *eye,* identity and sight, which Shakespeare explores with terrifying subtlety in his plays and sonnets, all of it summed up in the notorious pun, "when first your eye I eyed," which begins a sonnet that also contains one of his most remarkable quatrains, pivoting on the relation of the word, identity, subject and object, the look and the gaze:

Ah, yet doth beauty, like a dial hand,
Steal from his figure, and no pace perceived;
So your sweet hue, which methinks still doth stand,
Hath motion, and mine eye may be deceived.

If, then, that pronoun *I* and all it represents is either contemptible or deceitful, one can understand (notice that shifty *one*) why it seemed important to break up the whole signifying system of reproduction. For, if traced through the sinister traces of its economy of exchange, whose principle is specularity, it turns out to be—with illusions looking like nature—a structure of domination and power. If it has extended its hegemony over the face of the earth, as phallocracy or imperialism, it has also colonized the space of the unconscious, the terrain that Beckett works, it all, it all, the familiar chamber where no one sees the motion but the motion, the rudimentary construct of a repressive psychology, that which goes with the I (both eyes), the autonomous self or imperious ego, neither of which can quite break up because they never really existed, occulted as they were in the libidinal economy of the West, mythic and untenable as the Federal Reserve—or at least, in the world of leverage buyouts and arbitrage, an independent and rational monetary system.

Now if Gogo—pressed by Didi to remember what happened a moment ago—says, "I'm not a historian," Beckett obviously makes no claims to being an economist, nor—despite *Catastrophe,* the play he recently dedicated to the dissident Czech playwright Václav Havel—does he have a specific interest in politics. Although he was active during the war in the French Resistance (while playing chess at Roussillon), I remember his saying years ago that political solutions to the world's problems are like going from one insane asylum to another. Yet that doesn't prevent him from reading, daily, the socialist paper *Libération.* Nor did it prevent *Waiting for Godot*—that plaintive elegy of catatonia in which nothing happens, twice—from becoming the greatest political drama of the fifties, a virtual preface, as an exemplary model or paradigm of *waiting,* to the passive resistance of the early sixties that was waiting in the wings, along with the strategies of indeterminacy and activated forgetfulness that characterized the Movement, before it lost its patience, and its historical memory, in the Days of Rage. (Postscript: when I visited him recently on returning to Paris, the front page of *Libération* was spread out on the writing table, with the picture of the unknown Chinese student, waiting, confronting the tanks alone.)

What all of this suggests is not merely another image of the poet as prophet but the degree to which, perhaps, my own thought—long intimate with the plays, and the prose, which seemed from the beginning to be intimate with what, much younger then, I didn't quite know I thought—remains inhabited by Beckettian ideas and images. I should add, however, that as with any intimacy (and this seems Beckettian too) I have also found myself resisting this tendency of my own mind that, over the years, seems inseparable from his thought, so that I'm no longer sure when reading his work, or seeing it staged, that what I see is really there or, like Lévi-Strauss with the Bororo Indians, merely a projection of my own mind. No matter, Beckett might say, for in any case we are dealing with what, in his precocious essay on Proust, he described as dissynchronous systems of perception, and, no matter whose thought it is, it's what in the process of being thought fails us anyhow.

Which brings me back through these rather expanded and circuitous prefatory remarks (questions are remarks, said Wallace Stevens, but remarks are questions too) to the collage of Beckettian thought with which I thought I'd start but which has, I think, already started, delaying the start,

Beckett, after all, *not* I, and "the brain still . . . still sufficiently . . . oh very much so! . . . at this stage . . . in control . . . under control . . . to question even this. . . ." Meanwhile, in the circuitry of what follows—or circulation, leaving much to be desired—I will, as I said, be moving theoretically to aspects of Beckett I haven't questioned yet, as a result of the labors left unfinished, as this talk may be, perhaps, "finished, it must be nearly finished," what seems to come back, it all, it all . . . or "the semblance. Faint though by no means invisible in a certain light. (*Pause.*)," from the Enlightenment to deconstruction, "the light the light the light of the labors lost," as Lucky says in his torrential disquisition, the monstrous enunciation in a remotely remembered logic of the dissolution of Western metaphysics from the (im)personal, aphasic divinity uttered forth by Aquinas to the waste land of T. S. Eliot. "It has a structure," Beckett said, over our Bushmill's, "empty heavens, diminished man, abortive stones"—that's what I heard, *abortive* stones, and who can doubt it, though Lucky says *abode,* "abode of stones who can doubt it I resume but not so fast I resume. . . ."

It was very strange when it first came on the scene, the babble of Beckett, neither a bang nor a whimper, but a whisper a rustle, making a noise like leaves like ashes like leaves (*pause*) the heap the little heap, finished, it's nearly finished, yet arising from the silence in Babylonian proportions, they whisper they rustle they all speak at once, and what do they say? "Where now? Who now? When now? Unquestioning. I, say I. Unbelieving." But you better believe it, and you better question it, the forlorn pronoun of a delinquent identity, *I,* say I, the signifier slipping in a world of becoming, the metonymic erosions and macerations "up to the mouth" and the grievously exquisite shift into a visible language, funny then no longer funny, because "something is taking its course" that only makes it worse: the running sores, the wounds, the mutilations, the abortive stones and slimy abortions, the stumps the stanchers I resume the skulls and, when it seems to be subsiding, no need for the painkiller, the leak in the fontanelles, "never but the first and last time curled up worm in slime when they lugged you out and wiped you off," that time, extruding life through the *pensum* into the merest fraction of being. Or, if less can be imagined, then less, the least, "the all of nothing," as in the entropic cylinder of *The Lost Ones,* the permutations of near extinction, "in cold darkness motionless flesh," if not exactly insentient, with "unceasing eyes," declining through "old craving" by "insensible degrees."

"What I'd like now," said the narrator of the book that Beckett's wife brought to forty-seven publishers before it was accepted, "What I'd like now is to speak the things that are left, say my good-byes, finish dying. They don't want that." But after years of exile, silence, and relative anonymity in the shadow of Joyce, Beckett has become, with the Nobel Prize, the one indisputable venerable figure among us, and as he syncopates the dying through the excruciating successions of lessness they always seem to want more. I remember that time, however, when his plays were first performed and people who now swear by Beckett—including actors in my company in San Francisco who refused to be in *Godot*—were not only taken aback or confounded but revolted by his vision. Still, it remains a curious thing that sometimes the know-nothings are on to something, in their unrepressed resistance to what most of us disguise. Were they right to begin with? "Nothing to be done"? Really, when you think about it, who wants to live with that? Yet just before I left Paris there opened at Beaubourg, the Centre Pompidou, a retrospective exhibit of the Situationist Internationale, the ecological movement of politicized anarchism that anticipated the sixties, and which, by the way was never intended to end up in a museum, no more than Beckett was expected to be performed, as he is now being performed, at the Comédie Française, which has always been execrated in the French avant-garde and would be, if the Situationists had had their way, mere rubble, a heap, blown up, a little heap. While they rejected virtually the whole tradition of Western culture, and all its artists with few exceptions, Beckett was one of them, exemplary and exempt.

Nothing to be done: it hardly seems like a prescription for radical change. Yet today, wherever you go, Beckett is almost universally admired, as if he were beyond all partisanship or ideology, for the integrity of the babble, the inexhaustible documentation at the level of the drives of what, by any other measure, is an encyclopedic mess. A miniaturist of impeccable patience, he has endowed us with the monstrous elegy of the sado-masochistic facts of life in a doomsday book of humiliation. There may be a sense in which what is also beguiling in Beckett has desensitized us to what he shows, which accounts for various productions, say, in which—when it's not mere brainless response or selective inattention—they're eager to laugh him off. But through all the hilarious figurations of the comic geometry of behavior it's still an appalling vision, as Didi says, "APPALLED"—and not even the wan and lyrical stasis that, at certain ineffable moments, seems to envelope the wounds makes them any easier to endure.

Endurance is the elemental issue in Beckett that could exhaust this entire session, but lest that get too painful, let us turn, in the evasive way of theory, to what I deferred before, the omnipresent subject and surreptitious operations of the look and the gaze.

The look and the gaze—the distinction between them and their relations with the unseen visibility of desire—are among the more mystifying concepts in recent theory. But they are no more mystifying than that seeing body on the theatrical scene, the specular accretion called the audience, which materializes in the space between the look and the gaze. The look in its dispossession seems to be, if not a renegade, an avatar of the law. For it is out to make distinctions and, like the Furies of classical drama, on the hunting path of truth, which circles back upon us—as in Beckett's dead imagining or the recurring dream of Freud's Wolf Man—as "the eye of prey," that cross-eyed subjectivity where the look becomes the gaze.

"Why shouldn't I go hunting, too?" says Hilda Wangel, in Ibsen's *The Master Builder,* when the haunted Solness "*looks deep into her eyes.*" "Get the prey I want? If only I can get my claws into it!" In the hunting pack as conceived by Elias Canetti (in his startling book on *Crowds and Power*) the one who sights the game may be honored in its distribution as much as or more than the one who made the kill. "But even those who were only distant witnesses of the kill may have claim to part of the prey. When this is the case, spectators are counted as accomplices of the deed. . . . Whatever the way in which distribution is regulated, the two decisive factors are the *sighting* and the *killing* of the prey."

The case of the Wolf Man offers a paradigm, however, of that inverted voyeurism in which, at some primordial level of desire, the child's dream of being silently stared at (by wolves in a tree) is a cover-up for his own staring presence at the primal scene, the decisive sighting of the prey in which the kill is yet to come. It is part of the self-conscious tradition of theater that its hypnotic power is derived from the transposition of the primal scene, a reversal which also seems to remember that, when we came into the world, we occupied the center of the stage. Jonas Barish is invoking this tradition when he asks these questions in *The Anti-Theatrical Prejudice:* "Does the greediness of our gaze point to a buried memory of the earlier thirst to be gazed at, and our satisfaction when that thirst was slaked? Is our desire to sit as beholders merely the other side of the coin of our wish to be beheld, our unacknowledged exhibitionism? If so, perhaps the antitheatrical prejudice reflects a form of self-disgust brought on by our conflicted longing to occupy the center of the stage once more." As Beckett suggests, more likely than not.

In a theatricalized society the prejudice—residual puritanism or insis-

tent Platonism—may itself be repressed. For we may see the conflicted longing in the manifest content of the theater through the evolution of its drama
and the devolution of its heroes. Storing up alms for oblivion, the economy
of the theater seems based upon the conversion of overinflated characters
into objects of self-liquidating perception: from Agamemnon to Richard II
to Flamineo and Danton, Ibsen's Borkman and Pirandello's Henry IV, and
never more intensely than in the liminal figures and corroded heroes of
Beckett's anti-plays: above all, Hamm, who sits with supreme disgust in the
center of the stage, eminently conscious in his "blindness" of seeing and
being seen; or, with all the grandiloquence of an easily punctured vanity,
the tyrant Pozzo, out-Heroding Herod, who asks as he performs whether
everybody is looking at him; or in the blind relay of the diminishing look,
the unslaked babble of the Mouth of *Not I,* with its silent Auditor; or, as
the buried memory bottoms out: "No eye. No mind"—the talking heads in
the funereal urns, stabbed by light and repeating themselves in *Play:* "Am I
as much as . . . being seen?"

The line is designated by Beckett to be repeated at the closing of the repetition of the play, which implicates the observers in the plaintively cunning
question, if we want to check it out. But in order to do that we have to repeat
ourselves—an impossible proposition at the repetitive heart of theater that,
for all the repetition, is never what it *was.* Yet, if we engage in the repetition,
we are deeper in collusion with the obtrusive and imperious light, giving
sanction to its inquisition, whose partial objects we've become. In whatever
ontological or economic ways the I is *as much as* being seen, we have to be
there to see it, if it is to be even the vaguest approximation to what was seen
before. (Not to mention, as they do in *That Time,* that it was "never the
same, but the same as what for God's sake did you ever say I to yourself in
your life come on now [*Eyes close.*] could you ever say I to yourself in your
life.") In this respect, we are trapped by the repetition, like the disarticulated
creatures in the (im)memorial urns. Thus, we find ourselves, uncannily, in an
archaic and familiar part, as audience, forced to play it again but not quite
knowing how to do it, and still very much in the dark—"all dark, all still, all
over"—about the dispersed and vanishing subject of the incapacitated I: "I
mean . . . not merely over, but as if . . . never been—."

If the light forces the issue in *Play,* the blind but specular Hamm does
the forcing in *Endgame*—though he attributes the necessity of the repetition, when Clov makes an issue of that, to the *dialogue.* Himself a figure of
speech, Hamm sees through every thought like the preying eye of a camera
obscura, observing the nuances of each word as if it were an object. If
there's something dripping in his head that requires a painkiller, it seems—

at the very quick of perception—as if the dripping were a brain scan. Narcissistic as he is, he also seems to perceive at the level of primary process, with an ear for the pun in prey, as we may see in his mordant pieties. "Let us pray," he says, archly cloying, and all the more clawing for that. Hamm materializes to our attention like a ruined totem, in black specs, doubly veiled, the handkerchief under the cloth like a Veronica on his face. The *I* which encounters the gaze encounters the gaze as object: "Me—(*he yawns*)—to play." The grammar specifically articulates, over the yawning identity, the estranged contingency of the subject. We are at the very onset at the depleted limit of the scopic field (gray, zero), as if the world were exhausted by being seen and the theater by too much sight.

In his staged blindness Hamm is a kind of sadomasochistic mockery of the entirely hidden gaze:

HAMM: Did you ever see my eyes?
CLOV: No.
HAMM: Did you never have the curiosity while I was sleeping, to take off
    my glasses and look at my eyes?
CLOV: Pulling back the lids?
(*Pause.*)
No.
HAMM: One of these days I'll show them to you.

In the S/M business Clov is no slouch either, as we can plainly see, who stare in fascination at the pregnant pause. What he seems to be remembering in case we have forgotten is that if the eye is seen we do not see the gaze. If the voyeur—the viewing subject as pervert—is looking for some shadow of presence behind lid or curtain, a fantasy to admire, what is encountered here is a stalemate, not the phallus but a fetish.

Now, as we know from Freud, the power of the fetish is that it both reveals and blocks the discovery of a fundamental wound or loss; which is to say, castration. And what we have in the conception of Hamm is a sort of insidious reification of the castrated subject. For he is not only the thing on display but the teasing voyeur as well, for whom, as Lacan says of the *exhibitionist*, "what is intended by the subject is what is realized in the other." But how can he be the voyeur if he is really blind? (Of course he is not really blind, since he is only an actor, pretending to be blind. Which raises the problem, if we pursue the riddle of acting further, of whether it is a true pretense or a false pretense. But this is an enigma over which for the moment—as it might be escalated to the point of vertigo by Genet—we shall mercifully pass.) If we take Hamm on faith, then the voyeurism is displaced. It moves into the ear, spiral to the eye's sphere. He watches by listening, with the seductive intimations of the acutest vigilance. If he has been somehow victimized, he is "the victim as referred to some other who is looking at him." As to the condition for which he requires the painkiller, it comes in the sadomasochistic drive when, as Lacan speculates, "the loop is closed, . . . and the other has come into play when the subject has taken himself as the end, the terminus of the drive. At this moment, pain comes into play in so far as the subject experiences it from the other."

There are times in *Endgame* when it appears that Hamm, with his stethoscopic ear, is monitoring feedback from the audience, as in the cryptic sufferance of the last rites when, the circuit of pain restored, he seems to acknowledge another presence abjected onto himself. "You . . . remain," he says, as he recovers himself with the handkerchief in the brief tableau before the curtain. In the concept of *aphanisis*—the term used by Ernest Jones for the disappearance of sexual desire—the movement of disappearance is, most radically, the manifestation of the subject. (As the abolition of sexuality is not identical with castration, so aphanisis is the object of a fear even more profound than castration.) If the veil itself—"Old stancher!"—does double duty, that's because, in this unabating, relentless, corrosive play, not even finished when it's finished, the vanishing of the subject seems more lethal than before. Meanwhile, who/what it is that remains remains an open question, which partially depends—as it certainly did, prior to Beckett's canonization—on whether *you* are still there in the audience.

(1989)

9

The Less Said

Astride of a grave and a difficult birth . . . he made it hard in mourning to mourn him, fittingly, in anything but his own words. For who was it, after all, that wrote the text of mourning. Or, in its sepulchral orchestration, even hilarious, mourning and melancholia.

The problem has always been, since we discovered that he was funny, to take him at his word, funny, but then no longer funny, from the recursive lamentations over the nothing to be done to the last obsessional and fractal testaments to the ubiquitous void:

"Say for be said. Missaid. From now say for be missaid." From now, surely, be what it may.

But how could it ever be anything but missaid, since he was always addressing the void (within the postmodern the postmortem condition), speaking as it were not astride but, so to speak, from the mouth of the grave or, bespoken perhaps, from somewhere beyond it. "No future in this. Alas yes." The gravedigger puts on the forceps.

But wasn't it he who told us at the risk of contradiction—or was it aporia? aporia pure and simple—that it's all a matter of words, speak no more about it, speak no more. ("I should mention before going any further, any further on, that I say aporia without knowing what it means. Can one be ephectic otherwise than unawares? I don't know.")

I suppose I should say something about what he meant to us in the theater, what he meant to *me*, that time, that time I mean when he didn't for those who walked out of the theater seem to mean anything at all. Or that other time, in the nursing home, the last time I saw him, the bed, the floor, the wall, "the familiar chamber," the indispensable door, the kind of floor, the kind of wall, which, having seen, you have seen it all, and he: "*What do you think of recurring dreams? I have one, I still have it, always had it, anyway a long time. I am up on a high board, over a water full of large rocks. . . .*"

But as I see myself slipping, "though not yet at the last extremity, towards the resorts of fable," it occurs to me that it might "be better to keep on saying babababa, for example," or like a charm to certify the raising of the dead, reluctant as he may be in the existence uttered forth, quaquaquaqua—

And so it goes, as the forceps slip, with the vicissitudes of the void. "A pox on void. Unmoreable unlessable unworseable evermost almost void." Almost? There he is again, hedging his bet or bearing it out to the edge of doom, like "it's finished, nearly finished, it must be nearly finished," with the dubious imperative of the consummation, if we can trust his predilection, devoutly to be wished.

"*I have to dive through a hole in the rocks.*"

Now that he's gone it's hard to believe that if death is not the end of him birth was the death of him. Or that even in the imagining (imagination dead imagine!) he "gave up before birth," like the voice of one of his fizzles, farted out, "at suck first fiasco," a failure before it began.

Was he writing about writing or was he writing about the self? Or the inseparability of (his) writing, "vasts apart," from the outside diminishing prospect of its remotest possibility, the "meremost minimum" guesswork of a self? And what, as one tries to think of *him,* can one possibly say of *that,* in the slippage of the signifier, not this, that, the unmoreable unlessable uttermost inadequacy of all this *otherness,* the shadow of a cenotaph, "one minute in a skull, and the next in a belly, and the next nowhere in particular."

Now, who wrote that? I mean: what are we to say of the identity of an author, now dead, something more, surely, than metonymically dead, who became an institution, but as a virtual penance, or "pensum," given "at birth perhaps, as a punishment for having been born perhaps, or for no particular reason" (which is if anything worse), wrote himself into a fiction, "a life worth having [*pause*], a life at last," as a mere agency of language? Which he never thought much of anyway, unless "efficiently misused."

As he said in a little-known letter published in his *Disjecta,* with a high imperious residually elitist equivocally modernist disdain for words: "As we cannot eliminate language all at once, we should at least leave nothing undone that might contribute to its falling into disrepute."

In this regard, his best was not sufficient. Or rather its *insufficiency* was such, the nothing undone and remaining to be done, the exhaustive enumeration of its "infinite emptiness," that it left the language renewed, if only minimally, "like a little bit of grit in the middle of the steppe" or, "grain by grain, one by one," the echolocation of "the impossible heap," or the dripping in the head, "splash, splash, always on the same spot," an artery or vein perhaps, "ever since the fontanelles," when it seemed there might be an end to speech.

Alas yes, it's not possible otherwise, "birth there had to be," though it might have been another "who had a life," not he, "a life not worth having," he'd write, "because of me," and what are we to make of that? aside from the fact that we have to *make* it, as he long ago warned us we would, with nothing but the words, "all words, there's nothing else" as, failing again, failing better, he's entered at last (perhaps) the unnamable's dream of silence, "a dream silence, full of murmurs, I don't know, that's all words," a pox on void, and the signifiers too. . . .

(1989)

10

Remembering Beckett
An Interview

(The following interview was conducted in Paris, at the apartment of Bernard Vincent, editor of the journal Sources, *in September 1996. The interviewer is Marie-Claire Pasquier, professor of American literature at the University of Paris X.)*

Let me start with an incidental question. Did Beckett ever read anything that you'd written about him, and did he react to it?

In all the time I knew him, a little over thirty years, I never gave him anything I ever wrote—except toward the end, once. In the early years, supposition was that Beckett never read anything written about him, whether by friends or by anyone else. That was just a fiction. It was soon apparent to me that he did. But I never gave him anything. A while before he died my wife, Kathy, berated me about it. I had written about him incidentally and sometimes extensively, but it was shortly after I had published two longish essays—the one on deconstruction and another on Beckett and Barthes—that I decided to bring him a book. He was already quite ill by then, over at the nursing home off the avenue du Général Leclerc. I gave him *The Eye* of *Prey.* I know he was very moved by the gesture, but I didn't see him again after that, and so I never really knew whether he actually read the essays.

Kathy berated you for doing what exactly? For not showing them?

Yes, for not showing him anything, not even what I'd written about my work on his plays as a director. He was so moved, though, by my giving him the book that he got up with some difficulty—his arthritis, at that point, was severe—made his way over to a bureau, and took out a manuscript. It was a manuscript of *Comment dire,* which he gave me.

What I would like to know is when you read your first line by Beckett, when you were first introduced to his work, and when you first met him, and how long ago that was.

I came across Beckett early in the fifties, a couple of years after my theater started in San Francisco. I was also teaching at what was then San Francisco State College (now University), which had one of the two major poetry centers in the United States. It was started by a woman named Ruth Witt-Diamant. She had been in Paris, saw or heard about *Godot,* and first mentioned him to me. She also talked about his fiction, which I remember vaguely—I may have seen something before. But she gave me a copy of *En attendant Godot,* which she said I must read. I forget exactly what year that was. It was probably about 1954 or 1955. Shortly after, we did the production of *Waiting for Godot* in San Francisco.

So you knew the play in French before you got the English version?

Yes. Before we did the play, however, it was produced with peculiar notoriety by Michael Meyerberg in New York. Because they were afraid that the work might be prohibitive, they advertised, as I recall, for "ninety-six thousand intellectuals." Or whatever number it was they needed to break even at the box office. Actually, it was produced first at the Copacabana Playhouse in Boca Raton, Florida—or was it Coral Gables?—with Bert Lahr and Tom Ewell. It was a disaster. Alan Schneider directed it there. He was shattered. But people would have walked out on Beckett in those days anyhow—as they did in Paris and when he showed up in San Francisco—but down there in Florida, it was just totally. . . . Anyhow, in those days it was impossible to get the rights to a play that was being set up for production in New York. So we had to wait it out. The production in New York—directed not by Alan but by Herbert Berghof—got a little respectful attention and then pretty quickly disappeared.

And I suppose that Beckett in those days was not as particular as he became about controlling every single production. Since he was not well-known, he didn't have the authority he later acquired.

That's exactly so, or so it seemed to me. He at least pretended indifference to what was being done to his plays then. Moreover, he hadn't yet directed. When we did early on a production of *Endgame,* I sent him some pictures. It was just before I met him. The pictures were quite stunning, but the setting revealed was probably not what he had in mind when he called for gray walls in his stage directions. Our walls were gray, but with a sort of sumptuous poverty, shades of gray, textures of gray, an assemblage of materials that—as Hamm and Clov made their tour to the hollow in the wall, counterclockwise around the room—suggested, subliminally, the entire history of Western culture, in reverse. One would think that later on, had he seen the same pictures, he might have objected to the scene design. But I have a letter which indicates that he found what he saw quite splendid. So far as I knew then, he approved of what we did.

Have you ever seen any of the productions by Beckett as a director? And as a director yourself, can you make any comment on what you thought of them?

No, I was never there when he was actually directing. I was here in Paris, however, when they were filming the productions, which he presumably approved. The series is called "Beckett Directs Beckett." Actually, the staging was done by another director, but following diligently Beckett's instructions or repeating what Beckett himself had done. In all frankness, I found those productions rather banal, too straightforward and not terribly imaginative. I mean, they were pretty much what might be done off the page if in fact we sat here today, read the play, and said, "How should we put this on?" And did the obvious. No, there was nothing extraordinary, and that, I think, is unfortunate, because what's recorded on film will be taken as the authentic. Actually, a former student of mine had gotten the film or video rights, and I'd been invited, along with a couple of other people, to comment on those productions. It was very difficult to say much about the stagings, which more or less literalized what's apparent on the page.

As a more general principle, what do you think of this right to control productions that Beckett, the author, considered he had? And now that he is dead, do you think that directors should be allowed more freedom in their interpretations of Beckett? For instance, I'm thinking of what we are going to see at Peter Brook's theater this week (Oh, les beaux jours!). *We don't know what it's going to be, but we will probably see evidence of such freedom. What is your opinion on the principle of freedom?*

I think such control is just untenable. There are no longer any grounds for it. Actually, if the ground went out from under, you could say that was in some measure Beckett's fault. After all, when we ask, who is Godot? and have no answer—"If I knew who Godot was, I would tell you," he said—we're into the indeterminacy of origins that, from Pirandello to deconstruction, would seem to jeopardize authority and virtually surrender copyright. Anyhow, I happened to be here in Paris some days after we had heard that Beckett had stopped the production at Bob Brustein's theater in Cambridge, at Harvard. The director was JoAnne Akalaitis, who was associated previously with the Mabou Mines. JoAnne had been with our theater in San Francisco, so I'd known her a long time. Actually, several others in the Mabou Mines (Lee Breuer, Ruth Maleczech, Bill Raymond) had also been nurtured on those productions in San Francisco. They'd been virtually weaned on Beckett. Later, they themselves had done work that he was aware of.

Anyway, he and I were meeting at that place he frequented on the boulevard Saint-Jacques, a café in the Hotel PLM. I asked him about the controversy. I had not seen the production. I was already here in Paris when I heard that he had stopped it. The tone was probably critical when I asked why he did it. He immediately became flustered, even a little angry. I pressed the issue. "Look, JoAnne grew up with your work. She's thought a lot about it, knows it deeply. That's no sign of disrespect, her taking some unorthodox approach. . . ." He wasn't in the mood for that. It was very difficult. I'd never had any arguments with him. We could discuss almost anything, and sometimes we disagreed, but there was never anything like a real argument. But the more I tried to discuss it the more distressed he became. Normally, if there were something of an impasse, I could joke him out of it. Which I tried. "Look, Sam, we're in Paris, what are you worried about? People have been talking about the 'Death of the Author. . . .'" Another time he would have laughed, I know it, but it backfired, made him angrier. Maybe I should have let it drop, but. . . .

He had been disturbed when he heard that I'd stopped working in the theater, and, when I did see him, he'd always ask about when I'd start directing again. That led me to say, when he seemed less agitated, "Well, maybe after all Alan was your best director." Because Alan Schneider was very, very dutiful in doing the plays. He would fly over, talk to Sam, get his word about what something meant—I would never dream of doing a thing like that—and then he would produce it, at least to his mind, as Beckett would have wanted it done. . . . Alan, you know, is dead now.

And he died before Beckett died, I think.

Yes, he died before Beckett, in a terrible accident in London, stepped off the curb looking the wrong way. . . . But in any case, I said, "Maybe Alan was your best director." Then I reminded Sam that he had wanted me to direct again. "But if I were to do that," I said, "the only thing I could assure you of is that I would never direct one of your plays so long as you're alive." I couldn't do it. Not with any guarantee that it would be faithful as he wished.

How did he react to that? Was he hurt?

It was hard to tell. He took it, it seemed, calmly enough. After all, there were plenty of others to do the plays. It's very hard to reconstruct the atmosphere. It was quite tense.

There was a sentence he said when he heard a biography was going to be written about him. He said, "I will neither help nor hinder." Why didn't he have the same attitude about his theater?

Well, biography first. Not the more or less authorized one that just came out, by Jim Knowlson. The one you're talking about was by Deirdre Bair. Beckett was equivocal about cooperating. He may have thought of it as a wise passivity, but maybe it was a little unwise, because it really upset him afterwards. In any case he did cooperate with Deirdre Bair's biography, which was done some years ago. She was a relatively young woman when she presumed to do it, and you have to give her credit, though there are those who still resent her. She was quite enterprising. If she didn't get it all right, she nevertheless got a lot of material together, and if he didn't hinder, he did help. As for the theater, he eventually looked upon his texts as virtual musical scores, with more or less absolute notation, from which you departed at risk. It wasn't that he went to see the other, objectionable productions, he never did. But there were others around who served as guardians of the ring hoard, the text, alerting him to deviations.

I would like to come back to your first meeting. You say it was after you had produced your Endgame, *right?*

Yes. He was aware of our work by the time we met. We had done the production of *Waiting for Godot,* and while there were other things to be said for it, it became notorious because that was the production we took to San Quentin prison—the first time a production had ever been done in a maximum-security prison. Almost immediately after that, Martin Esslin—who was completing his book on the theater of the Absurd—turned up in San Francisco, saw *Godot,* and referred to the San Quentin performance in a kind of prologue. That made it widely known. Beckett knew about it. We had actually corresponded between the production of *Godot* and the production of *Endgame,* and then we met. Just before that first trip to Paris, I had directed two productions at once: along with *Endgame,* a play by Sean O'Casey, *Cockadoodle Dandy,* which he also wanted to hear about, because he liked O'Casey.

Did the fact that you were working on O'Casey at the same time make you more conscious of Beckett as an Irish dramatist?

We were certainly aware when we were doing O'Casey that we were dealing with two Irish dramatists, but Irishness in Beckett was never a big issue with us. What we did with *Endgame* was quite unusual in other ways. In any case, it was right after I finished those two productions that I went abroad for the first time. It was at the end of the fifties. We had made an arrangement to meet, and Beckett came to pick me up at my hotel on the rue Monsieur-le-Prince, right across from the Polidor. The hotel's no longer there. He was very gentlemanly, very courteous. He would always come pick me up at the hotel when we met, though I was over at his apartment on the rue des Favorites, when he was in Montparnasse—the first apartment where, next to the *poubelle,* there was the bicycle downstairs. There's a picture of that somewhere. I think of it as a sort of Cartesian bicycle, head above wheels—I forget exactly how he put it, I'm messing the image up, but like that in one of his novels.

So, he met you as a director, and as an American director. And when you produced Endgame, *you said, it was unusual. Perhaps you would like to talk a little more about it. But, first, had you seen any productions before you did any yourself? When you say unusual, do you mean as compared with other productions of the play?*

No, I hadn't seen any productions before. But we knew what we were doing was likely to be something more or other than what's prescribed in the text. I like to think, however, that we were scrupulous to a fault. I mean that ontologically, the fault line there, its rigor mortis. I actually did two productions of *Waiting for Godot.* The second one was done after we did *Endgame,* when I came back from Europe, and that one was extremely different from the first. That was partly due to what we'd done with *Endgame,* a more "clawing" play, as Beckett himself said. Perhaps I can put the distinction this way: in *Waiting for Godot,* you may recall, there's a moment when Didi—who is always in some sense trying to recapitulate what's happened—keeps badgering Gogo to remember any fact, any circumstance: the trees, the leaves, the fish bones, Lucky's kick. Didi wants to be located in space and time, but memory is always failing and there are lapses of consecutive thought. As he keeps assaulting Gogo with everything partially remembered that, moment by moment, keeps slipping away in thought, Gogo is merely bewildered and, except for the fact that he's hungry, only too ready to forget, even what happened a moment ago. "I'm not a historian," he says. Neither is Didi, for that matter. Now, there are certain advantages to that. Because they have no historical memory, and no continuity of thought, the activity of performance feels almost improvisational. And I'm being very conscious of the distinction between activity and action in *Godot.* I mean there is no action. In this two-act drama, as we've heard, nothing happens twice. There is, however, a great deal of *activity.* What accounts for that? Well, you get a lot of promiscuous doing, because with memory always failing they have to do it again, making up reasons for doing it as they go along. And because they don't know why they're doing it, or even what "it" is, the reasons failing too, they accelerate the activity, doing more to cover up.

In contrast, what's compelling to me in *Endgame,* focused in different ways in both Hamm and Clov, is that they seem never to forget anything. There is an almost remorseless continuity of self-excruciating memory. To see what that means: if I were to put my hand over this object, this remote control on the table, and at the moment I was deciding whether to pick it up or not to pick it up, at that moment two thousand years of Western history were to bear upon the prospect of action, containing all the reasons why I should and all the reasons why I shouldn't—the result is a kind of paralysis. If you can see all the motives for picking it up and all the motives for not picking it up, simultaneously present, what you have there, if in fact the action occurred, would be precisely that, an *occurrence,* a reflex, an abrupt or impulsive gesture against the incapacity to act. It would be an impacted version of the Hamletic impediment, the "ratiocinative meditativeness" that Coleridge described. When Hamlet finally *does* the deed, it comes, after all the wild and whirling words, as if in a sort of brain fever, as a violent reaction against the incapacity—as when he stabs Polonius through the arras: "Is it the King?"

Have you seen the movie by Resnais, Smoking / No Smoking? *This is also about picking up an object.*

No, I didn't see that. When we did *Endgame,* the distinction I just made determined how we investigated certain gestures or forms of behavior in the work—some of which were specified by Beckett, others we developed ourselves. For example, Clov is supposed to climb a ladder to one of the two windows at the back of the set, there like the eyes of the mind, split vision, one looking at the land, the other at the sea. He has to open some curtains. Now, it didn't actually last this long in performance, but in certain rehearsals it would sometimes take him as long as fifteen minutes.

You don't say fifteen seconds but fifteen minutes?

I'm saying fifteen minutes. Clov would literally stand up there, suspended over those curtains with an incredible tautness of the body, as if it were a moral issue to open or not open the curtains. When he finally opened the curtains—and, by the way, the curtains were suspended on a metal rod with metal rings—they were opened very abruptly, with a revulsion of feeling against the necessity of doing it, or with some reflex against the resistance to doing it, the overrationalized stasis I described before. When it was done, it was utterly shocking, literally shocking, because when the curtains scraped on the rod with their metal rings they made an extremely sharp sound. In the tight sequestered theater in which the play was staged, inescapably close, it felt like a scraping on the nervous system itself. I have said elsewhere, by the way, that Beckett's drama is like taking the spaces, silence, and stasis of Chekhov one step further: realism in extremis at the very nerve ends of thought. *Endgame* is a play I have seen since. It normally lasts an hour and a half. But certain of our rehearsals lasted as long as four hours.

This is the kind of thing you could impose on audiences in the late fifties, perhaps, or in the sixties. Do you think that an audience today would put up with it?

Now or then, it would be hard to take, but there was something mesmerizing about it. But, to be clear, the performance itself *didn't* last four hours. Actually, the production lasted something close to two hours. I'm saying that the rehearsals sometimes took four hours, because it was the ordeal of time that we were exploring. We *took* the time and then compressed it. Now, what did last, and what Beckett might very well have objected to had he seen it, was the fifteen-minute opening. Gray stage, dim light, a kind of materialization of indecipherable objects in space; among them, gradually seeable, a shape, a body, barely perceptible in the back: Clov. The walls, the ashcans, Hamm in the center under his shroud, you have to make all of that out, including on the walls, as if measuring time, empty time, gradations in the gray. As I say, it took quite a lot of time before anything materialized, the objects infinitesimally, and then Clov unveiling Hamm. Well, I've seen several productions where the actors just go more or less routinely through the task of taking the covers off of Hamm. With us the process was fastidious. First of all, there was the veil, the actual composition of Hamm under the veil. When the veil is meticulously, immaculately removed, we see a handkerchief like a Veronica over his face. You may have seen the picture at my house in Milwaukee—it's really quite beautiful. The veil itself looks antique and was in fact beautifully embroidered. When it was taken off, it was in the final precipitous moment almost the way a bullfighter might whirl with a cape. The gesture itself was quite beautiful, and it was done in such a way—out of slow motion, the one swift gesture—that the movement of lifting the veil also lifted the handkerchief, so that you got a little peekaboo effect on the face: now you see it now you don't. That quick effect was startling in the extruded action of unveiling Hamm—the twelve to fifteen minutes before the veil actually came off. The impeccable slowness of it, hardly a sound, minutes passing, that's excruciating in the theater.

When you said "Veronica," I thought of two things. You mentioned bullfighting, but isn't it the term used for the veil that Jesus had on his face? So this is maybe an allusion that was sensed also in the picture?

I suspect that is what Beckett had in mind. But, as I've indicated, when I met with him I almost never asked him what he meant by anything in the texts. We might talk about something he wrote, its implications, as a way of seeing, even philosophically, but mostly we talked about quite other things than the work itself.

You were wise because he would have answered that he didn't have anything to say, presumably.

He sometimes took that tack, but if you did ask him something specific, he would say something about it, as he did with Alan and others, and in his letters as well. But you're right, he could be reticent, or devious too.

He was helpful to some of his translators. His German translator could ask him questions, and he would answer so that it would be useful for the translation but not for the interpretation. I think you saw the recent production at the Bouffes du Nord of Endgame, *in which Hamm is sitting on a tire. Did you see that?*

No, I didn't.

Because that was an interesting change of image. I don't think that Beckett would have approved. What was amusing also was that it was performed by an actual son and father. These two great German actors. Their family name is Tenant. I think that's their name. And then another thing: in the dustbins there were actual dwarfs. They could stand in there because they were so small, and that had a stunning effect, but also anti-Beckettian. I don't think he would have approved. You say "clove." Is that how it is pronounced? Do some people say "cluv?"

No, we say "clove" in all productions in the United States. At least I haven't heard anyone pronounce it any other way.

You've written, as you say, "incidentally" about Beckett. He always comes up in your books. Among the recurrent figures there is Genet also, sometimes Ionesco, not so much though, and you also refer to Artaud. I know your cultural references by now, but one I'd particularly like to come back to is a quotation by Beckett from Confucius. Do you remember it?—"Better to light a single candle, than to curse the darkness." And your comment is this: "A Beckett play lights a candle and curses the darkness." Do you remember writing that, and could you comment further?

I wrote that long ago, in *The Impossible Theater,* but it's quite germane to things I feel about Beckett when I hear people discuss him today. There are those who have always tried to redeem him from his pessimism. The tendency in much thought about Beckett would be to reverse it and say, "Curse the darkness and light a candle," the implication being that the darkness can be redeemed. But I've always felt that Beckett puts things in the order in which he in fact perceives them. The order is the lighting of the candle and the cursing of the darkness. But it's the darkness which is dominant. I think that this has to be the premise of any approach to Beckett. Or not to *him,* but to the materials he left us and to the reality that these materials contain. Which is to say that whatever powers there are in the work of Beckett seem to consist of the really profound, essentially unrelieved, appalling perception of reality. That there is in some sense an impulse to move on, what Hamm says at the end, yes, is true, maybe (there's always a subjunctive in Beckett's thought), reckoning closed and story ended: discard, good, speak no more about it. But the capacity to move is minimal. It's not to be redeemed in the way productions tend to do it today by, for example, putting an indulgent stress on the comedy, so that there's an evasive sense of levity in the existential gloom.

So that when he was given the Nobel Prize, it seemed that they were doing exactly what you're saying, redeeming him from his bitterness.

Redeeming him, yes. He disappeared, you recall, at the time of the Nobel Prize, though I won't claim that was escaping redemption. Some of us, I suppose, were ready to claim it for him, as if the prize confirmed us too for supporting him early on. As it happens, Martin Esslin and I were actually in Canada together, having breakfast, the day we heard about it over the radio. We were in some sort of conference, giving talks, and after we heard it, we tried to get in touch with him. It was impossible. He had already disappeared.

On this question of pessimism or not pessimism you have another formula, which is your own this time. You call it the "last-ditch humanism of Beckett." That's a wonderful formula because it's an oxymoron in a sense. Could you say more about it.

First of all, there's the "ditch." And sometimes the ditch is an abyss, a crevasse. It's deep, it's a big rift in reality. But the "humanism" is there, beyond all denial, *in the denial,* crucially there. I think it distinguishes him, particularly when distinctions are being made between the modern and the postmodern. If you get involved in the debate as to whether there's continuity or a breach between the modern and postmodern, it seems to me that Beckett is really the pivotal figure. While many of the writers that we associate with postmodernity have similar strategies—parataxis, discontinuity, dispersed subject, all of those things that are structurally identifiable in Beckett—the one thing that many of them don't have is simply the unrelieved poignancy. He has a way of saying in theoretical terms—he wouldn't put it in theoretical terms—that maybe authenticity is a fiction. Maybe origin never was. And yet, and yet . . . there is a kind of residual, unrelieved tenacity of memory that is inextinguishable in Beckett. He seems to be remembering something, with unappeasable longing for it, whether or not it ever was. And that's something one doesn't have, not with the same anguish, in most postmodern works. While the structural qualities are the same, the emotional content seems to me to be markedly different.

When you say emotional, would you be ready to say metaphysical, perhaps?

Well, metaphysical. It's one of those cases where you say, as Artaud would say, the metaphysics comes in through the pores, it comes in through the skin. It just seems to me a visceral metaphysics. It's not necessarily theological.

There's another formula of yours, dealing with this "inextinguishable poignancy." I think that's what you said. Here is something you wrote: "What we see in all of Beckett's writing is the trembling of perception at degree zero"—we remember Barthes here—"on the edge of its extinction." Could you explain what you meant by that?

There may be some combination there of what's in Beckett and what obsesses me, which is to say I've always been interested in the deception of appearances and the incapacity at some limit of desire to see what we want to see. As Lacan and others have said, we see in the shape of our desires. But what seems to me to have been always provocative in Beckett is very much what I was describing before, when the objects materialized in *Endgame*. It seems to me that what really happens in Beckett, and what is most moving to me, happens in those moments when you are precipitously about to see something which, in the very activity of perception, *disappears*, as if in fact exhausted in the energy required for you to see it. Almost as if there were a dramatization of the Heisenbergian principle: the very instruments of perception dematerialize the object; that is, the instruments of perception get in the way.

That is something I always found difficult to understand. Could you just take a little more time to explain what you mean? What is this principle? Because I think it is captivating but difficult to grasp.

Well, as I understand the principle—and usually we presume on scientific ideas, using them metaphorically—but as I understand the notion of indeterminacy there, the idea is that the very instruments required for perception determine the nature of perception. They both permit us to see and get in the way of seeing, so that they in some sense change the nature of the object to be seen. The problem with human perception is that the instrument is in part determined by want or desire, in other words, what we in some sense are looking *for*. And this both deranges the process and distorts the object of sight. But what, at a more basic level, has always interested me—and the same thing interests me in human experience, as in Shakespeare, or Beckett—is the whole question of appearance itself. You love someone. You think you know that person. The person should be transparent to you. And suddenly you look again, and there's something else there, it's not what it was. So the whole question of the deception of appearances seems to me to come into play, the object there, altered, with the look of being looked at. But Beckett gets at the issue in a particular way that has to do with the apparent materialization. It's like something in a photographic studio, presumably coming into sight, the image materializing from the processing itself, and just when you think you've brought it into focus, it disappears. What you thought you were seeing is there and then not there.

There's the movie Roma, *by Fellini, in which these frescoes are found. The moment the eye discovers the frescoes, the frescoes disappear, they vanish. It destroys them as it reveals them.*

I was once taken by Roberto Rossellini to see the frescoes at Cerveteri. You know, you have to open those tombs, which are sealed to visitors. But Roberto had influence: he said open, and they opened, and so we got in. But otherwise they keep them closed, because they are afraid that, if too much light got to them, they would disappear. Not only are the frescoes endangered by light but also, it seems, by the attritions of the look. Here the process I'm describing is very much like what was apparently believed in the Renaissance, that the eyes sent out energy. And it's as if the energy from the eyes erodes the object. In other words, as I look right now at Bernard Vincent, our technician today, the very energy of sight puts him in jeopardy, as an object subject to erosion . . .

Please don't erode our technicians! So we have come to perception after all. I won't keep you away long from specularity and all that. The Eye of Prey *is a wonderful title, and you once said it came from Beckett. Maybe you will explain where exactly it comes from. There is the essay on Barthes and Beckett, "The* Punctum, *the* Pensum *and the Dream of Love." How useful is Barthes in your interpretation?*

It wasn't so much that he was useful. They were just two people that I wanted to write about for various reasons (though the immediate occasion was that Barthes had just died, and I was asked to speak of him and Beckett at a testimonial symposium in New York). In any event, they permitted me to make an interesting distinction. At the time I wrote that essay, though I always admired Barthes, there was still the semiological retard or bias in his work. Remember that through the earlier part of his career he was at one level Marxist, always demythologizing.

Did you say "retard"?

Yes, brilliant as he was, a certain impediment. Perhaps it's my own retarding bias, but I thought it prevented him from seeing certain things. The semiological perspective, though it had certain assets, also had certain liabilities. If there was one fine difference between Barthes and Beckett, it's what Beckett couldn't contain in himself, which was precisely the emotional property that I was trying to describe before. Barthes always tried to displace that, emotions arising from privacy, subjectivity, depth. In the dialectic of surface and depth Barthes preferred surface, and it wasn't until later on, with *La Chambre claire,* when he withheld the fetishized picture of his mother, never showed it, kept it hidden, that it seemed to me something did surface that, for some reason, Barthes prevented himself from exposing before.

To put it a little crudely, you seem to take two people, one of whom was a creative artist and the other more of an exegete and interpreter, but who never pretended he was an artist. Is that distinction, to you, irrelevant?

It's irrelevant. With Barthes, of course, the issue of what constitutes an artist seems to dissipate in his prose. Here you have two writers: they both write superbly. They write in different genres, but I was in some sense examining, I suppose, my own disposition, temperament, and instincts. At some final property of thought, they are, all told, a little more on the Beckettian side. And that's what I was trying to clarify.

Could you imagine directing a piece by Barthes? Could you imagine turning it into a stage piece?

I can imagine directing anything if I'm interested in it. When I first started to work in the theater, there were certain prescriptions about what was possible and what was not possible. Certain things, they said, could not be put on stage. I tried dutifully to understand that, but after a while I realized that there's nothing living or dead, under heaven or on earth, that can't be put on stage—if you have the right idea.

So now we come back to The Eye of Prey *and this extraordinary expression.*

The "eye of prey" comes from *Imagination Dead Imagine.* And, by the way, that in itself describes a distinction between Beckett and the Barthes of the semiological period. The Barthes of that period could not allow himself the second *imagine.* You'd say *imagination dead,* because imagination is a "transcendental signifier." Therefore it's out, along with *genius* and all those other terms that are no more than metaphysical derivations. Beckett critiques that critique in the title, *Imagination Dead Imagine.* In other words, you have to understand that imagination is dead before you can start imagining again. But imagination is like the leaves on the tree in *Godot,* going to sprout again, dead but always living. I think the later Barthes would have had to accede to that. As the eye of prey occurs in *Imagination Dead Imagine,* it has to do with what, say, Lacan might have talked of—through Saint Augustine—as the *envenomed eye,* the eye which is always searching, or inquisitional. It's like the difference between the *look* and the *gaze.* The eye of prey is the one that looks, it's the analytic eye, it's the eye that's incisive, that surgically cuts. It's the eye which is on the other side of the eye which is slit in the Buñuel film. It's the animal, predatory eye.

You say at one point, the "envenomed stare." I take it this is a translation from Lacan?

That's the phrase that Lacan gets from Saint Augustine. There's a passage in Saint Augustine where the child is looking at his sibling, the younger child, and the "envenomed stare" suggests that the older one wants to kill the younger one.

You use the phrase "the cutting look," and you say for Beckett there's no look that is not cutting.

There is no look that's not cutting. I think that's an interesting proposition, the notion of the cut in the look. Most people in fact don't like to be looked at. Why that should be so seems to me an issue of metaphysical proportions. By the way, I can explore this in any number of ways, but I remember vividly—since you know my daughter Jessamyn—an occasion involving her. But first, consider the parents' relationship to the child when, for example, the child is crawling on the floor. There you are standing above, a sort of monolithic figure. It's still hard to decipher what a child, as an infant, may be feeling about the immensity of the towering figure. But there is also, of course, the acquisitive or appropriative aspect of the gaze or the look. I'm collapsing the two at the moment. You look at the child, presumably with tenderness and love, but in fact the very look also contains the desire *to be* loved. In other words, I look at you, I love you, but I really want you to tell me that you love me. Now I remember one time, when Jessamyn was in the crib, and I was looking down at her. I'll come back to this in Beckett, but I remember looking at her, or was it gazing at her? I suppose there must have been something like the appropriative gaze, and I remember the first moment where she literally—I'll have to show it to you—where she literally began to flail her arms in front of her, like this, as if she were saying, "Don't look at me!" Now why that should be is something that requires extraordinary reflection.

Just one anecdote of my own. When my son was small, I would crouch next to him so that I would be his size, and he would see me crouching, and he would crouch too.

Exactly. But to stay with the unobtrusive or intimidating look: Beckett has another memorable phrase—I think it's in *The Lost Ones*—where he speaks of the "nesting stare." Children, you know, before their necks are sufficiently formed so that they can keep the neck erect, tend to turn their heads around, a sort of wobbling pivot, as if they're looking behind. Beckett speaks of that turn as if they're looking back, so to speak, to the mother's breast. Thus, the nesting stare. It's as if they're staring back to where there was perfect accommodation . . . perhaps to the womb itself.

I would be tempted to understand the nesting stare as the opposite of the cutting stare. That would be the protective stare, or the stare seeking protection?

The desire for that which is utterly protective and nurturing. Freud once said—and Beckett was very much interested in analysis; he worked with a Freudian analyst, Bion, although he was also very impressed with Jung—Freud said that all thought is a long detour from the memory of gratification. The nesting stare, it seems to me, is related to the memory of gratification. It is something other than the eye of prey, but speaking of that, and also of children, let me recall an incident which I referred to once before in something I wrote, a variation on the eye. In the year that I first met Beckett, we saw each other several times and, as I said, he would come to pick me up at the hotel on the rue Monsieur-le-Prince. My first wife was with me in Paris, and our three children, they were there. When he came to pick me up, the two of us would go out and walk or go to dinner or whatever, but he always expressed interest in my children. I thought that this was more or less formulaic at first, but from the questions he asked about them it became clear that he was really interested in the children. He said more than once he would like to meet them, and my wife, so we eventually made an arrangement to go out to dinner together, my wife, he and I, but he would meet my children before we went. So, he came to pick me up as usual, and as I came down the staircase, he was down at the bottom, looking at me, puzzled, because I was coming down alone. "They're all sick," I said. "They all have the flu. Everybody has the flu." He looked at me as if he could hardly believe it. But we went out and took a long walk. We had dinner somewhere, and when we came back near midnight he looked upstairs—we had two rooms in the hotel—the light was out in one room but was still on in the other. "I guess my wife is still up and the kids are sleeping," I said. Again, a puzzled look, almost disbelieving. "Next time you come to Paris," he said, "you must produce your children for my eyes of flesh." Twenty years later he used that phrase in *Imagination Dead Imagine,* or at least that's where I first saw it. Some years after that I actually brought Jessamyn to meet him, and said, "I've now produced a child for your eyes of flesh."

And he remembered saying that?
No, he didn't quite remember. I reminded him.

There is a sentence by him you quote, which is, "Am I as much as being seen."
That's from the play called *Play.* It has to do with the verification of being by sight. It's like when Pozzo says, "Is everybody looking at me?" It's as if I have no confirmation of being unless I am seen. But you have to play

with that phrase too. "Am I as much as *being* seen?" "Am I as much as being *seen?*"

There is the same ambiguity as in Imagination Dead Imagine. *You've been around actors a lot. Do they take pleasure in being seen? Are they different from other people in that sense, in that they want to be watched?*

I think that that is the most complex ontological problem of theater. We speak of such things as "stage fright." Why should that be? It has always occurred to me that the real issue in theater always pivots upon displacement. If there's pleasure in being seen, what's being seen is no pleasure—if you really think about it. For the person performing in front of you is dying in front of your eyes. If you're sufficiently patient, it will happen. You will see it, but it will not be visible.

Could you repeat that? Because this is quite a paradox. I want to take it in. Could you repeat it?

Well, it seems to me that it's existential truth. It's undeniable. The person performing in front of you is dying in front of your eyes, as I am right now. That's literally true, invisibly so. But if you are sufficiently patient, you will see it . . .

Unless you die first . . .

Unless *you* die first, right. But it is not sufficient. It may be more or less covered up by various forms of theater or mimicked in horrid splendor as it is in *King Lear,* but even when it appears to be empty, there is always death in the center of the stage. That's what's very powerful in Beckett, his consciousness of that, specifically dramatized in the very few seconds of his little play *Breath.* That consciousness is elaborated and mordantly focused in Hamm, who is being stared at and, through black spectacles, seems to be staring back at us, subject/object, returning the gaze—and all the deadly implications of the structure of being watched. Again, in a very literal sense we're close to what the theater is: the seers being seen.

Would you say that the curtain is a shroud?

Oh yeah. But well, I'll come back to the curtain in a moment. The curtain is really an interesting phenomenon. Yes, it's a shroud, and many other things besides. It's a veil, a baffle, a blind, a shroud.

Hamm is supposed to be blind. Because he says, "One day you will be blind like me" . . .

"One day you'll be blind," that's what he *says* . . .

And maybe that's what he sees . . .

All of it pointing, sometimes painfully, to what we cannot see. "There's something dripping in my head," he says. You can't see that either, right? Something dripping in my head. But where was I before, I was trying to say something . . . Oh yeah. In *Waiting for Godot,* if you are following Beckett's stage directions—and in fact we did follow the stage directions in the first production that I did of it—the two tramps have to divert themselves from the impasse at which they appear to have come. There's nothing happening, so with increasing panic in the diversion, they resort to playing games. At one point they're moving desperately back and forth across the forestage, looking out, presumably, into the maw of the auditorium, into the reversed and darkling perspective of what appears to be nothing there. That nothing, of course, is the audience. Which is—that body of conventional absence—*breathing death,* you see. Now, you might say this is the postwar existential aspect of the play. Even Winston Churchill shared its sense of reality. He spoke of this "great charnel house of Europe" at the end of the Second World War. The experience of the war and the nature of theater seem to merge in the immediacy of the play. The tramps move across the front of the stage, pointing in horror at the darkness where the audience is, saying, "A charnel house! A charnel house!" And that, in brief, is Beckett's view of it all. "You don't have to look." "You can't help looking." Which is what makes it theater.

You said you would come back to the question of the curtain, which separates the audience. But relative to the performance strategy in Beckett, going from the womb to the tomb, perhaps, is the issue of the audience as an absence. I don't quite understand why you mentioned the audience as an absence.

You've got a lot of questions there. Which one do you want me to talk about first?

We'll start with the curtain.

Conventions of the theater are best approached if you try to imagine their not having been. Meaning, you try to imagine how, first, they came into being. For example, in almost every theater history I've ever read, if you look up *curtain,* it'll say something like this: "The Romans invented the curtain, which was called the *auleum.*" And then they pass on. Yet it always occurred to me when I read things like that, well, yeah, that's interesting, but why did they do that? Who did that? Or how did it materialize? Try to imagine. Here we are, we're all looking at each other, right? Nothing between us. And then this phenomenon intervenes. Whether somebody invented it or it materialized at some time, what phenomenologically and psychically changed in human reality to warrant this intervention? In other words, how . . . ?

Except that you use it exactly like a mask . . .

Well, that's what I was just going to say. A curtain is a shroud, a veil, a mask . . . but once you begin to reflect upon it, it can operate in various ways: you realize you can do this . . . you can do that . . . or you can do this . . .

All kinds of things . . . lifting, opening . . .

You can part the curtain, you can raise the curtain, you can move it from side to side. You can, of course, have a half-curtain, the way they do in the Kathakali, so you can see the headdresses above. Brecht had, similarly, a visible curtain line. You can have feet exposed below, like the Italian futurists did, or swag it to frame a boudoir. I once did a production of Brecht's *Galileo* in which the curtain was raised high over the heads of the audience, a vast canopy of resplendent blue. It hovered there like the sky itself, and, when released, it came down floating, like a great minstrel galleon's enormous sail. But just as it was rustling to nest, a film suddenly came on, zap, and it was a movie screen. On the other hand, in the second production of *Waiting for Godot* that I did, the curtain was neither so gorgeous nor so adept. It was done in a smaller theater, and I wanted it performed in almost perfect silence. So the entire stage was foam rubber. When the actors moved, you couldn't hear them, and then, more often than not, you not only couldn't hear them, but they sort of sank into the stage. Whenever they walked they kept sinking into the stage. The curtain for this production was a shabby, see-through curtain. It had tattered holes in it like the clothes of the tramps themselves. It was a debilitated curtain. And, moreover, this curtain, which was supposed to rise, couldn't, as we say, "get it up." So, as it tried to rise, it would go halfway, then twitch and jerk, and then fall down. It would go limp. It lay there on the stage like a ruined convention at the dead end of history. Even so, you can do a lot with a ruin when you think about it.

You can also decide to have no curtain. And then for the audience, what is present is the absence of the curtain. Also, what you said about the see-through curtain . . . I mean, there's a whole transparency . . .

Opacity or transparency, the question is, why is it there? And why, historically, did it appear in the first place? By the way, that's what I think all my writing has been about. I've always been interested in the materialization of theater from whatever it is *not*. Life? reality? whatever we call it, the assumption of something other than theater, from which theater materializes, or out of which we make it, the thing which it is not. But, back to the history books. We're told, say, that theater came from ritual. When I read that somewhere, I always raise my eyebrows: "Who said so?" I mean, what had priority, ritual or theater? And is there any other reality except the reality which already has over it an integument of theater like a curtain or a film? After all, that's what the theater itself, or at least the drama, has traditionally wondered about. It's always been raising the question as to whether there is anything but theater. "Life is a dream." "All the world's a stage." Maybe so, maybe not. But that's the thing in question.

You say, raising your eyebrow, what comes first? But where does the audience fit in all this, as a metaphor linked to gazing?

You asked about the audience as an absence. If the audience is not an absence, it's not a reliable presence. Think of even the conventional play: the reality that's dispersed through characters on the stage. Whatever may be improbable, impermeable, indeterminate about the characters, they are nevertheless there, featured on the stage. They have a certain palpability, embodied, carnal, spoken for. The one really indeterminate aspect of any performance, in some sense absent or unaccountably present, is the audience, particularly when it's dark. We don't really know who's there, you know. I always make an issue of this in relationship to *Hamlet*. "Who's there?" "Nay, answer me. Stand, and unfold yourself." It's as if the text itself were speaking to the absence.

*You remember—I know the title in French—*Outrage au public, *by Peter Handke, in which they address the public directly. . .*

Offending the Audience. Well, offending the audience assumes, in fact, that somebody is there who can be offended. But what's interesting to me about *Hamlet* is that, first of all, there's a kind of reversal, which is to say that the person approaching the ramparts is the one who asks the question, instead of the guard, who should. "Who's there?" It comes out of the dark like a challenge from the text, a challenge to identity. "Nay answer me, stand and unfold yourself." It's as if the unfolding is required for the audience to materialize. Without answer, no audience. But there's another play that I always refer to, which, for me, defines this whole issue as deeply as anything I know. It seems a sort of poetic justice of history that in the only existing Greek trilogy the first character to materialize—as if, you might say, from primeval darkness into Platonic light—is the Watchman. The first play is the *Agamemnon,* in which the Watchman awakens into the Enlightenment, so to speak, from ten years of waiting and watching. Internally, dramaturgically, he is responsible for the exposition, what's happening in the House of Atreus. For good reason, given the collusion of Clytemnestra and Aegisthus, he's very nervous about that. Speaking elliptically, warily, he positions himself in the cosmos, before "the grand processions of all the stars of night," vaguely suggesting what's going on. And then he concludes by saying—I don't read Greek, but in all translations it amounts to this— "I speak to those who understand, but if they fail I have forgotten everything." It seems to me that those who understand are the audience, who already know, the story known, what it is that they have to acknowledge. And anybody else who assembles before the curtain, as in the open sky at Epidaurus, is sort of irrelevant, they may never understand.

You call him in English "The Watchman" and, of course, to watch has a double meaning, which we cannot grasp in French, but "Watchman" is particularly interesting.

Another critical representation of this idea is the famous "mousetrap," again from *Hamlet,* where you have the watchers watching the watchers watch. It's that aspect of theatricality that's always interested me. And Beckett's very attuned to it, for all his apparent indifference, conscious of the audience, or its absence. What always struck me is how attentive the plays were to precisely that. In *Waiting for Godot,* for instance, those wonderful lyric duets of Didi and Gogo: they make a noise like wings, like ashes, like leaves. . . . They all speak at once, what do they say? They say . . . well, what are they referring to? What is the referent? Who are *they?* As they speak, the actors are listening as if they had a stethoscope to the heartbeat of the audience.

When you said the actors, you mean the characters. Or do you really mean the actors?

I mean the actors, at least as it was in our production. I'm almost differentiating the actors from the characters. That distinction seems to me to be critically important. In *Endgame* too. Take the one who is playing Hamm, presumably looking straight out toward the emptiness in front of him. Yet he may be more attentive to what's happening in the audience than the audience is to what's happening on the stage. He is a register of every sensation out there before him. It's as if he records the emanations of the gaze. He's like a sensitive photographic plate. In the deepest performance, he registers it all.

I was expecting you to use, at some point, and you haven't, Lacan's expression, "the scopic drive." This is also something which is important in your reflections on the theater. Do you feel like mentioning it?

There's a chapter in *The Audience* which is entitled "The Most Concealed Object." Lacan's treatment of the scopic drive, the desire to see, raises the question: to see what? Whatever there is to see that hasn't been seen. That's always in relationship to the taboo. What's interesting about the taboo, as we open up one taboo after another, is that the taboo is ingenious, the taboo always recedes. When you think you've got the taboo, it goes somewhere else. So the compulsion *to* see is, as Freud first suggested, an obsessive compulsion which is always and forever unrelieved. The most concealed object, as Lacan says in reworking Freud, is in some sense the drive itself. One wants to see the drive, but as Ben Jonson said in a masque, as if talking of time or death, the taboo within the taboo, no one sees the motion but the motion. The drive itself is the most concealed object.

You quote Lacan as saying, "There are eyes everywhere, I see only from one point, but in my existence I am looked at from all sides." Could this be used to refer to the relationship between actors who see from one point, while they are looked at from all sides by the audience, so many eyes watching them?

"Is everybody looking at me?" Again. Even now, is everybody looking at me? What's interesting—think here of Genet—is the sensation that, even when there appears to be nobody there, we're incessantly being watched. We are under surveillance. And, of course, notions of shame and guilt are attached to that. Even when we are alone. To the degree that one feels guilt or anxiety or something else unnerving. What is that about? It's as if we are still being watched, and there's nobody there, right? That, of course, permits Freud to construct a notion such as the *superego*.

You know in books I used to read in my childhood, the little boy would say, "The eye of God is watching me." He's looking at chocolate, and the eye of God is watching.

That, by the way, comes up in *Waiting for Godot*. Gogo keeps looking up there to see whether somebody is watching him, who's utterly indeterminate.

You quote Shakespeare, a beautiful sentence, which is relevant to what you were saying before. Gloucester says in Henry VI, *"I'll slay more gazers than the basilisque. . . ."*

No, that's Richard II . . .

Richard II? OK. So, did he really write that?

Who else could write that?

Say it again . . .

"I'll slay more gazers than the basilisque." It's as if Richard, with circuitous or devious vision, is an expert at the gaze. If anybody is inside the gaze, if anybody understands it as a phenomenon, he is it. "I'll slay more gazers than the basilisque." It's as if he has perfected from birth the envenomed stare, confronting the gaze with the gaze, as if it were lethal coming from him. He walks downstage at the beginning, he talks to the audience, virtually baits them: you can observe me all you wish, gaze at will, judge, you will never know me.

I have a question which is not directly connected to what we said before but which I would very much like to ask you. And it's about the relationship between the theater and visual arts, such as sculpture. You mentioned Giacometti, and you said he was Beckett's favorite sculptor. I would like to ask you, as a director, if you think that a director working for the stage works in a sense like a sculptor, like a visual artist.

Without that capacity you don't have much of a director. But there are visual artists and visual artists, and how they detail and contour space is obviously a big issue. In the case of Giacometti, he figured in the way we were trying to conceive *Endgame.* What is compelling about the sculpture is the strength of its seeming fragility, submitting only as much metal to the air as the air needs to surround it. There would be less if it could be an intact structure, if it survived the severest diminishment. There would be even less, a desire shared by Beckett, who wrote the terribly moving *Lessness.*

You know, I saw the other day an exhibition at the Jeu de Paume. One sculptor put a figure kneeling against the side of the wall, and he said, "This sculpture is made of plaster, paint and air." Air is part of the sculpture. So, is it true on stage also?

Well, most of the stage is air. But this suggests something else I've always wanted to do in the theater. It has to do with what might be thought the opposite of air. Have you seen Picasso's *Death's Head?* It is, I think, one of his greatest pieces of sculpture. It looks like a great globule. If one can imagine the objectification of a black hole, the black hole in space, about which we say the mass is so dense that it impacts upon itself, in some sense implodes, gravity reversed to come out some other side—Picasso's *Death's Head* is like that. I wrote about it in *Take Up the Bodies.*

Une tête de mort?

Tête de mort, yes. That head is so dense it seems immovable, a totalized object. But theater is a temporal form. Now you see it now you don't. One of the reasons I never liked videotaping or filming the theater work I did is because it was meant to disappear. The desire to preserve it, I think, is a factitious sort of notion. It's a thing in passing that, once passed, not only shouldn't but can't be there. That makes for certain problems when publishers ask for pictures in my books, or even when, suddenly, I want them myself. But even in the fashion book I'm writing now, I like to describe things, and the idea of documenting them with pictures I always have mixed feelings about. I like the language to evoke it rather than illustrations. And that may come from some theatrical tendency. In any case, the theater's a temporal form. It moves through time, and therefore it changes and dissipates, and disappears, through time. Conceding that, the mind then moves, sometimes resolutely, in the opposing direction: to stop time, to make it all hold still. Imagine creating a theater work with all the obduracy, the gravity, of Picasso's *Death's Head.* Now and then, I believe, I was close to imagining something like that onstage, with the illusion of achieving it. It was the doing of *Endgame* that initiated the idea, because of its stasis, its paralysis. The paradox: I wanted to create a theater work about which you would feel that it moves through time and disappears, utterly temporal, yet absolutely sculptured in space, immovable, an absolute object. Obviously, that's impossible. But the idea of doing that . . .

Slowing down, slowing down the action, as you did with the curtain in Endgame, *would that be part of the effect?*

Endgame had no curtain in our production . . .

No, I mean the curtain . . . drawing the curtain . . .

Well, that had some relationship to it, but I felt that—the desire to objectify the temporal—about almost anything that I ever did, and very markedly in what I did with my KRAKEN group much later.

By the way, KRAKEN, did that mean something?

The actual term comes from *kraken,* the Nordic sea monster. The reason we took the name is that we were interested in the relation of surface and depth. Tennyson wrote a poem about the kraken, which died when it surfaced after being fathoms deep. I got it, actually, not from Tennyson but from Melville, who was corresponding with Hawthorne, after finishing *Moby-Dick.* Hawthorne asked him what he would be doing next. And Melville said, "I'm after bigger fish." The bigger fish would be the kraken. We Americanized and called it "krayken." The KRAKEN group did do certain work which addressed the problem, the fantasy, of achieving something marmoreal, thus memorial, in a temporal form, as if the movement were frozen solid. A work we did, *The Donner Party, Its Crossing,* literally moved from beginning to end, over two hours, unceasing motion in the form of a square dance. I mean unceasing motion, intricate and exhaustive, even when the figures in the crossing, that fatal journey, were buried twenty feet beneath the snow. We wanted the materiality of the event to feel so dense that it virtually arrested time. That's essentially what I'm talking about, the illusion of immovable substance in this apparently dispersed form.

(1996)

Astride of a Grave; or, the State of the Art

(This essay was written for a performance studies conference on "Theaters of the Dead," at the Graduate Center of the City University of New York, in March 1998. Since I knew I was departing from the more anthropological expectations in that context, or the ritual manifestations of such a theater, I thought a preface was in order. I've included that here, as it was there.)

There may be times in what I'm about to say when I'm not quite sure what I'm saying—if not quite incoherence, a feeling of disjuncture, because some of what I'm saying was prompted, more or less directly, not by theaters of the dead but by death itself, whatever that may be. None of us, of course, is an authority on the subject, though I did have the peculiar impression, when Elin Diamond called and invited me to speak, that it was partially because my qualifications were improving.

In any event, it's a subject which I've talked about before, as you will see, and, in quoting myself, I will sometimes be eliding what I said then into what I'm thinking now, with no guarantee that my thinking is more mature. There are certain passages where it may seem that I'm departing from the issue, but there I'll be referring to or explaining one or another relationship moving these reflections, which may have begun, actually, more narcissistically, when I was still in my teens and wrote a story about doing what may seem a little strange to have been doing at that age, or any age for that matter, though in a sense we do it in the theater. The story was about my staring into a mirror in order to watch myself die, which I did with a certain solemnity from time to time, though I never quite had the patience for the definitive moment—which, when the time comes, will probably escape me.

Let's start with the obvious. You get older, you think about death. If you've thought of it before, you think of it more. If you're lucky, you may have to think harder, for the moment, about the death of somebody else, which may be harder or easier than thinking of your own, depending on who it is, and in any case I'm not sure. As it turns out, I've had to think over a period of some years about the deaths of friends, and I wouldn't bring it up in this context except that three of them were important to my career in the theater, and the other as a theorist thought much of performance too. He was, besides, very much taken with an idea I've long had about the theater: that its power comes from the fact that the person performing in front of you is dying in front of your eyes, as I am now, ineluctably but invisibly, existential fact, and if you think of it for a moment, theater will have appeared, precisely because you think, from whatever it is it is *not*, and I'm not doing anything that I wasn't doing before.

But as some of you have heard me on this theme, I want to come back to my friends, about whom I'd been asked at each death to make a talk at a memorial ceremony or, for one of them, to write a sort of epilogue to a life that was written as death, or so minimally living that you could virtually write it off, or think of it only as written, it all, it all, as if its destiny were the *pensum,* that circuitous compulsion or echolocation of words, "all words, there's nothing else,"[1] the reality of the unnamable, which was the death of him after all. As for the words you hear in the theater or, for that matter, these words now—the words flying up, the body remaining below—it's as if he always knew that they were in their empty soundings the contour of silence and death, the unrepresentable ground of life, which—think of it as you will—can *only* be represented, the unactable, imageless, invisible thing itself that, however perversely, we nevertheless want to *see*. (In that regard, the theater itself may be, as Euripides seemed to understand in his devastating reappraisal of the festival of Dionysus, the institutional form and purveyor of that perversion, endorsed by the lethal god who, multiply imaged but imageless too, seems to exist in the gaze.) "Astride of a grave and a difficult birth," and as "the grave-digger puts on the forceps," the imminence of specularity: "At me too someone is looking,"[2] and there's something deadly in that, grievously so in the theater of Beckett, where there's the equal and opposite fear that nobody's looking at all.

As I wrote of it in *The Audience,* there are cryptological moments when the absence is unbearable, although there's something there in the dark, and you can still hear it breathing, it whispers, it rustles, like ashes, like leaves, like "the awful stench of history, which is an echo chamber of death. . . ."[3] But you're now familiar with that and can even laugh it off, we after all know the jokes, although when we first started doing Beckett he was hardly known at all, and some people would leave the theater—"A charnel house! A charnel house!" (*Godot* 41)—still scandalized at the thought that, particularly in the theater, to which they'd bought a ticket, they were something less than alive, sitting there breathing death, which is why the entire history of the theater could be pared down to a generically desolate image, a sort of zero sum of a phenomenological reduction, on the dispeopled stage of Beckett's synoptic *Breath*.

Is that merely Western theater? The ritual forms of other cultures might seem to be otherwise, though I've tried to suggest elsewhere that there is no mode of performance that does not hinge upon a breath, and a shadow's breath at that, which moves through all appearance, like *shakti, chi,* or *pneuma,* or the phantasmic passage of the *yugen* of the Noh, while "there is in the disappearing space of performance something of a cemetery too," as well as a sense in which "the performer is always imagining his own death," projected into the future as the memory that comes from behind, "as if it had already happened."[4] If that's basic metaphysics in a theater of the dead, it was congenital reflex with Beckett, in or out of the theater, more or less on the principle that, with imagination itself in jeopardy, it's likely to be most enlivened (imagination dead imagine) by imagining death.

To be sure, there are times when certain figures in Beckett seem to be overdoing it, not only imagining but, if not reliving, relieving life in death. So it appears with the narrator in the early story "First Love," for whom "the smell of corpses" at his father's grave, "distinctly perceptible under those of grass and humus mingled," is not at all "unpleasant, a trifle on the sweet side perhaps, a trifle heady, but how infinitely preferable to what the living emit, their feet, teeth, armpits, arses, sticky foreskins and frustrated ovules." The narrator is, true, not necessarily Beckett, but we may suspect a shared sentiment when he says, "Personally I have nothing against grave-yards, I take the air there willingly, perhaps more willingly than elsewhere, when take the air I must"—all the more so as "the living wash in vain, in vain perfume themselves, they stink."[5] We can, of course, laugh this off too, as death's-head humor, merely part of a dramatic tradition, as in the corro-sive jokes of Jacobean drama or the grotesque of Yorick's skull, though the stink has pervaded the theater, which, from whatever noxious beginning, smells of mortality, maybe only a trifle, and distanced by specularity, but for Beckett's Hamm as for Shakespeare's Lear a headier odor than that, cut-ting to the brain, as if it were the stench that is the essence, the manic obses-sive foundation, of the thought of theater itself.

"Do you smell a fault?" (*Lear* 1.1.15). That's Shakespeare, not Beckett, but the fault line runs like a lesion of the reality principle below the premises of any stage—in any configuration: proscenium, thrust, or round—or any culture, and even when the stage is dispersed, there we are, breathing death, with fabled ingenuities of forgetting, as in a festival or a carnival or as in the celebrations of the sixties, the "participatory mystique" trying to cover it up. As they persist in performance studies, burial rites, ancestral worship, or theaters of the dead are—as perceived by a scholar-ship derived from the sixties—usually haunted by the illusions of commu-nity, but whatever it is that haunted Beckett as he wrote impeccably for the theater, there was never sufficient identity, singular, no less collective, to ever suffer from that: "Am I as much as . . . being seen?" says one of the figures in the funerary urns of *Play,* awakened from the dead by the inqui-sitional light, with thoughts of "penitence, . . . at a pinch, atonement,"[6] but very little faith in "the occult origin" of their exclusion, no less the capacity to summon "an imagined community into being"—about which wish-fulfilling prospect, particularly for the colonized or oppressed, Joseph Roach has written so vividly in *Cities of the Dead.*[7]

If there is in such a figure anything approaching what Roach calls a "plausible surrogation" (40), a sort of vortex of "cultural self-invention" (28) restoring forgotten behavior, that would appear to happen with no lit-tle jaundice and, as always in Beckett, something like default. As for the mortuary ritual in which "the three-sided relationship of memory, perfor-mance, and substitution" are most "acutely visible" (Roach 14), in which we might feel—in a presumable unity around the body of the dead—the uncanniness of surrogation, Beckett tends to be, with the fastidiousness of a connoisseur, a little more dubiously down-to-earth. "With a little luck," says the narrator in "First Love," "you hit on a genuine interment, with real live mourners and the odd relict rearing to throw herself into the pit. And nearly always that charming business with the dust, though in my experience there is nothing less dusty than holes of this type, verging on muck for the most part, nor anything particularly powdery about the deceased, unless he happens to have died, or she, by fire. No matter, the lit-tle gimmick with the dust is charming" (12–13).

About these grave matters, the narrator offers, as he eats a banana sit-ting on a tomb, a certain self-deprecating, if mordant expertise. As he wan-ders "among the slabs, the flat, the leaning and the upright, culling the inscriptions," he reflects on the epitaph he has written for himself, with which he is "tolerably pleased." Unfortunately, "there is little chance of its ever being reared above the skull that conceived it," he says, "unless the State takes up the matter. But to be unearthed I must first be found, and I greatly fear those gentlemen will have as much trouble finding me dead as alive" (12). Alive or dead, there is in the apparent cynicism an acutely visible sense, as the death wish passes onto the corporeal space of the theater, of something taking its course that—despite a performative ethos of available otherness—no performance can relieve. We now speak of constructed identities, subject positions, and the subversive acts of "bodies that matter," but for the narrator whose corpse is not quite "up to scratch" (16), the game of identity politics—with its masks and masquerades and purported "crisis of categories"—would be, young as he is, a sort of callow indulgence, since any way you look at it identity is a double bind, if not entirely delusion: "it is painful to be no longer oneself, even more painful if possible than when one is. For when one is one knows what to do to be less so, whereas when one is not one is any old one irredeemably" (18). In the theater of the dead as Beckett construes it, the irredeemable, of course, is the name of the game, as it was when the tramps first came on to the stage, where everything's dead but the tree, with an inconsolable sense—just before the activist sixties—of "Nothing to be done" (*Godot* 7). I have pointed out before that the bleak and passive drama of *Waiting for Godot* may have turned out to be, politically, in its apparent renunciation of politics, the most energizing play of the period.

As for the narrator's epitaph, though he is revolted by his other writings as soon as the ink is dry, that still meets with his approval: "Hereunder lies the above who up below / So hourly died that he survived till now" ("First Love" 12). However that may have applied to Beckett himself, it's not what marked his grave in Montparnasse when I presumed, soon after his death, to write an elegy in a voice that somewhat merges with his own, while thinking of his survival as a birth astride of a grave. "Alas, yes, it's not possible otherwise, 'birth there had to be,' though it might have been another 'who had a life,' not he, 'a life not worth having,' he'd write, 'because of me,' and what are we to make of that?"[8] I'll come back to what I made of it then, but let me bring in my other friends, not necessarily in the order of their deaths, but with a rather embarrassed consciousness that, as I spoke in memento mori, the death of each of them was somehow absorbed into, or seemed to confirm, what I had been developing, since *Take Up the Bodies: Theater at the Vanishing Point*, as an ontology of performance, which lives on borrowed time or the attritions of time, as a "space of amortization" ("Universals" 170)—time, then, with a wallet at its back (referred to now as an "economy of death")—whose substance is appearance consumed with disappearance, drawn thus to the vanishing point.

First of all, there was Jules Irving, one year older than me, who was my partner in the theater, in San Francisco and New York, for just about twenty years. Then there was Robert Corrigan, one year younger than me, who founded *The Drama Review* when it was still at Tulane and published some of the first pieces I ever wrote on the theater, starting with a letter that I had written in Berlin, where I'd been invited by Helene Weigel after we'd done Brecht's *Mother Courage* (in 1957, its first production here). The letter was to the company of The Actor's Workshop of San Francisco, a sort of sizing up of our theater against what I'd seen in Europe, where I also met Beckett, after having directed *Endgame* as well as *Waiting for Godot*. Despite the notoriety of that production after we brought it to San Quentin, Jules and I were still dealing with a certain restiveness among the actors because there was, as I remarked from abroad, "too much European despair in our repertoire,"[9] if not what Beckett once called, with a certain necrophilia, "the issueless predicament of existence."[10] At the first rehearsal of *Godot* (in which two of our best actors refused to play) I had emphasized that, though audiences might find it strange, even repellent, as some did, no modern drama was—in its apparent interiority, on the selvedge of solipsism—more seductively aware of the presence of an audience, or its absence, all the more so when it appears to be there.

Whatever was there beyond the stage, its very heartbeat is revealed—with an almost diabolic precision in its delicate dying fall—in that exquisite threnody on desire, mortality, and time that, giving a definitive turn to the ideal of alienation, virtually defines in a pure lyric a theater of the dead. Listen to it again, as Didi and Gogo listened, looking into the maw of the audience, to whatever there in the charnel house may have been stirring still:

All the dead voices.
They make a noise like wings.
Like leaves.
Like sand.
Like leaves.
Silence.
They all speak at once.
Each one to itself.
Silence.
Rather they whisper.
They rustle.
They murmur.

They rustle.
Silence.
What do they say?
They talk about their lives.
To have lived is not enough for them.
It is not sufficient.
Silence.
They make a noise like feathers.
Like ashes.
Like leaves. (40)

The plaintive tension of the lyric is probably broken by a laugh, with the repetitive line about the waiting for the inscrutable Godot. What strikes me now, however, as we've grown accustomed to the comedy, is the degree to which I attributed it to "the remorseless pessimism of Beckett," with the drama proceeding on a datum of nothingness, indelibly marked by its elegiac tone. After an altercation with the State Department about having that production represent the United States (in 1958) at the Brussels World's Fair, I wrote another letter asking the actors, who were playing in New York before they went to Brussels (I stayed behind in San Francisco to rehearse another play), for "the proper intensity of desperation," and warned them against playing it for laughs, a tendency conspicuous in productions since. Despite his own positive thinking, what Corrigan might very well have responded to in this letter was the following passage: "Didi and Gogo are incurable patients linked in an eternal Patience, sad, lonely, dreadful, without avail, two hands clasped in numbed fear and trembling."[11] In that period of existentialism, nothingness was not Bob Corrigan's thing, but there was enough of a theological stink in what I was saying that appealed to his sensibility—he was, after all, the son of a bishop. And he liked the last line of the other letter, drawn not from Beckett but from T. S. Eliot's *Family Reunion,* a play in which the living appear to be observed by the dead. The line was used as the title when it was published: "Meanwhile, follow the bright angels."

We tried to do that, too, when many years later—after I left Lincoln Center and he had started the School of the Arts at NYU—we virtually became partners, while conceiving from the beginning, with $58,000,000 of Disney money (and a vast new building) to back it up, California Institute of the Arts, of which he was the president and I the provost and dean of the School of Theater and Dance. There was a serious impasse between Bob and me when I resigned from Cal Arts, protesting interference by the Disneys, but I won't go into that, except to say that when I left I never expected to see him again. He was wise enough to see that I did. What I did see, however, very soon after, was the beginning of his dying, or, if the beginning was always already, as we've come to say in theory, its distressingly visible symptoms, what, when I was younger, I couldn't quite see in the mirror. That occurred, fortuitously enough, at a television studio in Paris where Bob and I, my wife, Kathleen Woodward, and Martin Esslin—who had used our San Quentin production as the talismanic image of *The Theater of the Absurd*—were being interviewed about the videos they were making of Beckett's plays. As Bob responded to a question, I noticed one hand clenching the other, and though he tried to disguise it, when I insisted at a break that he tell me what was wrong, he said it had been diagnosed as Parkinson's disease—then grabbed his hand again, to keep it from shaking. It was the same hand that, once, in leaving Cal Arts, I had refused to shake.

"Whatever this may say of me," I said at his memorial, "it was he who reached out, as I'd seen him do before, time and time again." What followed was a view of Bob that, with the demand for definition that only comes with death, I had always taken for granted, but with a consciousness too of the theatricality of the occasion, wanting to get it right, in commemoration, while telling it as it was, though I couldn't tell it all. If there was always a subtext still unuttered, there is, I suppose, in any sort of theater, not exempting theaters of the dead, where the taboo that appears to be broken only recedes and mourning is mixed with other emotions, some of them not exactly ceremonial, if telltale about some who are there. "What was curious about Bob," I said, "is that he could also reach out to a facsimile of friendship, where bad faith was registered like a fact of nature. This is not meant to imply that Bob was ingenuous and merely taken in, for," confronted in actuality with the enigma of appearances (of which death after all is the apotheosis)—"he had a kind of genius for sizing things up in passing, with a sort of winning ease, taking the measure of possibility even against the grain. Which is to say, if exceptional talent or imagination were there he could overlook a flawed character or forgive a lot of faults. That is, without theorizing it, a kind of aesthetic, not exactly in fashion today, rather high modernist, so far as it accedes to the primacy of value in the claims of art when art, in practice, can justify its claims." Bob would insist, as he did in *Theater in Search of a Fix*, that whatever it did in practice the art with the strongest claims could also make them, canonically, across the fact of death—that fact, in theater, determining the state of the art. He would speak of theater as an act of faith, which he defended to the end in tragic drama, where "[heroic] spirit lives on long after the corpse has been interred."¹² If it isn't quite the same spirit as in other theaters of the dead, for which we have, after all, ideological criteria, Bob was never embarrassed, so to speak, by the transcendental signifiers.

Jules Irving rarely thought in such terms, or if he talked of faith or spirit, it might have been as a matter of expedience or desperate improvisation, to raise morale when the theater was in trouble. When the signifiers hollowed out, there was the saving grace of a sense of absurdity, quaquaquaqua, rather like Lucky in *Waiting for Godot,* the role he played in our production—as if, astride of a grave, saying whatever it took to keep from falling in. Actually, there were times when he and I seemed to resemble Didi and Gogo, though I can't tell you which was which. "One of the thieves was saved. (*Pause.*) It's a reasonable percentage." Or is it? "What is the theater," I had written in *Take Up the Bodies,* "but the body's long initiation in the mystery of its vanishings?"¹³ Speaking of mystery, if Jules were to return from the dead, as I said at his memorial, "he'd be an immeasurable cultural resource, better than Lazarus, and certainly funnier, because nobody was better at distilling calamity into hilarity. His illnesses, as he told about them, were legendary among us, epic—and when he warmed to the subject, Rabelaisian. One of his more triumphant moments was when he appeared—he thought about it as a performance and performed it, telling about it—before a medical symposium as a demonstration case. Wouldn't you know that his kidney stones were rare? He dissolved them with more water than they use for the irrigated miracle of Los Angeles [where the memorial was taking place, at the Mark Taper Forum]. As we rocked with laughter and he winced with pain, we thought he would outlive us all."

Jules was an inveterate gambler, he loved to gamble and used to say that, if he had to die, it should be at the crap table in Las Vegas. As it turned out, he had the attack that killed him at the crap table in Reno. When I asked Priscilla (his wife) why he was playing in Reno, which he always declared he hated, she said he was certain the odds were better. (Well, wasn't the theater itself predicated on catastrophe theory?) Mostly he knew the odds, which he always turned, as a means of inspiriting himself, into a premonition of disaster. For him it came sooner than we thought, which is why I thought he might appreciate what his dying caused me to think about, while "wincing," as I said, "at the implication of our common sham." Jules was not a theorist, he only knew what's what, and while he would rather not have died to make a point of it, I think he would have agreed with this, which made some who were at the memorial somewhat uneasy at the time. "Most plays," I said, "are the kind that are already interpreted before they are performed, leaving almost nothing left over for the actors but what they already know, though they don't always know it—most rehearsals being mere illusions of discovery, if not the discovery of that particular (and essential) illusion. When we have any doubts about that, death comes to dispel them; and we realize all over how unprovided for we are, how speechless despite the necessity of speech, the saying by means of which we know what we cannot say, even with all the scenarios and texts and the memories of great performances that, theoretically, should have explained it all. Tomorrow and tomorrow and tomorrow, we remain as ignorant as we are today."

But Jules knew, even before it came up in the mausoleum of appearances in Genet's *The Balcony,* which I staged in San Francisco in 1961, that whatever else they fantasize all the scenarios end in death. Which is what caused me to say, as I thought about his: "Whatever it is that appears to be real, like this dying, is what we have to explain, not reality itself, which we can never. And if it's only appearance, then, that we're talking about, as the great dramas suggest, when they claim that life is a dream or an insubstantial pageant fading, then we must ask—if there is any implication that appearances are a deceit—why does reality, whatever it is, choose to play false? Why do I say false? Because—for all the resignation of the ages about the inevitability of dying—even the more expected death than that of Jules Irving causes us to feel conflicted, at odds with ourselves, divided emotionally, wishing to assent to some knowing necessity in the shape of things, yet for one undisguised moment at least feeling somehow it is at best a cheap trick of the inexplicable, which is redeemed, but never entirely, by bringing us together for another hopefully undisguised moment to pay tribute, not merely to Jules, but to the mystery, in a baffled gathering of something like love."

Reading back over this now, it seems to me I was somehow defining, through Jules, what I had long been coming to think about the theater, conventionally designated a social or communal form, confirming a collective identity, but which really discovered its powers not in any unity but the unity of separation or—as I said at the memorial service, before hundreds of people we'd worked with over the years—"in the one inviolable community of death." It's a community that, on the face of it, I'm not too happy to join, as there was always an ambivalence about working in the theater, about which I have written that, practiced in deceit and illusion, it has a long history of distrusting itself. There is something in the theater, I've said, which resists being theater, as if the factitious energy of appearances—what is most entertaining, beguiling, seductive about it—were the recursive fascination of the death drive itself.

The ambivalence I speak of was discerned by my friend Michel Benamou, who brought me to the Center for Twentieth Century Studies, where the first talk I gave, at a conference on performance, was entitled "Missing Persons." When Michel became one of them, though a few years younger than me, too young if we were older, the emotion I experienced was nothing like "simple grief," for it was as if the death drive, too, had been outwitted, tricked, accelerated, when he died suddenly of a brain hemorrhage on a return to France. If you were trying to imagine then what a theater of the dead should be, it would be nothing but a lie if death weren't felt as obscene. What I spoke about, thus, at the service was still related to that, "the emotion I instinctively feel whenever I'm confronted with the lethal opacity of things—pure unmitigated rage," the rage itself as a form of transcendence, and never mind the critique of the signifiers or, for that matter, the critique of the oedipal drama or Brecht's critique of tragedy, where all the scenarios end in death, unalterable, inexplicable, irredeemable, but precisely because of that, producing the kind of emotion that I've always felt—without any need of the Alienation-effect—not at all as incapacitating, far from disempowering. I once wrote a manifesto called *The Impossible Theater,* whose power and prospect came, as I thought then and still think, from the fact that it *was* impossible, nothing more than that arousing the will to do it, as it did in Beckett with his notion of failing better[14] or, when it couldn't get any worse, the impulse to say, as one of his characters does, "Fuck life." Which impulse increased as friends began to die, though a sense of it as less, lessness, didn't keep him from writing a play like *Catastrophe,* in which the Protagonist like a corpse conveys as much of a political message as he ever put on stage—though so far as it was a message impairing the play for me.

As for Michel, when I saw him last I had read to him from the book I was finishing then, in which, as I also said at the service, "the image of dead bodies is very much in the center of the stage, along with the idea of vanishing. Michel had one reservation about what he'd heard. He knew that I wanted to make my way through all that unanswerable dying, but he worried that I was putting—even if there was no solution—too much stress on the dissolution. Maybe so. But neither will I use Michel's vanishing against him, to make my point—which is, through the sense of vanishing, more like what he wanted me to make. I can't say. I'm still asking the questions over and over, which are spilling out of the book. I wish he had lived to read it, instead of disappearing into the questions."

Yet that seems to me now the function, if it has any function at all, of a theater of the dead, at least today, as we approach the millennium in a world of globalized information with stocks that are rising and falling but, as part of the order of things, more than its share of gratuitously dead bodies: since it can't provide the answers, no less a correct politics, to disappear into the questions, so that the questions are never forgotten. That's where, I think, Beckett disappeared, although nobody knew more painfully that we are born into the questions too, "or was it aporia? aporia pure and simple," though "I should mention before going any further, any further on, that I say aporia"—mingling mine with Beckett's words—"without knowing what it means. Can one be ephectic otherwise than unawares? I don't know." What I do know, as I said in the elegy entitled "The Less Said," is that "the problem has always been, since we discovered that he was funny, to take him at his word, funny, but then no longer funny, from the recursive lamentations over the nothing to be done to the last obsessional and fractal testaments to the ubiquitous void: 'Say for be said. Missaid. From now say for be missaid.' From now, surely, be what it may. But how could it be anything but missaid, since he was always addressing the void (within the postmodern the postmortem condition) speaking as it were not astride but, so to speak, from the mouth of the grave or, bespoken perhaps, from somewhere beyond it." Though he had fought injustice when history required it, history still weighs like a nightmare on the brain of the living, and it was afterward that he wrote: "'No future in this. Alas yes.' The gravedigger puts on the forceps" (217), then "little by little . . . you begin to grieve."[15]

That's why I said it was "hard in mourning to mourn him, fittingly, in anything but his own words." For he had, after all, just about written the text of mourning or, "in its sepulchral orchestration, even hilarious, mourning and melancholia" ("Less Said" 217). The fizzles, the fractures, the farts, the fiasco at first suck: life seen as failure even before it began or, in the unabating plenitude of our insufficiency, "the unmoreable unlessable uttermost inadequacy of all this *otherness,* the shadow of a cenotaph, 'one minute in a skull, and the next in the belly, and the next nowhere in particular,'" or then again, "dripping in the head, 'splash, splash, always on the same spot,' an artery or vein perhaps, 'ever since the fontanelles'" (219)— when a word like that becomes, like the exhaustive enumeration of "an infinite emptiness," an overwhelmingly imponderable source of rage.

What is all this about a theater of the dead? We are just finishing the twentieth century. "The whole place stinks of corpses" (*Endgame* 46). There are other kinds of theater, sure, but until the dead bury the dead, I'm talking of the bottom line. "Use your head, can't you, use your head, you're on earth, there's no cure for that!" (53). So why should it be represented, since it's always represented, despite the desire to abolish or appropriate representation, in carnival, festival, alternative forms of theater, as anything more than the dream of something else? "Look! There! All that rising corn! And there! Look! The sails of the herring fleet! All that loveliness!" Where did that come from? "Oh way back, way back, you weren't in the land of the living" (44).

(1998)

In Short
The Right Aggregate, the Grand Apnoea, and the Accusative of Inexistence

For all the untenability of a singular character or a unified ego or coherent being, and the swallowing up of identity in a serial negativity, there is hardly a body of work in modern literature with so unitary a vision as Samuel Beckett's, along with the readily identifiable tonality of a perpetual voice, stuttering or aphasic, embracing dissolution, affirmed by abrogation. Thus: "Imagine a place, then someone in it, that again," knowing that whoever was there, if he was, he won't be, "Saying, Now where is he, no, Now he is here,"[1] wondering always, as now, where he's gone, "where been how long how it was,"[2] or in the end if he'll ever be, no matter, be sure, no end. The corporeal body on the stage, even if just a mouth, is a slight impediment to what, manic-obsessively on the page, is the anomalous disclaimer of a compelling fiction that anyone can be, and if so, better not, including, presumably, the one who created or perpetrated the fiction, or to whom it happened, overheard, in being "dreamt away," letting himself be dreamt away, "listening trying listening," where there's nothing to be heard, "nothing to listen for no such thing as a sound," nor anyone to hear it if there were, in the vanity of listening, a self to be discovered, "where no such thing no more than ghosts. . . ."[3]

In the incontrovertible absence of a "self so-called,"[4] its gasps and spasms or dissociated logorrhea, the irony is self-evident: word by word, or a torrent of words, in all their actuated invalidity, Beckett's identity is there beyond question—"Unless another still. Nowhere to be found. Nowhere to be sought. The unthinkable last of all. Unnamable. Last person. I. Quick leave him"[5]—as singular in permutation as any identity can be. Who would fail to recognize its grievous incapacities or, failing thus, the failing better with such distinction that rupture, fracture, dislocation, or syntactical bits and pieces seem, through relentless denegation, the formal cause of authenticity, and all the bereft or spectral figures, dubiously heard, maybe never seen, no more than accretions or aggregations of the Beckettian presence itself.

When push comes to shove, Pim to Bom, all the avatars of "I" and Other, or of the "I" in, out, and of itself, there is only one identity and that one is, by whatever name, or pronominally, still Beckett, first person, last person, Beckett still, "to and fro in shadow from inner to outershadow," to be sure "by way of neither," traversing the lapse of borders, while asserting, hedging, denying differences that might—were the sentence, the *pensum,* inflected another way—not exist at all. But then again they don't, except in the words that in asserting, hedging, denying, insistently posit a referent that, as none is, there is none, wasn't meant to be, though the words that say so are perhaps "too strong,"[6] if not noiselessly breaking wind, or plaintively up in the air, or parsing the "unheeded neither,"[7] syntax upended or gone to hell, "You know that penny farthing hell you call your mind,"[8] or (Dante always remembered) the hell of unknowing at the center of thought—"Thoughts, no, not thoughts. Profounds of mind"[9]— devoid of itself, pellucid, in an apotheosis of doubt. "Careful."[10] There is in all this, with the discretest sublimations of an always potential violence, "gently gently" (*Ill Seen* 52), something circumspect, a quality often described in Beckett's own behavior, as if—along with the disarming courtesy and reserve—he had to be on guard against something abrupt, forbidding within, "a great wind suddenly rising," or the inclemency of being itself.

"Nice fresh morning, bright too early," he wrote at the quickly unsunny beginning of *From an Abandoned Work.* "Feeling really awful, very violent." Which causes him (or the first-person, "young then," not-quite narrative voice) to prefer to "all moving things," a bird, a butterfly, "a slug now, getting under my feet, no, no mercy," things without motion. "Great love in my heart for all things still and rooted, bushes, boulders" and yes, no doubt on certain days, "even the flowers of the field," which otherwise in his "right senses" he would never touch, no less pluck one. Soon he is talking of dying, but by nothing so tranquil as a natural death, by drowning perhaps, or fire, "in fire, yes, perhaps that is how I shall do it at last"—the *doing* it quite important, no passivity here—"walking furious headlong into fire and dying burnt to bits." For this gratuitous martyrology, or suicidal impulse, his mother is no help, there in the window still waving, "just waving, in sad helpless love," and then—"enough of my mother for the moment"—he recalls "at a great distance a white horse followed by a boy," and then "just white, the thought of white, without more," which seems to put things in abeyance, "just the violence and then this white horse, when suddenly," he says, "I flew into a most savage rage, really blinding," unaccountable, and equally so, feelings of violence all day without the rage, and other days quiet, just that, "No, there's no accounting for it, there's no accounting for anything, with a mind like the one I always had, always on the alert against itself," or trying "to get relief by beating my head against something."[11]

Now and again, rereading Beckett, I am struck by the degrees and gradations of repressed, subdued, deflected, rising, released violence. Notice how many stage directions come to that: *Violently.* Or *Wildly.* Despite the sentimentality that Beckett himself alleged to be in *Krapp's Last Tape,* he nevertheless said of Krapp that, while there's something frozen about him, he is "filled to his teeth with bitterness," potentially violent, "like a tiger in a cage."[12] Or there's Henry in *Embers,* not merely his imprecations against "some old grave" he can't tear himself away from, or, after remembering "ADDIE's *wail amplified to paroxysm,*"[13] his own "Roaring prayers at God and his saints." I'm thinking, rather, of the sequence immediately after, when Ada suggests there's something wrong in his brain, and Henry bursts out "(*Wildly.)* Thuds, I want thuds! Like this!" then comes up with two big stones from the shingle and "(*Starts dashing them together.)* Stone! (*Clash.)* Stone!" And then, the clash of stone amplified, he throws one stone away and says on the sound of its fall: "That's life! (*He throws the other stone away. Sound of its fall.)* Not this . . . (*Pause.)* . . . sucking!" (*Embers* 100–101).

If things subside into the sucking, the ooze, the mire, the muck, Beckett also developed, like the man in his first story, *Assumption,* a sort of ferocious rigor against the "wild rebellious surge" (*Prose* 4), as if keeping the muck itself from heaving into violence or the sucking into sounding another cry of rage, with "his remarkable faculty of whispering the turmoil down. This whispering down, like all explosive feats of the kind," had its own repertoire of "subtle preparations: all but imperceptible twitches of impatience, smiles artistically suppressed, a swift affection of uninterested detachment" (3). Subtle as they may be, in whatever state of imagined being, these preparations are in vain. Even in *The Calmative*—the story that starts with "I don't know when I died"—the effort to remember when that occurred, disturbs the dead body with the same reflective violence as might be reserved to life: "For I'm too frightened this evening to listen to myself rot, waiting for the great red lapses of the heart, the tearings of the caecal walls, and for the slow killings to finish in my skull, the assaults on unshakeable pillars, the fornications with corpses" (*Prose* 61). Speaking of lapses of the heart, there is also the harrowing question, raised by Mr. Rooney in *All That Fall*: "Did you never wish to kill a child? (*Pause.*) Nip some young doom in the bud" (*Plays* 31).

And so it goes, gently, gently, the incipient fury and more than latent violence. That the pimp who stabbed Beckett was named Prudent seems only appropriate, with a kind of poetics to it if not poetic justice. That he should have said, when Beckett asked him in an anteroom of the Palais de Justice, why he did it, "I don't know," is appropriate folklore, even if true. Not knowing is, of course, the ground rhythm of Beckett's thought, which turns over and over the epistemological burden of knowing too much of an impermeable too little, no less the daunting question of how, or from whence, it is known at all: "Dim light source unknown." Thus, too, in a surplus of the unknowable, the adjuration to "Know minimum." As for the prospect of knowing less, devoutly to be wished, even the reductio ad absurdum must have a sense of proportion: "Know nothing no. Too much to hope."[14] As in the cylinder of *The Lost Ones*—"Vast enough for search to be in vain"[15]—Beckett has always had a remorselessly circumscribed niche in the ethos of less is more, with lessness as possibility, but "at most mere minimum. Mere-most minimum" (*Worstward* 91), with nothing as minimum's maximum never to be known.

To speak of doubt in Beckett is, then, vastly, to underestimate the case, though he may have done so himself early on, in the elliptical periodicities of "Dante . . . Bruno . Vico . . Joyce," when he spoke of Joyce's recognizing "how inadequate 'doubt' is to express a state of extreme uncertainty," replacing it with "in twosome twiminds,"[16] which still seems a long binary way from the painful indeterminacies or capillary confusions of Beckett's own divided mind, or "in the succession of transmutations," the circular convergence there of minima and maxima, the "particular contraries" that are, as he took the idea from Bruno, "one and indifferent" (*Disjecta* 21). What Beckett brought to the circularity was an evolving microphysics for the successive transmutations, the compulsion of exactitude, as in *Imagination Dead Imagine*, "No way in, go in, measure" (*Prose* 182), all the more so as what was measured was imperceptible, whether an "infinitesimal shudder instantaneously suppressed" (185) or, in the movement from a pitch-black freezing point to its reverse in heat and whiteness, where "the extremes alone are stable," the distressing gradients of "feverish grays" (183). Over the years, however, this notion was maintained: minima and maxima coincide. As "maximal speed is a state of rest," so "the maximum of corruption and the minimum of generation are identical; in principle, corruption is generation" (21). It is a principle that permeates every aspect of behavior and form, scene and seen, murmured, echoed, sight unseen, in the particle physics or psychic accretions of his own transmuted successions. So, as contrasted with the "familiar chamber" of . . . *but the clouds,* there is the "Unfamiliar room. Unfamiliar scene" of *Ohio Impromptu,* "Out to where nothing ever shared. Back to where nothing ever shared. From this he had once half hoped some measure of relief might flow" (*Plays* 285). But it was only to be expected, through whatever subtle successions: the unfamiliar chamber turns out to be familiar, the only thing shared at the extremities being the absence of relief, with no relief from absence, of which no end . . .

Some time ago Wolfgang Iser, considering Beckett in terms of a "fiction of the end," remarked that "the negativeness of these texts would seem to consist in the fact that they refuse to satisfy our elementary needs." But what *are* these needs? And even if, as Iser adds, "whenever we think we have found something definite to satisfy our needs, we are made to realize that what we have found is only a fiction,"[17] what else did we expect to find? There is, to be sure, the long history of fictions pretending to be something else, while not quite purging or disguising the sometimes uneasy conviction that fiction itself is an elementary need, if not, indeed, an ontological datum even prior to need. ("What complicates it all," as Beckett himself remarked of the urge or obligation to invent or to create, "is the need to make. Like a child in the mud but no mud. And no child. Only need.")[18] The temptation to think so is already confounded, however, with the notion of higher value, including the equal and opposite need to undo the fiction, bringing it as close to the real, or the real's need for itself, as language can conceivably be, which then confounds need with the origin of value, itself confounded by the uncertainty of origin, the possibility of its being, as a delusive function of factitious existence, merely another fiction, that source from which—is it tropically or toxically?—all things proceed.

"With so much life gone from knowledge how know when it all began, all the variants of the one that one by one their venom staling follow upon one another, all life long, till you succumb." To what, succumbing, may also never be known, since there appears to be, with all its venom, a beginning to begin again, or in the very absence of origin its incorrigible repetition. "So in some way even olden things each time are first things, no two breaths the same, all a going over and over and all once and never more" (*Abandoned Work 162).* The never more persists, or the desire for it, "until nothing," again, why think about need, "there was never anything, never can be, life and death all nothing, that kind of thing" (163). All his life Beckett surveyed, indeed measured, with uncontainable dispassion, the needless inconsequence of things, so much so it seemed a need, though no matter what it seemed, the inconsequence was all, so much so, no point in going on, on, lashing out against it, never letting go, or crawling into the future, if that should happen to be, since crawling was destiny, unless it were something lower, as it appeared to be, down among the water rats, in the mini-saga of *The End.*

With gulls ravening at the mouth of the sewer, in "a spew of yellow foam," filth gushing into the river, "and the slush of birds above screaming with hunger and fury," the narrator—snug in the box he made, a boat in the "liquid world," for waiting out the end—puts the summary question: "But what does it amount to? Howling, soughing, moaning, sighing. What I would have liked was hammer strokes, bang bang bang, clanging in the desert. I let farts, to be sure, but hardly ever a real crack, they oozed out with a sucking noise, melted in the mighty never." Which seems to be taking the measure, too, of Beckett's terminal fiction, which in the mighty never one might call *interminable*, like Freudian interpretation sucked into the dream's navel. "As for my needs," Beckett writes, "they had dwindled as it were to my dimensions and become, if I may say so, of so exquisite a quality as to exclude all thought of succour" (*Prose* 97). Which is not exactly the case with the waiting for Godot. "I'm hungry," cries Gogo,[19] returning need to basics, in ordinary terms, as elemental as can be, where a carrot is no more than a carrot, though equally basic, it seems, is the hunger of Didi for meaning, as if—mingled with the slush of birds, the air "full of our cries" (*Godot* 58)—the child's cry at birth, the primordial hunger, is in that umbilical wawling instant a transvaluation of value, where hunger, meaning, and fiction are inseparably elemental, one becoming the other in the somatic thrust and psychogenesis of need. That includes the need to believe that the one who has the need is something *more* than a fiction, or at least as much, though we may come to wonder in Beckett, through the astringent formalism, or form-lessness, the systemic reductions or generic residues, of his later prose and plays, if it's even as substantial as that, no less that there's someone there who might conceivably hear the cry. And if there were, where would that be?

Toward the end of *The Interpretation of Dreams* Freud speaks of the "first psychical activity," which, in earliest childhood, produced a "'perceptual identity'—a repetition of the perception that was linked with the satisfaction of the need," the mnemic image of which, recathected, and thereby reinvoking the perception itself, quiets the hungry baby screaming and kicking helplessly. If the reappearance of the perception is the fulfillment of what we call a wish, something occurs, however, that changes this "primitive thought-activity," deterring satisfaction and making the need persist. When Freud refers to it—rather unexpectedly, almost shockingly in context—as "the bitter experience of life,"[20] that's the point at which we may realize, however we may wish otherwise, that the real subtext, the reality principle of the method that Freud has been articulating through his career, is the bitter experience itself. That persists in his view of reality all the way through from the founding of psychoanalysis to *Civilization and Its Discontents,* by which time, for all the heuristic genius and its lifelong promise of healing, he might have acceded to Beckett, whose own bitter experience, and unaccountable discontents, confirmed the limits of therapy or, as at ground zero of Hamm's afflatus ("use your head, you're on earth, there's no cure for that"),[21] anything like the "talking cure." The irony is, however, that the garrulity of the unconscious, which prompted never stops, might be the basis of an aesthetic, or, in its "incoherent continuum, . . . the corrosive ground-swell of Art."[22]

About that, Beckett hardly wavered from what Belacqua said to the Mandarin, in *Dream of Fair to Middling Women,* about Rimbaud and Beethoven, "the terms of whose statements serve merely to delimit the reality of insane areas of silence, whose audibilities are no more than punctuation in a statement of silences." Belacqua then muses about writing the book that Beckett wrote over and over, in which the experience of the reader was to be "between the phrases, in the silence, communicated by the intervals, not the terms of the statement," with the experience being, "'the menace, the miracle, the memory, of an unspeakable trajectory.'" In the pantheon of this trajectory Rembrandt also appears, with the miraculous "dehiscing" of a "dynamic décousu," whose "disfaction" or "disaggregating," returns Belacqua to Beethoven, and the "punctuation of dehiscence, flottements, the coherence gone to pieces, the continuity bitched to hell because the units of continuity have abdicated their unity, they have gone multiple, they fall apart, the notes fly about," like the words in the later Beckett, especially when accelerated on the stage, by the inquisitional light in *Play* or—brain flickering away like mad, "quick grab and on"[23]—the voluminous stream of the Mouth, "a blizzard of electrons; the vespertine compositions eaten away with terrible silences" (*Disjecta* 48–49); in Beckett, sometimes funnily, the pitiful respite of the appalling (*Pause*).

As far back, then, as *Dream of Fair to Middling Women,* in which Beckett's youthful self-punishing arrogance displays itself in the neologistic artifice of rather baroque profusions, we can find a philosophy of composition that obtains—with a proportionate darkening of the vespertine—

through the most parsimonious austerities or minimalist mathematics of the shorter plays and prose, where "the tense passional intelligence, when arithmetic abates, tunnels, skymole, surely and blindly (if we only thought so!) through the interstellar coalsacks of its firmament in genesis, . . . in a network of loci that shall never be co-ordinate." How, then, does creation occur? Down there in the firmament, surely and blindly (even if we think so!), that remains obscure; all that can be known by the creative mind, in the "recondite relations of the emergal," is that it arises "from a labour and weariness of deep castings that brook no schema." What we have, as when the gravedigger puts on the forceps, is a sort of mortuary aesthetic, where the mind, "suddenly entombed, then active in anger and a rhapsody of energy," scurries and plunges "toward exitus," with the momentum of a "proton, incommunicable" and the insistence of an "invisible rat, fidgeting behind the astral incoherence of the art surface" (44–45), with exitus as quietus before resumption of the particle physics. In these short or spastic pieces, as in the French of a final poem ("folie— / folie que de— / que de"),[24] it's as if language itself were reaching not only to what is primal or aboriginal, at the level of sensation, but to the biological mechanisms of the mind, no mind, but to what before it existed was nuclear or neural, of which there's a fidgeting semblance in the invisible rat. (Nothing quite like this occurred to me at the time, but it seems there was a semblance when, in the recondite relations of the emergal, over forty years ago in San Francisco, I brought to our first rehearsal of *Waiting for Godot* the remarkable drawing by Paul Klee of an Egyptiac sibylline figure with a rat coming out of her head.)

As the fidgets turned into *Fizzles* over the laborious course of the years, the astral incoherence became an entropic Möbius strip, or an occluded stream of thought, whose compulsive permutations are folded back upon each other, thought abrading thought as if it were metabolic. On the bafflement of identity there's nothing better, even Kafka, and the voice is unmistakable, even when fizzling out, or thought to be impossible, to "have thoughts," no less a voice. "I gave up before birth," it says (I almost said "he"), "it is not possible otherwise, but birth there had to be," and then another disclaimer, or separating instance, "it was he, I was inside, that's how I see it," for the rather perverse reason that—in "a life not worth having"—keeps repeating itself, impossibly so, of course, to tell "the tale of his death," which is never quite enough ("not enough for me"), maybe "his burial if they find him, that will be the end, I won't go on about worms," though that seems impossible too, "perhaps he'll drown, he always wanted to drown, he didn't want them to find him, he can't want now any more," but as long as thought continues ("he won't think any more, he'll go on") now is never the end of then, for which he'll never forgive himself. Yet if "because of me," says the insatiable voice, "there's nothing left in his head, I'll feed it all it needs."[25]

What persists in Beckett, then, as if it were identity's measure, is the pulsing specificity of self-excoriation, its last unending judgment, for not knowing where he is, or who, amid the always vociferous "figments" incessantly longing for silence, which, as he says, "talking," keeping the figments talking, "can only be me."[26] There really is, no denying, something redundantly manic about it, that is, the ceaseless iteration of denial denying itself, and the almost predictable psychopathology in the shifting identity of absence—"who would I be, if I could be, . . . who says this, saying it's me?"—or, more precisely, "the same old stranger as ever, for whom alone accusative I exist, in the pit of my inexistence" (*Texts* 4 114). As with everything grammatical in Beckett, like the sentence itself, the inexorable *pensum*, there is a double meaning to *accusative*, or rather a double case, linked to the direct object but implying an accusation, "in the toils of that obscure assize where," as in the judicial system of Kafka, "to be is to be guilty," which is why "one is frightened to be born, no, one wishes one were, so as to begin to die" (*Texts* 5 117). So far as that goes, "you may even believe yourself dead on condition you make no bones about it," which of course he does, echo's bones, over and over, from beginning to end, from afar, still waiting afar for the story, of which "no need, . . . a story is not compulsory, just a life," then there it is again, a far story, "to begin, to end, and again this voice cannot be mine. That's where I'd go, if I could go, that's who I'd be, if I could be." Which for an unlikely moment may seem "restored to the feasible," which in truth could never be, surely when he was living, "yes, living, say what he may," now that he's "dead like the living" (*Texts* 4 115–16), but dead, truly, say what he may have said.

And small consolation in that, though it remains unutterably there—indeed, a "place of remains"—taxing the patience of those who don't like a story beginning, as it does in *Fizzle 8*, "For to end yet again skull alone in the dark the void no neck no face just the box last place of all in the dark the void" (243). As if there were levels of void, there may seem more solace in *Endgame*, "reckoning closed and story ended," with its last withering vision of an unendurable patience, the "last million last moments," as Hamm prepares his stancher and, resolving to speak no more, first person, last person, invokes the second person: "You . . . remain" (83–84)—Clov? the audience? in the split infinitude of a self, some indeterminate other?

"Who asks in the end, who asks?" (*Company* 17). Don't ask, for it might be you, and you're still not sure who is asking. "The hearer. Unnamable. You" (28). In the remorseless solipsism of Beckett's shorter prose the presence of an other, objectively there, seems if at all tenable almost unbearable; but that a pronoun can be so promising, with minimal promise, no promise at all, is a matter of relativity in the accusative of inexistence.

Thus it is when one moves from the final fizzle—"through it who knows yet another end" (*Fizzle 8 246)*—to *Heard in the Dark 1*: "You see yourself at that last outset leaning against the door with closed eyes waiting for the word from you to go. You? To be gone. Then the snowlit scene." To be sure, the scene with its "expanse of light" is only seen "in the dark with closed eyes," and it's not destined to sustain a promise very long, even though, when the door clicks and the steps start, "you are on your way across the white pasture afrolic with lambs in spring," strewn as it also "with red placentae" (*Prose* 247). There is, in this, a sort of romantic irony that Beckett, as he grew older ("no older now than you always were"), never outlived, nor the one who is heard in the dark, who, in using the second person, appears to be addressing himself, "As if there were no other anymore. For you there is no other anymore" (248). Or so he says, taking his course across the pasture, "which is a beeline for the gap or ragged point in the quickset that forms the western fringe" *(247).*

This is one of those pieces in which the affect is unaccountable, the emotional memory, though it alludes to the "father's shade . . . not with you anymore," and the gathering for "the return," to who knows what, no quickset there, the interval longer than it was before (once "three to four minutes," now "fifteen to twenty"), foot falling "unbidden in midstep or next for lift cleaves to the ground bringing the body to a stand. Then a speechlessness whereof the gist," shifting then to the plural from the second person: "Can they go on? Or better, Shall they go on? The barest gist." Whatever the case, or persons, the beeline continues, from the origin that maybe never was to the identity yet to be, "The unerring feet fast. You look behind you as you could not then and see their trail. A great swerve." A clinamen in the void. And, as it was in *Endgame,* when Hamm returned through his feverish gray chamber to the hollow in the wall, the movement is counterclockwise, "Withershins. Almost as if all at once the heart too heavy. In the end too heavy." Which also has the capacity, if you've come "halfway across the pasture on your beeline to the gap" (248–49), the pit of inexistence, to nearly break your heart.

Nostalgia is the menace in Beckett, the pathos in the red placentae, if birth there had to be, and then in some "speechless misgiving" (*Heard 249)* an unlivable afterbirth. Given the way it is, was it really meant to be, no telling what it was? "Well, I'm going to tell myself something (if I'm able)," he had written in *Texts for Nothing,* "pregnant I hope with promise for the future, namely that I begin to have no very clear recollection of how things were before (I was!)," but again it seems like wish-fulfillment after he or whoever's speaking (words confused with tears, "my words are my tears, my eyes my mouth") insists that the past has thrown him out, gates slammed behind him, "all memory gone" (*Texts 8* 131–32). If there has been, as we're told, nothing since but fantasies, nothing in the imaginary is more fantastic than that, as if memory, overburdened, were always protesting too much, while lamenting indelibly all that it forgets. Amnesia, said Freud, is the deepest form of memory, and what seems in Beckett unforgettable is some unremembered offense, "to be punished in this inexplicable way," in a suffusion of words that break the silence, like a single endless word, "all is inexplicable, space and time, false and inexplicable, suffering and tears, and even the old convulsive cry, It's not me, it can't be me" (133). As it turns out, having raised the question—relative to saying what happened, where, when, whatever it was, it all, the reiterated unsayable, "patiently, variously, trying to vary, for you never know, it's perhaps all a question of hitting on the right aggregate"—there he is, as if moving to the end that gives a meaning to words, "panting toward the grand apnoea" (asphyxia, breathlessness) at that terminus of the grand boulevards, the place de la République (where, in our Paris apartment, this essay first emerged), "at pernod time."

Meanwhile, through it all, this other question persists: "But am I in pain, whether it's me or not, frankly now, is there pain?" If there is we wouldn't know it, because "there is no frankness" here, and maybe no feeling at all, but no, can it really be doubted, though the text (insidiously) says, "all I say will be false, and to begin with not said by me, I'm a mere ventriloquist's dummy," and so it goes back and forth, in a trajectory of contraries, yes I am, no I'm not, the gap or pit between, or in "bowler hat" and "brown boots lacerated and gaping," maybe simply the pits, between whoever it is and "the other who is me," who may never have seen "the light of day, any more than he, ah if no were content to cut yes's throat and never cut its own" (133–34), which still wouldn't dispose of the tortuous pronouns, thus merely letting (it?) be. As for the right aggregate in the unbroken flow of words, "there are four million possible, nay probable, according to Aristotle, who knew everything" (134), though perhaps, despite the treatise on tragedy, not all that much about pain, to which all words point in Beckett, even in ribaldry just the same. "What I understand best, which is not saying much, are my pains," says the self-calumniating narrator of "First Love." "I think them through daily, it doesn't take long, thought moves so fast, but they are not only in my thought, not all." Swift as thought may be, the subject of pain is elusive, even when physiological, like phantoms of the brain. Between this earth, "the shitball and heaven's high halls," there isn't much he understands, about women, or men, or animals, "But even them," he says, "my pains, I understand ill. That must come from my not being all pain and nothing else. There's the rub. . . . To be nothing but pain, how that would simplify matters."[27]

But since nothing is quite so simple, not even, with bowler hats and gaping boots, the "Nothing to be done,"[28] is there anything, then, like a facsimile of relief? As we see in *Waiting for Godot,* the Beckettian moment(um) is such that thought moves fast with failing memory back to forgetfulness, or—there's the rub—the illusion of lapsed memory as a refuge from pain, if not the dream of a time when the pain is all over. "I mean . . . ," say the voices in *Play,* "not merely all over, but as if . . . never been—" (*Plays* 148). While the mise en scène is as strange as ever—heads protruding, stabbed by light, necks held fast in the funereal urns (147)—the not-at-all comforting fiction of the imaginary *as if* appears to have a context that is in the corpus of Beckett almost conventional: instead of Aristotelian tragedy, the adulterous plot of a boulevard melodrama. "Peace, yes, I suppose," says M, "a kind of peace, and all that pain as if . . . never been" (152). Here, as elsewhere, the words resonate beyond the scenario in a self-reflexive way, or between one fizzle or text for nothing and all the disconsolate others. Thus it is, too, with M's fatalistic "There is no future in this" and W2's remark, after the swivel of light, about the danger being that things may "disimprove," with the attendant feeling that you can certainly count on that. It's not only the dramaturgy, then, that causes W2 to say: "Is it that I do not tell the truth, is that it, that someday somehow I may tell the truth at last and then no more light at last, for the truth?" Of course, the liability of this ultimate telling is no doubt next to zero. "I know now," says M, "all that was just . . . play. And all this? When will all this—" (153), the indeterminate referent upping the ante on pain that, far from never, has always inevitably *been,* and if anything will be, whatever the "momentum coming" (155), will "never have been . . . just play" (153).

No more than it is with the panting figure, breathless, bent over—"what is this I see, and how, a white stick and an ear-trumpet, where"—back again on the place de la République. "The vacancy is tempting," a version of the void, as the bowler hat and boots, the now-familiar "insignia, . . . advance in concert, as though connected by the traditional human

excipient, halt, move on again, confirmed by the vast show windows."
With hope held out, by the level of the hat and ear-trumpet, for the Beckettian hero "as a dying dwarf or at least hunchback," the only thing undiminished is the indefatigable voice: "shall I enthrone my infirmities," it
asks, "give them this chance again, my dream infirmities, that they may
take flesh and move, deteriorating round and round the grandiose square
which I hope I don't confuse with the Bastille, until they are deemed worthy of the adjacent Père Lachaise" (*Prose* 134), where Proust is buried, and
other worthies, but not Beckett, whose remains, to use that word, lie with
his wife, Suzanne, under a polished black marble slab in the cemetery at
Montparnasse. Their names, the dates, no more, no insignia other than
that.

"I am dead enough myself, I hope, not to feel any great respect for those
that are so entirely," said Mrs. Williams in the unfinished play about
Samuel Johnson and Mrs. Thrale, apparently to be entitled *Vanity of
Human Wishes*.[29] If there was, nevertheless, always in Beckett's work an
elegiac strain, there were times when it appeared that, mourning before the
fact, with a dying fall, the echoing lamentations were feeling out an epitaph.
"Over, over, there is a soft place in my heart for all that is over, no, for the
being over, I love the word, words have been my only loves, not many."[30]
As for the words that remain, our legacy, over, over, or "from deep within
oh how and here a word he could not catch" (*Stirrings* 3 264), they don't
quite make it to the being over, the infirmities still enthroned, and going
from bad to worse, can you imagine, almost unimaginably so. If one speaks
of the imaginable in existence, what is possible among us because we're
human, yes, that's possible, even in the Beckettian inexistence, anything is
possible, including possibly what you can't imagine, no, unspeakably
worse, "so on unknowing and no end in sight. Unknowing and what is
more no wish to know," though "he would have wished the strokes to
cease and the cries for good and was sorry that they did not" (*Stirrings* 2
263). So far as we can see in Beckett, if it were not exactly steady state, the
worst is yet to come, or would be if, in the extremity of imagining, it
hadn't happened already—"whence when back no knowing . . . where been
how long how it was"[31]—which is the condition, surely, for its being imagined, whatever the words for that, imagination dead imagine, that, too, all
over again.

But then, to make it worse, suppose it wasn't imagined. Is there not,
after all, something like fact in the world? Or something like the world, in
fact, "a world to leave, . . . a world to reach," yes, even Nagg concedes,

reaching out of the ashbins, that there *is* a world elsewhere, though not, no, by any stretch of imagination, up to the measure—"a snug crotch is always a teaser" and, "at a pinch, a smart fly is a stiff proposition" (*Endgame* 22)—of the bespoke trousers in his own creation myth. Facts are facts, though with the accusative of inexistence they tend to occur by negation, if not quite, aporetically, canceling each other out. So: somewhere between the graveyard and "the prisons of Arcady," the fact remains that, "with creatures, with words, with misery, misery," there is something like the world, indeed, in which, "Ah, says I," there might be a way out, and even a way in, somewhere to come from, no, a point of departure, there might have been a mother and other faces on the way to the tomb, though none to be recalled, proving nothing whatever, if proof could ever be. "But the fact that I was not molested, can I remain insensible to that? Alas I fear that they could have subjected me to the most gratifying brutalities. I won't go so far as to say without my knowledge, but without my being encouraged, as a result, to feel myself there rather than elsewhere." Despite the onerous suggestion of those imagined gratifications, there is in all this an obsessive return of the same, "all unaware of any break or lull in [the] problematic patrolling, unconstrained, before the gates of the graveyard," or—"what vicissitudes within what changelessness"[32]—the sense of immersion within, or even the protoconfusion, there rather than elsewhere, with "other spaces, other times, dimly discerned, but not more dimly than now, now that I'm here, if I'm here, and no longer there, coming and going before the graveyard, perplexed" (*Text 9* 139).

However it goes wherever it goes, the problematic patrolling, the intolerable redundancy of its measureless ways, "it comes to the same, for it's not that either," and assured of certain certainties (along with the elegiac, there has always been in Beckett an Eliotic strain: the words slip, slide, will not hold still, decay with imprecision, as precise in failure as words can be) you can surely be certain of that, which is "something else, some other thing, or the first back again, or still the same" (139), and so on, on, you can almost write the words, though inexhaustibly, to be right, no, not quite those but just the same, if you have the endurance, his words, yes, are there any other, in the never-ending turpitude of words, or what he called in *Molloy*, "the long sonata of the dead"? About the "nameless things" and "thingless names," in a world that's dying "foully named,"[33] the drawn-out stammer of the living dead, Bataille remarked—in an early, percipient essay on Beckett—that in the language which "calcifies that calculated world" to which culture, behavior, and institutions attach significance, "the word is no longer the signifying factor, but rather the crippled form that death, in its indirect way, must inevitably take."[34] In fact, however, now and then in passing, an estranging word will appear that may take us by surprise (unless we recall, accompanying the invisible rat, the fidgeting ostentation, not a little supercilious, in the earlier vespertine language of the astral incoherence), *oestruation, introrse, divellicate, vomer, deasil, herpetic,* if not quite as enchanting as Hamm's rapturous *fontanelles,* still odd, technical, rarely used words, like the grand *apnoea;* or the *dehiscence* that later became familiar through the oedipal fracture ("coherence gone to pieces") of the mirror stage of Lacan; or, "if they could open, those little words, open and swallow [him] up," the *desinence* before the silence that in the end will never come (*Text 8* 132).

If words have been his only loves, not many (many loves? or many words?), there has also been in Beckett a congenital rage against the commiserable rage of words, the inadequate aggregation. "It's because I haven't hit on the right ones, the killers, haven't yet heaved them up from that heart-burning glut of words, with what words should I name my unnamable words" (*Text 6* 125), or better, out of revulsion for the heart-burning glut, an apocalyptic vision, or, since it comes from "the head and its anus the mouth" (*Text 10* 141), never mind the vision, call it excremental: "That's right, wordshit, bury me, avalanche" (*Text 9* 137). Heart, head, anus, mouth, and sometimes "a voice without a mouth, and there's a kind of hearing, something compelled to hear, and somewhere a hand, it calls that a hand, it wants to make a hand, or if not a hand something somewhere that can leave a trace, . . . no, that's romancing, more romancing, there is nothing but a voice murmuring a trace" (*Text 13* 152). What the reality is, remaining, through the "last everlasting questions" of a regressively aging dehiscence, "infant languors in the end sheets, last images, end of dream," is still another question, question mark forgotten, along with the origins that are (*avant la lettre* in Beckett, before French Freud or Derrida) nothing but a trace, a trace in the faintest murmur of all the metaphysical lies: "And whose the shame, at every mute micromillisyllable, and unslakable infinity of remorse, . . . at having to hear, having to say, fainter than the faintest murmur, so many lies, so many times the same lie lyingly denied, whose the screaming silence of no's knife in yes's wound, it wonders" (154).

And there's much to wonder about. After a generation of literary study, purging itself of remorse—along with nostalgia, one of the presumed lies of an elitist modernism—it may be well to remember that, when Beckett first appeared on the scene, we were about to go, through a rabid distrust of language in a developing counterculture, into a period of body consciousness, and thence, when the nudity subsided with the dissidence, into the (deconstructively) self-denying, (often) self-enamored, discourse of the body: the body this, the body that, the libidinal body or desiring machine (for which, in Deleuzian schizoanalysis, the bicycle horn of *Molloy*, like Schreber's "solar anus," was worked into a model),[35] or parsed out as historical constructions, the ideological body, which is not quite the body that Beckett had in mind, nor there in the inexistent darkness of *Not I*— "imagine! . . . whole body like gone" (*Plays* 220)—the existential body that has to endure the Mouth. Given the recurrent torments of his own biological body, the cysts, the boils, the eczema, we might well understand why— aside from the whispering abscess that caused a racing heart—he might wish the body away, but now and again we find him wondering, "has it knelled here at last for our committal to flesh," or will we discover, perhaps, "a true one in pickle, among the unborn hordes," the one discounted in the discourse, the body that really matters (never mind the talk of transgression), "the true sepulchral body, for the living have no room for a second. No, no souls, or bodies, or birth, or life, or death, you've got to go on without any of that junk, that's all dead with words, with excess of words," through which he longs for "a voice of silence, the voice of my silence" (*Text 10* 142–43)—though, in short, like him, "For why or?" (*Company* 16), it's hard to leave it at that.

(1998)

Notes

Notes from the Underground

1. Following our appearance there, the inmates formed their own Drama Workshop and, after a year or so of preparation on other plays, performed both *Godot* and *Endgame* themselves. They also put out a Commemorative Edition of the prison newspaper (November 28, 1957) that originally contained reviews, commentary, and letters about our presentation of *Godot*.

2. In 1959 I went abroad on a subsidy from the Ford Foundation, in the first round of grants given by Ford in the arts, as a sort of preface to the awards made a year or two later to the developing regional theaters, including The Actor's Workshop.

The Bloody Show and the Eye of Prey

1. Samuel Beckett, *Not I,* in *Ends and Odds* (New York: Grove, 1976) 14. Further references to *Not I* and other pieces from this collection will appear in the text under their own titles with page numbers from *Ends and Odds*.

2. *The Unnamable* (New York: Grove, 1958) 170.

3. *The Lost Ones* (New York: Grove, 1972) 15–16.

4. *Molloy,* trans. Patrick Bowles, with Samuel Beckett (New York: Grove, 1955) 7.

5. *Waiting for Godot* (New York: Grove, 1954) 7.

6. John Ashbery, *Three Poems* (New York: Penguin, 1977) 46.

7. Theodore W. Adorno, "Trying to Understand *Endgame*," *New German Critique,* no. 26 (1982): 121.

8. *A Piece of Monologue,* in *Collected Shorter Plays of Samuel Beckett* (London: Faber and Faber, 1984) 265.

9. *Proust* (New York: Grove, n.d.) 54.

10. Jacques Derrida, *Of Grammatology,* trans. Gayatri Chakravorty Spivak (Baltimore: Johns Hopkins University Press, 1976) 5.

11. "Structure, Sign, and Play in the Human Sciences," in *Writing and Difference,* trans. Alan Bass (Chicago: University of Chicago Press, 1978) 292.

12. *Endgame* (New York: Grove, 1958) 44.

13. *From an Abandoned Work,* in *First Love and Other Shorts* (New York:

Grove, 1974) 39. Further references to this work and any other from the collection will appear in the text under their own titles with page numbers from *First Love*.

14. Roland Barthes, *The Pleasure of the Text*, trans. Richard Miller (New York: Hill and Wang, 1975) 66–67.

15. Jacques Derrida, *Speech and Phenomena and Other Essays on Husserl's Theory of Signs*, trans. David B. Allison (Evanston: Northwestern University Press, 1973) 15.

16. Christian Metz, *The Imaginary Signifier: Psychoanalysis and the Cinema*, trans. Celia Britton, Annwyl Williams, Ben Brewster, and Alfred Guzzett (Bloomington: Indiana University Press, 1977) 50.

17. Quoted by Ruby Cohn, *Back to Beckett* (Princeton: Princeton University Press, 1973) 125–26. (*Eléutheria* was not yet published when this essay was written.)

18. *Foirades/Fizzles* (New York: Whitney Museum of American Art, 1977), a catalogue of etchings by Jasper Johns on Beckett's text, unpaginated.

Barthes and Beckett

1. Roland Barthes, *A Lover's Discourse: Fragments*, trans. Richard Howard (New York: Hill and Wang, 1978) 12.

2. Samuel Beckett, *Endgame* (New York: Grove, 1958) 18.

3. *Roland Barthes by Roland Barthes*, trans. Richard Howard (New York: Hill and Wang, 1977) 51–52.

4. *Camera Lucida: Reflections on Photography*, trans. Richard Howard (New York: Hill and Wang, 1981) 75.

5. *Waiting for Godot* (New York: Grove, 1954) 58.

6. Sigmund Freud, *The Interpretation of Dreams*, trans. James Strachey (New York: Avon, 1965) 617.

7. *From an Abandoned Work*, in *First Love and Other Shorts* (New York: Grove, 1974) 47–48. Subsequent references to other shorts, appearing in the text, will be from this volume.

8. Antonin Artaud, *The Theater and Its Double*, trans. Mary Caroline Richards (New York: Grove, 1958) 52.

9. *Beyond the Pleasure Principle*, trans. James Strachey (New York: Norton, 1961) 33.

10. *The Unnamable* (New York: Grove, 1958) 31.

11. *Proust* (New York: Grove, n.d.) 29.

The Oversight of Ceaseless Eyes

1. Samuel Beckett, *Waiting for Godot* (New York: Grove, 1954) 59.

2. *That Time*, in *The Collected Shorter Plays* (New York: Grove, 1984) 230–31.

3. *Proust* (New York: Grove, n.d.) 6–7.

4. If the repetitions of the paranoia are consummately focused in the

drama of Beckett, there was until his recent death the double irony of his own protective vigilance over the integrity of his texts and the correct way to stage them. Since his drama has, in a sense, prepared the ground for revisionist performance, his rage over the presumptions of other productions—sometimes shared by reverent scholars—raises any number of theoretical questions about authorship and authenticity and the statute of limitations on the rites of theatricality.

5. Jacques Derrida, "Freud and the Scene of Writing," in *Writing and Difference,* intro. and trans. Alan Bass (Chicago: University of Chicago Press, 1978) 26.

6. *Endgame* (New York: Grove, 1958) 2.

7. *Danton's Death,* in George Büchner, *Complete Plays and Prose,* intro. and trans. Carl Richard Mueller (New York: Mermaid / Hill and Wang, 1963) 31.

8. Jean Baudrillard, "What Are You Doing after the Orgy?" *Artforum* 22.2 (1983): 42.

9. Samuel Beckett, "As the story was told," in *The Complete Short Prose,* ed. and intro. S. E. Gontarski (New York: Grove, 1995) 255.

10. Not only do we live in a time born to be photographed, but, as Walter Benjamin remarked in a famous essay, "Any man today can lay claim to being filmed" ("The Work of Art in the Age of Mechanical Reproduction," in *Illuminations,* ed. and intro. Hannah Arendt, trans. Harry Zohn [New York: Schocken, 1977] 233). With the immediate feedback of the electronic media, we can also lay claim to seeing ourselves being filmed.

11. The desire for such an unmediated moment, or the *singularity* of his grief, is what proves so moving in the book on photography written by Roland Barthes after the death of his mother, and which, as it turned out, seemed to be a premonition of his own death. Determined to be guided in the book only by the consciousness of his own feelings, he is also very conscious—as he approaches the *spectacle* of what-she-was in the photograph—that he has spent a lifetime as "observed subject" and "observing subject" in a world dominated by the visual image and without a "History of Looking" (*Camera Lucida,* trans. Richard Howard [New York: Hill and Wang, 1981] 10, 12).

12. Bertolt Brecht, "A Short Organum for the Theater," in *Brecht on Theater: The Development of an Aesthetic,* ed. and trans. John Willett (New York: Hill and Wang, 1964) 187.

13. If the effect can be experienced, even through boredom, it can also be produced quite spectacularly. For a commentary on the calculated estrangement of this ambiguously produced effect in the earlier work of Robert Longo, see Hal Foster, "Contemporary Art and Spectacle," in *Recodings: Art, Spectacle, Cultural Politics* (Port Townsend, WA: Bay Press, 1985) 79–96.

14. Guy Debord, *La Société du spectacle* (Paris: Editions Chamo Libre, 1971) n. 2. The book is a virtual formulation of the strategies, with a theoretical base, of the International Situationist group, whose critique of advanced capitalism in the early 1960s was inseparable from the critique of representation, which continues in theory with undiminished vigilance. First published in 1967, it was translated as *Society of the Spectacle* (Detroit: Black and Red, 1977).

15. Jacques Derrida, *Of Grammatology,* trans. and intro. Gayatri Clakravorty Spivak (Baltimore: Johns Hopkins University Press, 1976) 65.

16. A discussion of *Schaulust* can he found in Jacques Lacan's seminar "The Partial Drive and Its Circuit," in *The Four Fundamental Concepts of Psychoanalysis,* ed. Jacques-Alain Miller, trans. Alan Sheridan (New York: Norton, 1978) 174–86. After indicating that what is fundamental at the level of each drive is the reflexive movement outward and back by which it is structured, Lacan then says it is remarkable that Freud could disguise the two poles of this movement by a slight shift in verb forms that relates sight and pain: "*Beschauen und berchaut werden,* to see and to be seen, *quälen* and *gequält werden,* to torment and to be tormented.*"* The sadomasochism is implied in the circuitry of the two verb forms, Freud having understood from the outset that no part of the distance covered in seeing could he divorced from the circular character of the path of the drive, in which there appears what "*does not appear,*" a new subject that is the other. "It is only with its appearance at the level of the other that what there is of the function of the drive may be realized" (178–79).

Astride of a Grave

1. Samuel Beckett, *The Unnamable* (New York: Grove, 1958) 179.

2. Beckett, *Waiting for Godot* (New York: Grove, 1954) 58–59.

3. Herbert Blau, *The Audience* (Baltimore: Johns Hopkins University Press, 1990) 20.

4. Blau, "Universals of Performance; or, Amortizing Play," *The Eye of Prey: Subversions of the Postmodern* (Bloomington: Indiana University Press, 1987) 174.

5. Beckett, *First Love and Other Shorts* (New York: Grove, 1974) 11–12.

6. Beckett, *Collected Shorter Plays* (New York: Grove, 1984) 156–67.

7. Joseph Roach, *Cities of the Dead: Circum-Atlantic Performance* (New York: Columbia University Press, 1996) 14, 16.

8. Blau, "The Less Said," in *The World of Samuel Beckett,* ed. Joseph H. Smith (Baltimore: Johns Hopkins University Press, 1991) 219.

9. "Meanwhile, Follow the Bright Angels," *Tulane Drama Review* 5.1 (1960): 90.

10. Quoted by Anthony Cronin, *Beckett: The Last Modernist* (New York: HarperCollins, 1997) 141.

11. I included this passage in *The Impossible Theater: A Manifesto* (New York: Macmillan) 239.

12. Robert W. Corrigan, *The Theater in Search of a Fix* (New York: Delacorte, 1973) 8.

13. *Take Up the Bodies: Theater at the Vanishing Point* (Bloomington: University of Illinois Press, 1982).

14. "All before. Nothing else ever. Ever tried. Ever failed. No matter. Try again. Fail again. Fail better." From Beckett archive, MS 2602 (Reading), quoted by James Knowlson, *Damned to Fame: The Life of Samuel Beckett* (New York: Simon and Schuster, 1996) 593.

15. Beckett, *Endgame* (New York: Grove, 1958) 68.

In Short

1. *Faux Départs,* in *The Complete Short Prose, 1929–1989,* ed. and intro. S. E. Gontarski (New York: Grove, 1995) 272; abbreviated as *Prose.*

2. *Still 3,* in *Prose* 269.

3. *Sounds,* in *Prose* 268.

4. *Stirrings Still,* in *Prose* 265.

5. *Company,* in *Nohow On,* intro. S. E. Gontarski (New York: Grove, 1996) 17.

6. *How It Is* (New York: Grove, 1964) 115.

7. "neither," in *Prose* 258.

8. *Eh Joe,* in *Collected Shorter Plays* (New York: Grove, 1984) 202; abbreviated as *Plays.*

9. *Ohio Impromptu,* in *Plays* 288.

10. *Ill Seen Ill Said,* in *Nohow On* 50.

11. *From an Abandoned Work,* in *Prose* 156–57.

12. Beckett described Krapp in these terms while directing Rick Cluchey in Berlin in 1977; quoted by Anthony *Cronin, Samuel Beckett: The Last Modernist* (New York: HarperCollins, 1996) 484–85.

13. *Embers,* in *Plays* 99.

14. *Worstward Ho,* in *Nohow On* 91.

15. *The Lost Ones,* in *Prose* 202.

16. *Disjecta: Miscellaneous Writings and a Dramatic Fragment,* ed. and fwd. Ruby Cohn (London: John Calder, 1983) 28.

17. Wolfgang Iser, "When Is the End Not the End: The Idea of Fiction in Beckett," *On Beckett: Essays and Criticism,* ed. and intro. S. E. Gontarski (New York: Grove, 1986) 49.

18. This was said to Lawrence Harvey, quoted by Cronin, *Samuel Beckett* 389.

19. *Waiting for Godot* (New York: Grove, 1954) 13.

20. Sigmund Freud, *The Interpretation of Dreams,* ed. and trans. James Strachey (New York: Avon, 1965) 605.

21. *Endgame* (New York: Grove, 1958) 68.

22. *Dream of Fair to Middling Women,* in *Disjecta* 48.

23. *Not I,* in *Plays* 221.

24. *Comment dire* (Paris: Librairie Compagnie, 1989).

25. *Fizzle 4,* in *Prose* 234–35.

26. *Texts for Nothing 4,* in *Prose* 116. References will be to the singular *Text,* with number.

27. *First Love,* in *Prose* 32.

28. *Waiting for Godot* (New York: Grove, 1954) 7.

29. Quoted from a copy of the manuscript given to me by Ruby Cohn.

30. *From an Abandoned Work,* in *Prose* 162.

31. *Still 3,* in *Prose* 269.

32. *Texts for Nothing 9,* in *Prose* 137–38.

33. *Molloy: A Novel* (New York: Grove, 1955) 41.

34. Georges Bataille, "Molloy's Silence," in *On Beckett* 133.

35. Gilles Deleuze and Félix Guattari, *Anti-Oedipus: Capitalism and Schiz-ophrenia,* trans. Robert Hurley, Mark Seem, and Helen R. Lane (New York: Viking, 1977) 2–3.

Index

Page numbers in bold refer to photographs.

Ashbery, John, "Three Poems," 78
Assumption, 6; violence and rage in, 182
audience(s), 135, 149; absence of, 161; awareness of, 33, 161–63, 172; Beckett's relationship with, 66, 99; bourgeois, 91; confusion of, 121; and the desire to see, 123; Hamm's relationship with, 45; the look of, 91; offending the, 161; of popular theater, 58; postmodern, 121; responses of, 16, 37, 39, 40, 55, 143, 169; as spectacle, 116
Augustine, Saint, 155
authorship, 144; and authenticity, 180–81; and Beckett's authority, 66, 143–45, 146, 199n. 4; and the death of the author, 145; and freedom of directors, 144–45, 146
avant-garde, 4, 16, 21, 58, 117
Avignon, festival of, 57

Bair, Deirdre, 146
Balance of Terror, 124
Barish, Jonas, *The Anti-Theatrical Prejudice,* 65, 135
Barthes, Roland, 3, 11, 77, 58, 98, 142, 153, 199n. 11; on analogy, 107; and being named, 107–8; and binarism, 94–95; as Brechtian, 108; *Camera Lucida (La Chambre Claire),* 95–99, 103–5, 154; and the image of himself, 107; Imaginary of, 104; love and idea in, 94; *A Lover's Discourse,* 94–96, 99, 102–3, 105–7, 109, 111; mother of, 95, 96, 99, 106, 199n. 11; *The Pleasure of the Text,* 89, 103; *Roland Barthes by Roland Barthes,* 94, 104, 108; and Sartre, 104; and suffering, 96; "The World Thunderstruck," 103; and "writing aloud," 89
Bataille, Georges, 193
Baudrillard, Jean, 9, 118; "What Are You Doing After the Orgy?" 120
Beckett, Samuel: and audiences, 66; and authority over productions,

143–44; 199n. 4; and awareness of being observed, 104; and biographers, 146; Blau's correspondence with, 1, 70, 140, 144, 146; Blau's meetings with, 1, 5–8, 12–15, 17, 19–20, 29, 58, 65, 124, 132, 139, 142, 145, 146, 150, 157; and the body, 79, 142, 195; and category confusion, 2; comedy of, 94; and continuity, 20; and deconstruction, 92; despair of, 13, 24, 27, 28, 104, 125; as director, 63, 67, 76, 144; disappearance of, 151; and disdain for language, 128, 140; as dramatist of alienation, 28, 31; on "failing better," 177; and form, 30, 31, 185; on Freud and Jung, 17; grave of (Montparnasse), 171, 192; humanism of, 152; identity of, 180; and logos, 92; and loss, 96; memory of, 8, 157; and need, 185; nursing home of (Le Tiers Temps), 13, 139, 142; personality of, 35, 181; pessimism of, 151–52, 173; and the Resistance, 7, 132; romantic irony of, 189; stage directions of, 63, 70, 78–79, 159, 182; and subject desire, 114; and terror, 111, 125; on his texts, 21, 22, 26, 28, 143, 144, 146, 147; and the theater, 27, 65–66, 125–26; unitary vision of, 180. *See also under titles of individual works*
Beckett, Suzanne, 1, 20; grave of (Montparnasse), 192
Beckett Directs Beckett, 144
Beckett Society, 3
behavior, 43, 134, 170, 181
being, 82, 95, 132, 133, 180, 181; and being-filmed, 199n. 10; and being-in-itself, 7; and being-loved, 111; and being-named, 107–8; and being-perceived, 91; and being-seen, 85, 97, 157; privative, 91; project of, 21; remainder of, 93; rhythms of, 102; Weil on, 7, 30
Belafonte, Harry, 39
Benamou, Michel, 177
Benjamin, Walter, 9; "The Work of